P9-DXM-286

DATE DUE

NO 1 '04			
NO 22 '04			
FE 7 '08			

THE ARCHAEOLOGY OF ISLAM

Social Archaeology

General Editor
Ian Hodder, University of Cambridge

Advisory Editors
Margaret Conkey, University of California at Berkeley
Mark Leone, University of Maryland
Alain Schnapp, UER d'Art et d'Archeologie, Paris
Stephen Shennan, University of Southampton
Bruce Trigger, McGill University, Montreal

Published

ENGENDERING ARCHAEOLOGY
Edited by Joan M. Gero and Margaret W. Conkey

IRON-AGE SOCIETIES
Lotte Hedeager

THE ARCHAEOLOGY OF ISLAM
Timothy Insoll

CONTEMPORARY ARCHAEOLOGY IN THEORY
Robert W. Preucel and Ian Hodder

AN ARCHAEOLOGY OF CAPITALISM
Matthew Johnson

MATERIAL CULTURE AND MASS CONSUMPTION
Daniel Miller

METAPHOR AND MATERIAL CULTURE
Christopher W. Tilley

In preparation

THE RISE OF MESO-AMERICA
Elizabeth Brumfiel

ARCHAEOLOGY AS CULTURAL HISTORY
Ian Morris

ARCHAEOLOGICAL INTERPRETATIONS
Robert W. Preucel

THE ARCHAEOLOGY OF LANDSCAPE
Edited by Wendy Ashmore and A. Bernard Knapp

The Archaeology of Islam

Timothy Insoll

BLACKWELL
Publishers

…ied as author of this work has been asserted in
…and Patents Act 1988.

Oxford OX4 IJF
UK

Blackwell Publishers Inc.
350 Main Street
Malden, Massachusetts 02148
USA

British Library Cataloguing in Publication Data
A CIP catalogue record for this book is available from the British Library.

Library of Congress Cataloging-in-Publication Data
Insoll, Timothy.
    The archaeology of Islam/Timothy Insoll.
        p.   cm. — (Social archaeology)
        Includes bibliographical references (p.   ) and index.
        ISBN 0–631–20114–9 (hc.). — ISBN 0–631–20115–7 (pbk.)
        1. Civilization, Islamic.   2. Social archaeology—Islamic
    countries.   3. Material culture—Islamic countries.   4. Muslims—
    Social life and customs.   I. Title.   II. Series.
    DS36.855.I47   1999
    909′.097671—dc21   98–26727
                                                                                  CIP

Typeset in Stemple Garamond on 10.5/12 pt
by Pure Tech India Ltd, Pondicherry, http://www.puretech.com

Printed in Great Britain by TJ International Limited, Padstow, Cornwall

This book is printed on acid-free paper

This book is dedicated to Rachel

Contents

Figures

Plates

Acknowledgements

Various people have helped directly or indirectly in many ways to bring this volume to fruition, and I would like to take this opportunity to thank them. Particular thanks are due to Henri Medard for providing such a convivial environment for the initial idea to take shape in his flat in Paris; to the series editor, Ian Hodder, for his encouragement and faith in the project; to the six original anonymous reviewers for making this volume more cohesive; and to Rachel Maclean, Faraj el-Rashedy, David Edwards, John Alexander, Jo Brück, Ian Hodder, Helen Watson, and Andrew Petersen for reading and commenting on all or parts of the text. Louise Martin and Kevin Rielly provided much valuable information on faunal analysis; Venetia Porter (Department of Oriental Antiquities, British Museum) provided references on seals; and Talib Ali, then a student at St John's College, very kindly made possible my visits to the Cambridge mosque and introduced me to members of the Muslim community there, while the Manager of Cambridge Crematorium and Cemeteries kindly allowed me to see the plan of Newmarket Road Cemetery. Dr Abdullah al-Sharekh and the Reverend Steven Shakespear discussed various issues with me in the early stages of my research.

I have also benefited from discussions with Harry Norris, Paulo Farias, Robin Coningham and Jo Brück. For hospitality and assistance during various visits made while undertaking this research, I would like to thank: in Gibraltar and Spain, Clive and Geraldine Finlayson; in India, Vicky Singh; in Eritrea, Yassin Adem, Drs Yoseph Libsekal, Chris Hillman and Charles Spence; in Turkey, Dr Rachel Maclean; in Mali, Nafogo Coulibaly, Dr Téréba Togola, Massa Diarra, Jo Lee, Elmoctar Toure, Dr Klena Sanogo and Dr Mamadi Dembele. If I have neglected anyone who has helped, I apologize.

I am also grateful to St John's College, Cambridge, for funding various research visits, and to Nick Hollaway, and Abigail and Pamela Insoll for preparing the illustrations.

Every effort has been made to trace copyright holders. The author and publisher would like to apologize in advance for any inadvertent use of copyright material, and thank the following individuals and organizations who have kindly given their permission to reproduce copyright material.

For figures: 1.2 (Simplified chronology), courtesy of the Trustees of the British Museum. 2.2 (Types of mosque), courtesy of Martin Frishman and Thames and Hudson. 3.3 (San'a tower house), courtesy of the Centre of Middle Eastern Studies, University of Cambridge. 3.4 (Afghan structural evolution), courtesy of Garland Publishing, New York. 3.5 (Berber house), courtesy of Professor Pierre Bourdieu. 5.1 (forms of *Basmala*), courtesy of Professor Annemarie Schimmel and E. J. Brill Publishers, Leiden. 6.2 (Cambridge cemetery), courtesy of the cemeteries manager, Cambridge City Council. 7.2 (Round City), courtesy of Wayne State University Press, Detroit.

For plates: 2.1 (Almeria mosque), courtesy of Dr Peter Mitchell, Pitt-Rivers Museum, Oxford. 3.2 (Kazakh family) and 6.4 (Borneo cemetery), courtesy of the Cambridge University Museum of Archaeology and Anthropology. 4.2 (women cooking), courtesy of Dr Rachel Maclean. 4.4 and 4.5 (Qasr Ibrim objects), courtesy of the Egypt Exploration Society. 4.6 (war scene) and 7.2 (bathing scene) by permission of the Master and Fellows of St John's College, Cambridge. 5.1 (tombstone, Eritrea), courtesy of Dr Charles Spence. 5.2 (salt caravan), courtesy of Mrs Anna Bennett. 6.2 (*qubbas*), courtesy of the Library, Institute of Archaeology, University College, London.

Note on sources, orthography, pronunciation and dating It should be noted that the translation of the Qur'an used throughout this volume is that by Dawood (1993), while the spelling of Arabic words in English, italicization and capitalization largely follow Waines (1995). Likewise, for simplicity's sake, and following Lindholm (1996), no attempt has been made to include diacritical marks which would give the proper pronunciation of the Arabic words, except in a few instances. Readers are referred to Arabic–English dictionaries for correct orthography. The CE (Common Era), BCE (Before Common Era) dating system has been adopted, and all dates are CE unless otherwise specified.

1

Introduction

Have they not heard the histories of those who have gone before them?
The fate of Noah's people and of Thamud and Ad; of Abraham's
people and the people of Midian and the Ruined Cities.

Qur'an. Repentance 9: 70

Aims and Objectives

This volume takes as its starting premiss that the study of the material
remains left by adherents of the Islamic faith across many regions of
the world deserves to be better known by all those interested in the
past. It also accepts that Islam, the religion, exists as a definable,
cross-culturally applicable entity: a set of religious beliefs which
have been adapted and interpreted across the world depending on
cultural context. In other words, we can see Islam as a uniform
superstructure composed of the fundamentals of belief, with a diverse
substructure of practices, cultures and their material manifestations
below. Thus, the presence of a Muslim community should be recognizable in the archaeological record, for being a Muslim should generate certain types of material culture, specific to the faith, and
reflecting its doctrines and its requirements of the believer. This, in
turn, means that categories of archaeological evidence can exist, from
the Atlantic to Central Asia, which could indicate the presence of a
Muslim community. Yet how these categories are manifest will be
extremely diverse. This notion will be explored with reference to
how Muslim life is structured by the Qur'an (to Muslims, the Word
of God revealed to the Prophet Muhammad through the Angel
Gabriel), *hadith* (sayings and actions of the Prophet Muhammad as

remembered and recorded by his companions) and *shari'ah* (Islamic law): namely, is the ideal reflected in practical reality?

The oft-quoted maxim, usually from a secular Western viewpoint, that, 'Islam is more than just a religion but a way of life' has fundamental implications for archaeology, implying religious influence beyond the frequently considered domains of places of worship and treatment of the dead. This notion will be considered with specific reference to a wide range of material (much of which is frequently ignored). This includes the religious environment (the mosque); the physical environment (cities and other settlement types); the domestic environment (in all its many forms); death and burial; art, design, manufacturing and trade; and other aspects of Muslim life which are often neglected, including diet, pilgrimage, warfare and magic. As well as examining the issue of whether Islam can be seen to exert an influence on all areas of life as represented by material culture, attention will be paid to evaluating the evidence and its archaeological recognition from a practical perspective, thus demonstrating that Muslim communities are recognizable archaeologically. Yet it is not the objective of this volume to generate an essentialist image of Islam, Muslims and their material culture. Broad categories are considered, numerous exceptions exist and have existed, the pre-Islamic heritage is often considerable and great diversity is manifest.

The second aim of this study is to illustrate the richness and diversity of Islamic material culture through a series of case studies, but without recourse to providing typologies of monument forms, pottery types and so on, topics which have often been approached elsewhere. Our concern will be to place Islamic material culture within its social context, and the emphasis will be upon interpretation and the importance of studies of material culture as a way of furthering our understanding of Muslim societies in the past. To achieve this, we need to be selective and adopt a multi-disciplinary approach. In this respect, Islamic archaeologists are in a privileged position: a wealth of anthropological, historical and sociological evidence is available in addition to the archaeology; all can help in developing hypotheses and aiding interpretations. A further, and fundamental, advantage enjoyed by the archaeologist of Islam is the fact that Islam is a living religion and, although great changes are affecting contemporary Muslim material culture, the core doctrines have altered little since the first century of Islam, facilitating our understanding of the tenets of the religion. All this can help us to breathe life into the subject.

Finally, while many readers will know something of Islam, I hope that those with a greater knowledge of the religion and its history will excuse the stating of facts that are basic to the discussion. In many ways this volume has to assume a variety of identities: part textbook, part review and part theoretical study. It is also necessary to consider the present state of our knowledge, and the perspectives that I bring to the study.

Islamic Archaeology: a Brief Critique

Various criticisms can be made of Islamic archaeology as it presently exists, which impinge upon its position as an essential component of the discipline of archaeology. First, there has been an element of separation between the study of Islamic archaeology and other areas of archaeology through the simple fact that Islamic archaeologists have tended, perhaps not surprisingly, to be based within specialist departments, something which has both advantages and disadvantages. Scholars well versed in Arabic and other relevant languages are grouped together, and much admirable and often very specialized research is produced, but such departments can be seen as rather limited and there is an element of academic pigeonholing, with 'Islamic' and other 'exotic' archaeological studies placed away from the received mainstream and thus made to appear remote, inaccessible and different.

This separation of Islamic and other branches of archaeology is unfortunate as a closer working relationship would benefit all in a variety of ways:

- by reaching a larger community than those who consciously choose to study what is often perceived as the 'exotic';
- by realizing that the archaeology of such an influential religion is of great import and significance;
- by creating in European and American contexts an atmosphere of mutual understanding through learning from each other and drawing upon each other's experiences.

Thus improved methodologies could be developed for the study of all religions and for archaeology in general. Furthermore, it would help in appreciating that much of the past has been shared, rather than divided up into polarized insular, continental or regional blocks. Such closer working relationships might also assist in reducing criticism that a tradition of occidental scholarship within the 'orientalist' vein continues (Said 1978): a well-documented creation of Western historiography, evoking stereotypical images of Islam, for example in stressing decadence, luxury, the harem and bizarre sexual practices, and creating an exotic 'other' set in opposition to a superior Western world. Similarly, an isolated scholarly tradition does little to refute an alternative and increasingly common Western view of Islam, assisted by the media, as a religion of intolerance, restriction, radicalism and, stereotypically, associated with terrorism and Kalashnikov rifles.

Criticism can also be levelled at the way in which Islamic archaeology has developed. First, many studies have been inclined to concentrate upon one aspect of material culture (architecture, art and so on) or to be very site or regionally specific, without considering the wider context, even though the necessary data might be available for such a study to proceed. Where larger studies have been undertaken, frequently no attempt is made to integrate other forms of evidence, anthropological, historical or sociological. A multi-disciplinary approach is largely lacking, leading to a one-dimensional emphasis in research. Much new information about Islamic societies can be gained through the study of the archaeological record, but, unfortunately, excavation reports, the bedrock of research, often lack interpretation, their appeal is limited and hence are little used by the non-archaeologist. This further impedes the development of an Islamic archaeology which is multi-disciplinary in outlook, by restricting theoretical debate, a required starting-point. Secondly, the process of self-examination which has been undertaken in other fields of archaeology has largely passed Islamic archaeology by. Islamic archaeology has tended to fall behind those fields of archaeology where advances have been made in theoretical studies and in what is best termed 'social archaeology'.

However, these are not problems unique to Islamic archaeology. Medieval European archaeology, chosen as it is broadly comparable chronologically, has suffered, or in certain cases continues to suffer, from similar problems of theoretical and practical isolation, as well as a perceived inferiority of archaeological evidence to the written word (Champion 1990). The main difference, however, lies in the fact that medieval archaeology has carried out, over the past twenty years or so, a profitable process of self-examination (Hinton 1983; Austin and Alcock 1990; Austin and Thomas 1990). Methodologically sound, and interesting, archaeological research is now being conducted.

Other kinds of Islamic studies have gone through the process of re-examination and have progressed in theoretical leaps and bounds; for example, Islamic anthropology (see the classic studies of Geertz 1968; Gellner 1981; Gilsenan 1982) and socio-historical studies (Eickelman and Piscatori 1990). Although not everything put forward might be accepted, new ways of examining and describing Islamic societies are proposed. Indeed, within this vein of self-examination by related fields of Islamic studies, a recent paper looking into the use of material culture studies from a historian's perspective (Keddie 1992) has isolated the frequent absence of a multi- or inter-disciplinary approach. Archaeologists often ignore other available sources of evidence, and in a similar way the historian ignores material culture.

Further problems can be isolated. Whereas European medieval archaeology has been shown to be subservient to history, primarily textual, Islamic archaeology could in many cases be said to be subservient to art history. This point was indeed raised by Grabar (1971) over twenty-five years ago in one of the few evaluations of Islamic archaeology as a discipline that have been undertaken. But, unfortunately, this admirable sentiment was undermined by his statement that Islamic archaeology should have as its objectives: providing the exact features of standing monuments and the chronological and spatial setting of objects, with archaeology as 'an indispensable tool for the authentication, the dating, the localisation and explanation of works of art' (1971: 198). To be fair, this statement was somewhat tempered in a later, more substantial, review of both Islamic art and archaeology (Grabar 1976), but the emphasis on Islamic archaeology as involving cataloguing, classifying, collecting and recording, at the expense of interpretation and theory-building, still persists in this later paper and is accounted for by the fact that, among other reasons, 'the humanist fears committing himself intellectually until he is sure of himself, he fears hypotheses, mental gambles, and discussions' (1976: 260). This position is not adopted here – where hypotheses will be advanced and various 'mental gambles' taken in the following pages – and is, indeed, at odds with the examples of Grabar's elegant and 'socially aware' work which will be drawn upon in the following chapters.

Whole categories of archaeological evidence have been neglected owing to dated research designs and methods tied to the dictates of art history. For example, excavated material has contributed to our understanding of the formation and development of Islamic art, but we know very little about what was eaten in the Islamic world. The analysis of botanical remains and faunal assemblages from Islamic sites is under-developed, compared to the study of high-quality pottery, whereas the cruder everyday pottery is similarly neglected. Economic, demographic, landscape and environmental archaeology are all under-developed or under-utilized in Islamic archaeology. Neglecting such evidence inevitably limits our understanding of Islamic civilizations by reducing the possibilities of interpretation and

biasing the picture we present. Unfortunately, much Islamic archaeology is still not being done to accepted modern standards.

Emphasis within Islamic archaeology is still upon major monuments – the great mosques, palaces and so on – and the upper
echelons of society to the detriment of research into the bulk of the
population, the sedentary agriculturalist, the nomad and the lower
classes of city-dwellers. What is best termed a 'top-heavy' Islamic
archaeology has largely been the result, whereby our picture is
skewed in favour of palace-dwellers and consumers of prestige
items such as lustre pottery, rock crystal and ivory; whole strata of
society are absent or rarely represented. It is what Austin terms, in
the context of European medieval archaeology, the history of 'great
events' and 'great men' (1990: 10), and this is a great shame because,
as Keddie (1992: 34) notes, material culture is ideally suited to 'making the silent masses speak'. This preoccupation with courtly and
prestige production is further emphasized in the Islamic galleries of
most major museums where the exhibits, a fair proportion of them
provided by archaeology, rarely represent the everyday life and death
of most people. It is not true to say that this emphasis on the grander
objects draws the crowds and thus creates interest in the Islamic past
for in many cases it is the material culture residue of the ordinary and
the everyday with which people most identify. This aspect of the
recent Islamic past is sometimes found in the ethnography galleries,
even if obviously archaeological in origin.

The relative youth of Islamic archaeology is no excuse for the
existence of theoretically and methodologically old-fashioned techniques for, as already noted, comparable fields of archaeology have re-
evaluated themselves quite successfully. For Islamic archaeology to
avoid being marginalized and neglected it needs to adopt a higher
profile. The superposition of Islamic archaeological deposits with
other more 'fashionable' earlier ones is a case in point: archaeologists
frequently either wholly neglect or half-heartedly record Islamic
levels, in a rush to get at those beneath, the true aim of their investigations. Examining the theoretical and practical role of Islamic
archaeology is a necessary step in developing a more modern
approach to the archaeology of Islam, one concerned with all aspects
of the Muslim world and society.

But why is this of importance? To end this section on a positive
note, a modern approach is indeed being achieved by some Islamic
archaeologists, and there is absolutely no reason why Islamic
archaeology cannot make a contribution to, or fully enter, the mainstream of archaeological theory and practice. It is not through necessity a specialist backwater, but an area of study where exciting

possibilities for research are offered into the material culture remains left behind by a major, living, world religion, whose material culture, past and present, covers much of the globe.

The Role of the Scholar: Archaeology and Religion

Undertaking such a study also raises the issue of the qualifications of the researcher in observing and writing about Islam. The issues surrounding Western viewpoints and scholarship on Islam have been much analysed and debated (Said 1978; Hourani 1991). In essence, does one need to be a Muslim to study Islamic archaeology? It will be argued here that this is not the case (interestingly, support for this was offered by all my Muslim colleagues and friends who were consulted on the issue). Similarly, one need not be a Jew to study Jewish archaeology or a Christian to study Christian archaeology, though some would insist on just such a prerequisite. A more equitable perspective, as was proposed earlier, is that we should envisage the past as something common to us all, rather than attempting to appropriate great spatial, cultural or chronological blocks as somehow belonging to this or that group, with only members or adherents of the group being able to study it.

However, the charge can be levelled that something may be lost in interpretation through not being an adherent of the faith or belief system studied; one cannot see the complete whole through being detached from it. Conversely, something could also be lost by being an adherent of the faith or belief system under study, by making it more difficult to question established doctrines; in this way, the question of faith enters the equation. Essentially, there is no simple answer to this charge, and the issues of scientific rationality as opposed to belief are discussed in greater detail below. But it is certainly wise to proceed with sensitivity when dealing with extant beliefs, and to acknowledge that one is after all only an observer, albeit in a privileged position observing a living religion and ongoing processes.

The second major factor affecting the role of the scholar is how deeply he or she should be immersed in the area of archaeology which he or she is studying? Here, I should confess that I am not from an orientalist background, but from a general archaeological one. However, I envisaged that the present study would emphasize the advantages offered by exploiting archaeological evidence and be a contribution to the growing interest in the general archaeology of religion. In this context, I should admit that there are scholars who are better versed in many individual aspects of the subject – art history, architecture and languages. Nor do I claim that the book is all-encompassing and all-knowing; on the contrary, the shortcomings of this study seem all too apparent. However, I will consider the work to have succeeded if it generates some debate on the current aims, methodology and future of Islamic archaeology, and if it illustrates the unity, and at the same time diversity, encompassed in the terms 'Islamic archaeology' and Muslim, and demonstrates how powerfully, and socially constituted, material culture can be.

Thirdly, I hope that the relevance of this study might be felt by illustrating how, in the case of Islam, all facets of life can be structured by religion, and thus to separate out the religious element as something confined to a specific part or element of an individual's life is wrong. This could equally apply to Christianity, Hinduism, Buddhism, any major religion, besides Islam. To be a believer, to state 'I am a Muslim' or 'I am a Christian', should entail a life structured by particular spiritual codes, beliefs and outlook. Archaeologists have too often appeared to forget this, and while perhaps acknowledging that the individuals who made up the past communities under study were religious – represented, say, by a mosque, synagogue or church – see the other spheres of people's lives as segregated out, and controlled by other preoccupations, and accordingly study these as something separate.

But it is also correct to say that the archaeological study of religion in general is a complex affair, and for this reason is often avoided as a taboo subject, or hidden under the all-encompassing and difficult-to-define term 'ritual' (Renfrew 1994). It has been acknowledged that the archaeological study of religion lags behind other specialized fields, both theoretically and practically (Garwood et al. 1991: v). Elements of religion, sacred structures or burials are examined, but the bigger picture is often avoided, other than providing a historical overview (an interesting exception within the context of Islam is provided by Alexander's 1979 comparative study, and in general terms by Carmichael et al's. 1994 volume). This reticence is more understandable when it comes to considering the study of prehistoric religions (a notable exception is provided by the *Journal of Prehistoric Religion*), restricted as prehistorians are by the nature of their evidence, but it is less easy to understand when world religions or historically documented cult or ritual practices are under consideration archaeologically. Here the impact of religion upon all aspects of the archaeological record could be investigated in the pursuit of a more complete understanding of the role and impact of religion in different contexts.

A final point which must be considered is the validity of sacred texts and religious law as a guide to interpretation. In studying Islam, can the Qur'an, *hadith* and *shari'ah*, for example, be taken as a form of interpretative manual for the structuring of Muslim life in the past? The answer is yes, they act as a guide to all aspects of life, and a Muslim life should be structured by them. But we are dealing with individuals, and individuals are often selective; they make their own choices about their religious beliefs, and accept varying interpretations within the overall structure of the system of belief. Issues of non-observance must, of course, be considered. But in other ways the Qur'an and *hadith* do provide precise insights into why people do what they do, and thus why this or that might be found in the archaeological record. As such they should obviously not be dismissed as having no value as guides to everyday life, past and present.

To repeat, we can and indeed should, where possible, examine past life as a coherent whole, of which, within the framework of a major world religion such as Islam, all aspects of life can be structured by religion and can be approached and reconstructed by the archaeologist. That society and religion are inextricably linked, and that religion can serve as a means of perpetuating the structure of society, its norms and requirements, has long been recognized by anthropologists (see, for example, Geertz 1966). Within sections of the secular society which exists in contemporary Western Europe and North America this point could easily be forgotten: religion frequently holds little or no sway over many. Where it does exist, and this point will be referred to again later, it is often compartmentalized (Hubert 1994: 12), either physically or conceptually, as something placed within an allotted timespan, an hour in church on a Sunday, or the synagogue on a Friday perhaps. Religion as a guiding force in all aspects of life has been forgotten, and subsequently Western archaeologists, influenced by the prevailing social climate no matter how much they like to think of themselves as neutral observers, have likewise reflected this absence of an overall spiritual structure within their interpretations.

Islam and Islams

While acknowledging the overall existence of Islam as a structuring code to material culture, one stumbling block which has been encountered needs to be explained. This is the very existence of the notion of 'Islam' as compared to 'Islams'; in other words, the degree to which regional traditions, schools, sects and different nationalities within Islam and the Muslim world destroy, or at least encroach upon, the idea of the cohesive whole, the ideal Muslim, from the Atlantic coast of Morocco to Indonesia – diversity which might be reflected in the archaeological record.

The existence of regional traditions is in certain ways contrary to the notion of *ummah*, the world-wide Islamic community. In the course of conducting the research for this book, I was often told by various Muslim informants that, for arguments sake, a mosque congregation in London is not composed of different nationalities but is one community. This creates a contradiction as it is plainly apparent that our hypothetical mosque congregation is composed of different nationalities, from diverse cultural backgrounds. Yet at the same time these informants were wholly correct in arguing for the existence of the world-wide Muslim community, extending beyond and superseding national and cultural boundaries, the ideal Islamic community, which it is argued here is recognizable, in part, in the archaeological record. Perhaps by bemoaning the disappearance of regional 'material cultures', we are serving our own desires for a diverse and exotic tableau of Islam when, in fact, the creation of the single Islamic community is the ideal of most Muslims.

Antagonisms between universality and regionalism have been examined by various scholars. Eickelman and Piscatori (1990: xiii), for example, stress that 'universality competes with local communities and dogma with actualities', and that there is inherent danger in generating an essentialist view of Islam or of being Muslim, when it is difficult to predict the practice and significance of Islamic faith in any given historical setting from the first principles of dogma or belief (1990: xxii, 18). Similarly, Hourani (1991: 51) reviews these issues with regard to anthropology and how relevant the term 'Islamic society' actually is as a cross-cultural descriptive device, while Gellner has emphasized that it is simplistic to take 'Islam at face value' and naïve to think that 'because Muslim life is the implementation of one book and its prescriptions, therefore Muslim civilisation is homogeneous' (1981: 99). Although these important arguments have inevitably been simplified here, within the context of this study it is stressed that there is, of course, a departure point between ideals and realities, and in no way is Islam a bland uniformity across the whole of the Muslim world. Heterodoxy exists, as attested by the importance of Sufism in many areas, and by the existence of the two dominant creeds of Sunni and Shi'ah Islam (see below).

However, there also exists an underlying uniformity; otherwise the notion of the existence of a series of Islams, rather than a universal Islam, implies that the whole idea of a system of belief falls down, which is patently in opposition to the beliefs of the majority of

Muslims, Sunni or Shi'ah. This raises the question 'where then does one cease to be a Muslim?' Where do you draw the line about what is acceptable if you adapt your own Islam to just how you like it? It appears to be nonsense to chip away at the existence of a single Islam in favour of various regional Islams when one considers the essential input of faith in a universal belief system, compared with the observational rationality of usually Western social scientists. Furthermore, Gellner continues, from the point quoted above, that 'for all the indisputable diversity, the remarkable thing is the extent to which Muslim societies resemble each other' (1981: 99). The obvious existence of an Islam, even if only reduced to an acceptance of basic tenets, and thus of a Muslim, is further reinforced in my view by observational data collected away from the popularly perceived heartlands of Islam. In sub-Saharan Africa, for example, though great local adaptation of Islam has taken place, Muslims are immediately recognizable as Muslims, both today and in the past (Insoll 1996a,b,c). The point has been well made by Akbar Ahmed (1988: 25):

> the ideal would be recognisable in spite of differences of society, economy, social structure and organisation throughout the world, even outside the mainstream and established Muslim heartlands. It would be recognisable in the tropical jungles of Africa, in the steppes of Central Asia and in the humid forests of the Far East. Over 1300 years later it is recognisable in Muslim communities whether in Chicago, London, Cairo or Tokyo.

This is precisely what I argue for here, the existence of one Islam, rather than a series of disparate regional traditions, which lends itself to archaeological investigation. Yet within this whole there exists diversity, represented by different ways of life – nomad and sedentary, town- and country-dweller – ethnic, cultural and geographical factors, elements of non-observance, and varying interpretations and creeds. The notion of a 'flexible Islam in thought and practice', which is suggested by Eickelman and Piscatori (1990: xiv), is accepted here, and an attempt will be made in the following pages to show that assimilation between the superstructure Islam, its beliefs and practices, and local variety is possible, and indeed usual. For example, the existence of a Christian community would probably entail building a place of worship, a church or chapel, but within the categories of structure encompassed by the terms 'church' or 'chapel' huge variety exists, as it does equally within the category 'mosques' (see chapter 2). Archaeological investigation is well suited to shedding light both on local issues and on the larger questions, social organization, technology, urbanism and, of course, religion, across cultural and temporal scales.

Annales Theory and Archaeological Practicalities

A possible way of reconciling the problem of investigating universality and regionalism within the archaeology of Islam is provided by the approach of the *Annales* School of history as outlined by Fernand Braudel (1972). Here time is conceptualized as operating at a variety of levels, long, medium and short term, represented by '*la longue durée*', long-term forces, worldviews or ideologies, '*conjonctures*', medium-term structures operating over several centuries, and '*evenements*', short-term events, the 'fireflies' of time (Braudel 1972: 901; Bintliff 1991: 6–7). A theoretical approach such as that of the *Annales* School is not directly transferable to investigating this issue, but rather a 'mix and match' position can be taken, using elements of various models and ways of approaching the data in an attempt to breathe life into the archaeology of Islam. Yet the general notion of long- and short-term time scales as defined by the *Annales* approach ideally suits what we are attempting to explore here. Namely, the *longue durée* as the central tenets of Islam, structuring behaviour and remaining essentially unchanging, with regional traditions and events as the medium- and short-term cycles. This may seem an oversimplification, yet, as Sherratt (1992: 140) points out, 'while Braudel may be unsophisticated from the point of view of the fact-saturated modern historian or the philosophical subtleties of metahistory, his example may still inspire those with *bigger and cruder problems*' (my emphasis). In many ways, such a paradigm, alloyed with a none-too dogmatic position, allows the subject to be examined from a non 'culture-historic' perspective.

Three examples can be provided to illustrate how a framework involving *la longue durée* and the medium/short term can be applied to an examination of the archaeology of Islam. First, Muslim diet. Dietary rules exist, but there is no such thing as a Muslim cuisine. Food and drink are subject to fashions and regional traditions, but the underlying structure remains the same; for example, certain foods and alcohol should be avoided because of religious imperatives. Secondly, in dress and domestic architecture there is an emphasis upon privacy and modesty, but how this is obeyed is subject to myriad ways of expression without losing the core underlying prerequisites structured by religious doctrine and resulting social codes. Thirdly, the mosque usually contains a number of essential features, with primary among them the *mihrab* or prayer niche oriented to Mecca and indicating the direction of prayer (alongside a *minbar* [pulpit] in a congregational mosque, and usually a minaret of some sort for the call to prayer), yet the style of the mosque and its component parts – decoration, architecture, configuration – can vary greatly without losing the fundamental elements. *La longue durée* is represented by the Islamic structuring codes, immutable elements of Muslim faith; the *conjonctures* and *evenements*, either medium or short term, are represented by fashions, interpretations and regionalism (though this can exist over the long term, it is still set apart from the essentials), which create the diversity apparent within the overall entity.

Geographical, Temporal and Material Ranges

Having considered the reasoning behind this volume, it is necessary to define the limits of the material under discussion, for this study will of necessity range over a large geographical area. First, we must ask what exactly is meant by the Muslim world? This is difficult to define: as Grabar (1971) has noted, its extent has varied over time, fluctuating in size following successes and failures (the example of the creation and loss of Al-Andalus or Islamic Spain is a case in point). There was, and is, no unchanging entity (see figure 1.1). The spread or contraction of Islam has not been a uniform process, a perceived series of 'pulses' or 'waves' from a central place (though the early conquests sometimes appear to resemble this). The geographical borders of the Muslim world changed over time often leaving material culture remains for the archaeologist to decipher. Geographical blocks such as Christendom, and the Hindu, Jewish, Muslim and Buddhist worlds are tenuous entities, if really definable as such at all. They intermingle and mix, and have 'fuzzy' borders, with Islam, like the other great religions, drawing upon the material and even spiritual legacy of other religions and civilizations with which it came into contact over the centuries.

Fortunately, this volume is not concerned with charting changes in either the geography or history of the Muslim world, something which has been done on many occasions elsewhere (see, for example, Gibb et al. 1960; Lapidus 1988). Rather, the predominant concern with the theoretical implications that being a Muslim has for material culture means that examples can and will be drawn from wherever a Muslim community is found. This ranges from regions of the Muslim world as usually defined, from Morocco in the west to Indonesia in the east and from Central Asia to Central Africa, but also from regions not usually considered to be Islamic, including Britain and North America. However, their inclusion can be justified as there are

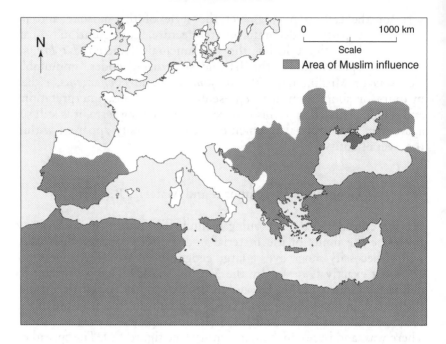

Figure 1.1 Map of approximate extent of former or currently Muslim-dominated areas in Europe (after Lapidus 1988: 243)

now substantial Muslim minorities within these regions, and to neglect the implications of their presence for the material culture record of the future would be wrong, as it is equally wrong to neglect that of religious minorities in Islamic regions.

In this context it should be noted that the term 'Muslim' rather than 'Islamic' will frequently be used as a descriptive device because it seems more flexible, admits diversity, recognizes the input of faith and, equally importantly, allows for the individual. 'Islamic' by contrast, certainly with regard to concepts such as the 'Islamic world', seems that much more impersonal and as if everything is dictated by religious doctrine alone, with individual choice removed, which is patently not the case.

Within the Muslim world, as has already been noted, both unity and diversity are found. Bearing this point in mind, we should avoid creating a distinction between the perceived 'pure' Arab heartlands of Islam (Arabia and the early conquered regions of western Asia and North Africa) and the 'impure' periphery (sub-Saharan Africa, South-east Asia). Great regional variation exists, but that does not necessarily mean that the Muslim living in Mecca is a better one than his or her co-religionist in Dar es Salaam. Both are members of the Muslim community. In this regard, general catch-all models such as those invoking a single centre and a vast periphery are inapplicable as an explanatory device when applied to the diverse phenomena present in a world religion such as Islam, incorporating many cultures and lifestyles. These include the Maghrib, land of the marabout or holyman and saint's tomb *par excellence*; Shi'ah Iran; Turkey with its Ottoman and Central Asian heritage; sub-Saharan Africa, where syncretism between traditional animist religion and Islam is often evident; the culturally diverse Indian subcontinent and Southeast Asia; Arabia and the Near East, the original lands of Islam; China, Afghanistan and Central Asia, home of numerous ethnic groups and lifestyles, Sinicized coastal Hui, descendants of Arab conquerors, nomadic and semi-nomadic Turkomen, Uzbeks and others, sedentary town and oasis dwellers; and the European frontiers of Islam, past and present, Spain, Sicily, the Balkans and the Caucasus. This is a vast area, with further diversity represented by the various schools of law, creeds and sects which have developed within Islam.

Although it is possible to define categories of material culture within the 'archaeology of Islam', their contents will vary both through time and space. The essential doctrines of Islam might have been largely established in the seventh century CE, and detailed ritual practices developed between the seventh and ninth centuries CE, but Islam itself is not a fossilized entity; Islamic material culture in all its forms was not fixed at that time. It has changed and evolved over the course of the centuries, with reference to custom and requirements. Perhaps one of the most significant periods of change is occurring at the present, and it would be wrong to regard contemporary developments as aberrations; rather, they are the continuation of the development process. A contemporary mosque in Bradford has as much relevance within the sphere of Islamic material culture as does the Dome of the Rock in Jerusalem. Although in many ways we are concerned with the ideal, the ideal Islamic city, house, burial and so on, this is not meant to infer that material culture is in any way static. Material culture is, of course, socially constituted and reflects the evolutionary process. Hence, where applicable, archaeological and other examples are also drawn from a wide time period, encompassing the origins of Islam in the early seventh century through to the developments of the late twentieth century.

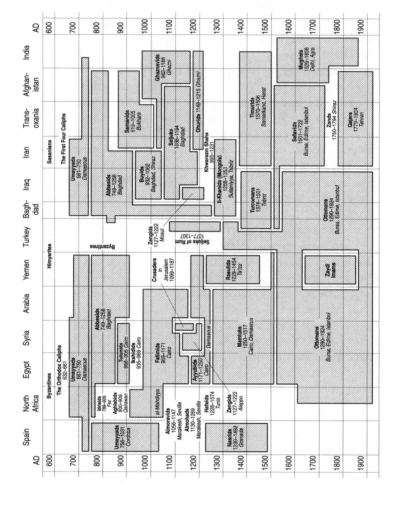

Figure 1.2 The Islamic world AD 600–1924: a simplified chronology showing the major dynasties (courtesy of the Trustees of the British Museum)

Islam: Origins, Requirements and Components

The origins and initial spread of Islam

The origins of Islam have been well studied and extensively discussed elsewhere (for example, Lapidus 1988: 21–36; Waines 1995: 7–32). Briefly summarized, Islam ('submission' to the will of God) originated in the Arabian peninsula when the Prophet Muhammad (born c.570 – died 632), an Arab trader from Mecca and the last and most important prophet (the 'Seal of the Prophets'), began to receive his first revelations from God, via the Angel Gabriel, in about 610. Muslim (those who have submitted) converts in these early years were few, but by 615 'Muhammad had become the leader of a community' (Lapidus 1988: 25). This nascent community was in Mecca, but conditions there were difficult, and in 622, having obtained a guarantee or pledge of safety, Muhammad and his followers moved to Medina in an event known as the *hijrah* or migration (year one of the Muslim calendar, 1 AH, *al-hijrah*). This event is of fundamental importance to Muslims (El-Rashedy 1997) as here the Muslim community (*ummah*) was formally established, and the *hijrah* is regarded as 'the transition from the pagan to the Muslim world – from kinship to a society based on common belief' (Lapidus 1988: 27). Conflict with the pagan Meccans continued until an armistice was signed in 628, and in 630 'the Muslim occupation of Mecca was complete' (Waines 1995: 20). In 632 the Prophet died in Medina, where he was buried.

The progress of Islam in the first century AH was swift. Muslim power in Arabia was rapidly consolidated, and under the Khalifahs or Rightly Guided Caliphs (successors to Muhammad) the Muslim armies spread into and conquered Palestine, Iraq, Syria, Egypt and large parts of Iran between 633 and 650. Under the subsequent Umayyad Caliphs, between 674 and 715, a Muslim Central Asian frontier zone was established with the conquest of Transoxania, and by the end of the first quarter of the eighth century, the conquest of the Maghrib (North Africa) and Al-Andalus (Islamic Spain) was complete. Further expansion was also made into southern Pakistan at the same time (Nicolle 1993: 3–5). Islam, the religion, accompanied the Muslim armies, and its social and religious codes and material culture were disseminated through conversion and conquest. Figure 1.2 gives an idea of the historical complexity of the events beyond these initial conquests (see also Gibb et al. 1960; Lapidus 1988).

The Qur'an and hadith

The Qur'an (literally, recitation or reading) is regarded by Muslims as the immutable Word of God revealed to the Prophet Muhammad via the Angel Gabriel in the form of verses, which are arranged in 114 chapters or *surah*. The precepts and principles of the Qur'an form the basis of the Islamic faith. Second only to the Qur'an as the source of *shari'ah* (Islamic law) are the *hadith* (traditions), the Prophet's sayings and doings, which were transmitted by either, or both, oral and written methods from their original source. Thus a *hadith* usually comprises the *matn*, 'or point it conveyed, and a chain of transmitters, (*isnad*)' (Waines 1995: 41), which enable verification. Six major collections of *hadith* are recognized by almost all Muslims as genuine, and are thus the most important. These were compiled by (in chronological order): al-Bukhari (died 870), ibn al-Hajjaj (died 875), ibn Maja (died 887), Abu Dawud (died 889), al-Tirmidhi (died 892) and al-Nasa'i (died 915). Together these form the *sunnah*, the Prophet's 'deeds, utterances and his unspoken approval' (Gibb and Kramers 1961: 552), thus comprising the way of the Prophet, which should form the example as to how to lead one's life for all Muslims. To quote Ahmed (1988: 24), 'across the world his followers would imitate the Prophet with affection in every kind of activity – abstaining from alcohol and pig's meat, colouring a man's beard with henna, using green for clothes and flags'. The Muslim ideal structured many aspects of life.

Shari'ah *and the Five Pillars*

The *shari'ah* is the law of Islam, which by its origins and nature is sacred in character, and which 'lays down an entire scheme of life whose aim is to make sure that good flourishes and evils do not destroy or harm human life' (Mawdudi 1986: 17). Besides the Qur'an and *hadith*, the other two main roots of the law are analogy through reasoning, *ijtihad*, and consensus or *ijma*. The essential principles of the Islamic faith as contained in the Qur'an and *shari'ah* are the Five Pillars of Islam, which are the requirements for believers. The first is the credo or *shahadah*, 'There is no god but God and Muhammad is the Prophet of God', which is the expression of absolute monotheism. The second is ritual prayer five times a day in the direction of Mecca (*salat*). The third is the fast (*sawm*) in the tenth month of the lunar year, Ramadan. The fourth is *zakat* (alms), giving between 2.5 and 10 per cent of one's wealth to the needy. The fifth is *hajj*, pilgrimage to Mecca at least once in one's life.

In fact, as will be discussed in greater detail later on, the Five Pillars lend themselves to archaeological recognition and are key criteria to the archaeological recognition of a Muslim community. The *shahadah* can be represented in inscriptions in many different media (chapter 5); *salat* by the mosque and other places of prayer (chapter 2); *zakat* by inscriptions and the system of *waqf* (endowments) of buildings, including hospitals, mosques and religious schools, by pious and wealthy individuals (chapter 4); *hajj* by pilgrims' hostels, routes, wells and milestones (chapter 4). It is only *sawm* which will be unlikely to be recognized archaeologically (chapter 4). Besides these fundamentals, many other aspects of life are codified in Islamic law, and guidelines provided to live according to Muslim ideals (see Schacht 1964), a life which draws no boundary between the sacred and the secular, and which has many archaeological manifestations.

The schools of law and the Sunni

Different approaches in interpreting the law led to the emergence of four legal schools (*madhabib*): the Hanafi, Maliki, Shafi'i and Hanbali, which are named after the scholar-jurists who founded them, and which were largely consolidated by the tenth century. All four legal schools are Sunni, meaning the adherents of *sunnah*, the way of the Prophet. Both the Shi'ah and the Kharijites (discussed below) developed their own laws, but these differ little from orthodox Sunni law, as both kept sufficiently close contact with the Sunni community in the eighth and ninth centuries, 'for them to take over Islamic law as it was being developed in the orthodox schools of law, making only such modifications as were required by their particular political and dogmatic tenets' (Schacht 1964: 16). For example, Shi'ah inheritance laws differ, and the institution of temporary marriage exists, which Sunnis do not allow (Momen 1985: 182). The four Sunni legal schools differ in how they interpret points of the law, which is the domain of learned men (*ulama*) and administered by the religious judges (*qadi*). But it should be noted that the existence of a class of learned and legal men does not equate with that of a priesthood, which does not exist in Islam. Even the Imam, here meaning the leader of congregational prayer, can be 'any respectable Muslim, sufficiently versed in the technique of *salat*' (Gibb and Kramers 1961: 165).

The majority of Muslims today are Sunni, probably as high as 90 per cent of the total Muslim community, and are found throughout the Muslim world. Which legal school is of importance varies according to geographical area (but they also often co-exist): predominantly Maliki in North and West Africa, Shafi'i in East Africa, South-east

Asia and southern Arabia, Hanafi in the areas formerly covered by the Mughal and Ottoman empires, and Hanbali in Saudi Arabia (Ahmed 1988: 48).

The Shi'ah

The other major Muslim grouping is the Shi'ah, historically associated with the Fatimids, and geographically associated today with Iran, but also found in the Gulf States, southern Iraq, India, Lebanon, East Africa and, more recently, in Europe and North America. Shi'ism has been defined as 'the general name for a large group of very different Muslim sects, the starting point of all of which is the recognition of Ali as the legitimate caliph after the death of the Prophet' (Gibb and Kramers 1961: 534). Thus from this it can be seen that the schism in the Muslim community which led to the development of Shi'ism occurred early in the history of Islam (the latter half of the seventh century), and developed primarily from politics, namely, conflicts over the nature of the caliphate between the family of Ali, the fourth caliph, son-in-law and cousin of the Prophet, and the Umayyad dynasty. Gibb and Kramers (1961: 534) again clarify this succinctly when they describe the split in the Muslim community as a consequence of the fact that 'Islam is a religious and a political phenomenon as its founder was a prophet and a statesman.' Thus how the relationship between political or secular and religious leadership was considered became of fundamental importance to the Shi'ah. Three paths are evident: the Sunni 'middle line', the Kharijite one of indifference to the caliphate, and that of the Shi'ah, with 'great religious value on the question of the Imamate'. Ali, who was martyred by his opponents, was viewed as the true Imam or caliph, and the martyr tradition in Shi'ism further increased in significance with the subsequent martyrdom of Hussein and Hassan, Ali's sons, who with the Prophet and Fatima, the Prophet's daughter and Ali's wife, form the five central figures to the Shi'ah, and the 'model family for all Shi'is to follow in their family interrelationships' (Momen 1985: 235).

But, essentially, Shi'ah doctrines differ little from Sunni. The Qur'an is central, the Five Pillars are the same, 'the Sunni ideal also holds for the Shi'ah' (Ahmed 1988: 57). However, it is in the position of the Imamate, or religious leadership, that the real difference lies. In the Shi'ite view, the caliphate became corrupted through the wrong succession. Ali was the first Imam designated by the Prophet, followed by a line of twelve or seven Imams depending on tradition. The majority 'Twelvers' believe 'that the Twelfth Imam (last seen in 873) was the *Mahdi* or "guided one" and is still alive, though hidden, waiting for God's instruction to appear and establish the kingdom of God on earth' (Bruce 1995: 82; see also Momen 1985). The 'Seveners' stop the line at the seventh Imam, Ismail; thus they are known as Isma'ilis. This obviously differs from Sunni beliefs, but in practice differences in rituals and customs are 'only marginally different to Sunni practice' (Ahmed 1988: 58), and have few material culture implications (exceptions, such as the Shi'ah focus on visits to martyrs' tombs and certain festivals such as Muharram, are discussed later).

Other Muslim groups and sects

Many other offshoots of Islam exist and, although all are of minority status, some are of greater significance than others. Primary among them are the Kharijites, who are in turn divided into a number of subgroups, the Nukkarites, Sufrites and Ibadites. The Kharijites have been described as espousing 'intransigent idealism' (Waines 1995: 106), and were democratic in outlook, believing that anyone could be elected head of the Muslim community, if they possessed the right qualifications. The Ibadi Kharijite group survives to this day in Oman, and in parts of North and East Africa. Elsewhere in the Muslim world numerous other Muslim sects exist or have existed (see, for example, Khuri 1990). More unorthodox than the Kharijites, and usually classed as non-Muslim by the majority of Muslims, both Sunni and Shi'ah, are the Druze of Syria, Palestine and Lebanon, a secretive religious sect broadly derived from Shi'ism and founded in the late tenth to early eleventh centuries. Of similar status and also found in the same geographical region (but extending into eastern Turkey) are the Alevi or Alawi, who emphasize the importance of Ali, and differ in many practices (lack of regular prayer and pilgrimage) from other Muslims. To these could be added the Qarmatians of the Persian Gulf and the Zaidis of Yemen, both offshoots of Shi'ism, and the Zikris of Baluchistan. This is by no means exhaustive but serves to show the diversity which exists within Islam, from a sliding scale of orthodoxy to heresy, depending upon the view of the observer.

Muslim Diversity: Mystics, Wahhabiyyah and Taliban

Three further and contrasting dimensions to Islamic religious and social practice are manifest by the Sufi tradition (mystical Islam) in all its divergent forms, and those represented by the Wahhabi Islamic

reform movement, and the Taliban. These examples have been chosen
not to exhaust all the possibilities of Muslim religious manifestation,
which they do not, but because they represent different points on the
scale of Muslim religious experience.

Sufism

Mystical Islam in various forms is one popular manifestation of
Muslim practice. Yet it should be noted that it is difficult to categorize too succinctly. The word Sufism is derived from '*suf*', Arabic for
wool, 'to denote the practice of wearing a woollen robe – hence the
act of devoting oneself to the mystic life' (Gibb and Kramers 1961:
579). Prior to the ninth–tenth centuries, the mystical tradition within
Islam was represented either by individuals who retreated from
worldly concerns or perhaps by a teacher and his circle of pupils.
After this, as Islam spread, more organized communities of mystics
began to form in lodges, with a religious master (*shaykh* or *pir*) at
their head, surrounded by a group of disciples. These *tariqah* (meaning path or way) took the form of brotherhoods or orders which were
usually male, and less commonly female, and followed sets of rules
which laid out behaviour, litanies and etiquette, the path to spiritual
understanding (Schimmel 1975). At the heart of Sufi teaching is the
'truth of the Divine Unity' (Nasr 1991: 3), and the spiritual 'path' for
the initiate is in a series of stages, whose number and sequence vary
between orders. Fundamental among Sufi rituals is the *dhikr*, 'the
repeated vocal invocation or silent remembrance of the name, Allah'
(Waines 1995: 140), and whose basic practice varies little between the
orthodox orders. Music, poetry and dance can also be used to attain
the ecstatic trance-like state which the *dhikr* can bring on. Numerous
tariqah have existed or continue to be found throughout the Muslim
world, most named after their founder. The *Shorter Encyclopaedia of
Islam* lists over 180, not including the branches within the main
fraternities (Gibb and Kramers 1961: 575–8; see also Trimingham
1971). However, all are united in their adherence to the mystical
path and in the similarity of their basic practice.

Saints

A second facet of Islamic mysticism is provided by the 'saint' or
'holyman' tradition, especially manifest in North Africa, though
saints' tombs are found in most regions of the Muslim world. The
cult of saints can perhaps be conceived of as more popularist in
outlook, and certainly less hierarchical and organized, than Sufism.

Gellner has proposed the terms 'religious orders and holy lineages' as a way of delimiting Sufis from holymen, but he correctly points out that their dividing line is indeterminate, as religious orders can be led by holy lineages, and holy lineages can become religious orders (1981: 160), a definition followed here. Around the tombs or houses of saints, settlements (in North Africa called *zawiyah*, and similar in certain respects to a Sufi lodge) often grow up, in which their descendants live. The intercession of the saint is sought by the populace for various things, with sacrifices or offerings made as a source of receiving *baraka* or blessings. But even this simplistic definition fails to cover the range of experiences and manifestations covered by the term. Even 'saint' is problematical, as Waines mentions (1995: 145): 'there can be no procedure for the canonisation of individuals since there is no authority to validate their sanctification.' Yet overcoming this handicap is straightforward by the simple expedient of remembering that Islamic mysticism covers a whole gamut of Muslim religious experience, alongside what Gellner describes as the *ulama*-led 'puritanical, unitarian, individualist' Islam (1981: 159).

Wahhabiyya

In direct contrast to mystical Islam is the Wahhabiyya Islamic reform movement. This Sunni movement, followers of the Hanbali legal school as interpreted by Ibn Taimal, was founded by Abd al-Wahhab in the late eighteenth century. Wahhabi written polemic has been described as 'almost entirely aimed at the cult of saints, as exhibited in the building of mausoleums, their employment as mosques, and their visitation' (Gibb and Kramers 1961: 618). The Wahhabis are thus obviously opposed to Sufi or holymen practices, and represent austere Islamic religious practice, attested in their simple mosques and tombs (see chapter 6). Geographically they are centred in Saudi Arabia, but their doctrines have spread to India and West Africa, a process partly facilitated by pilgrims returning home from *hajj* carrying their message. Thus, Wahhabi Islam represents another manifestation of Muslim religious practice and outlook.

Taliban

A third example of the variety of Islamic religious practice and interpretation is offered by the Taliban, of contemporary interest in the late 1990s as representative of 'fundamentalist' Islam. The Taliban, whose name is derived from '*talib*', as students from the Islamic *madrasahs* or religious schools in Pakistan, have recently taken control of large areas of Afghanistan, where they have proceeded to implement their own interpretation of *shari'ah*. Although the Taliban are currently condemned by both Muslims and non-Muslims, they are in fact continuing the age-old process of reinterpreting Islam, further illustrating the vibrancy of the religion. However, in the sum total of Muslim practice they are of little relevance outside a restricted geographical area.

Yet, it should also be noted that, with all the examples given, belief in the essential elements remains the same, the primacy of the Qur'an, the fundamental of belief. All are Muslims though they range through a spectrum, resembling perhaps, as a crude analogy, the diversity exhibited between a Presbyterian congregation in Scotland and a Catholic church in Italy, both classed as Christian. But, as will be shown in the following pages, the implications for diversity of material culture, though great, do not mean that common categories do not exist. All, for example, bury the dead according to Muslim rites – information which the archaeologist can utilize to examine the interplay between uniformity and diversity, ideals and reality.

The Individual and the 'Islamic Way of Life'

Having noted some of the major manifestations of group practice in Islam, it is also necessary to consider the implications of being Muslim for the individual. To quote Mawdudi (1986: 9), 'the chief characteristic of Islam is that it makes no distinction between the spiritual and the secular in life.' All aspects of life are governed by God's law, the *shari'ah*, and the 'Prophet organised all those who accepted his message into one community (*ummah*) charged with living in accordance with the teachings of Islam' (1986: 11). All spheres of activity, social, political, economic, and obviously, spiritual, should be governed by God's dictates and the moral code of Islam in creating a society above racial, national and class concerns: 'In brief, all his [man's] energies should be directed towards regulating the affairs of this world in the way in which God wants them to be regulated' (1986: 55). Here is stated, from a Muslim perspective, both the ideal of one Islam and also of our starting position – that Islam is a way of life. Anywhere in the Muslim world, therefore, devout Muslims could, quite apart from their formal religious observances, aspire to certain personal and family conventions which also demonstrate that they are Muslim.

Having ended this chapter on an idealistic note, we will now begin to examine how these ideals are made manifest materially and whether they are recoverable by archaeologists. The following chapters will therefore examine the image of Islam as displayed in material culture, and how this might be archaeologically recognizable. Essentially, we then return to the questions raised at the beginning of this chapter. Are religious universals rendered materially? And in the case of Islam do we have a complete set of data available to us as archaeologists to understand all areas of Muslim life?

2

The Mosque

None should visit the mosques of God except those who believe in
God and the Last Day, attend to their prayers and render the alms levy
and fear none but God. These shall be rightly guided.

Qur'an. Repentance 9: 18

The mosque has been chosen as the starting-point of this book as it is
an immediately recognizable symbol of Islam, to Muslims and non-
Muslims alike. It is a material personification of one of the Five
Pillars of Islam, the obligation to pray, as is stated in the Qur'an:
'Proclaim the portions of the Book that are revealed to you and be
steadfast in prayer. Prayer fends away indecency and evil. But your
foremost duty is to remember God. God has knowledge of all your
actions' (The Spider 29: 45), and thus at once brings us to the fundamentals of the religion. Furthermore, the mosque can be said to act,
through its various functions, both sacred and secular, as a creator,
unifier and perpetuator of the Muslim community (*ummah*), the
creation and maintenance of which should be the aim of all Muslims.
Rashid Chaudhri (1982: 2) expresses this when he remarks 'prayers in
a mosque teach us brotherhood and equality of mankind, as in a
mosque we find people of all races and classes standing shoulder to
shoulder without any discrimination of colour, rank, wealth or
office...all are equal in the House of Allah.'

The mosque is also a structure which is usually found wherever
communities of Muslims exist, which of course has major implications for the archaeologist interested in Islam as a key aid to the
archaeological recognition of the Muslim community. Yet, surprisingly, the archaeological recognition of the mosque and the criteria
which might allow this have never been adequately investigated. The

following discussion will not be concerned with charting the development of the mosque or providing a typology of mosque types, both of which have been exhaustively covered elsewhere (Frishman and Khan 1994; Hillenbrand 1994). Rather, attention will be focused upon assessing how the translation of Muslim religious essentials into material culture is achieved, how this might be theoretically approached, and the resulting implications for the archaeologist.

A twofold approach will be adopted whereby mosques can be viewed via different scales of analysis: what are termed 'structuring principles' and 'cultural diversity'. Examples of how places of prayer can be seen to serve various purposes will be provided to illustrate how the structuring principles are adapted to suit political and cultural context. The practicalities of archaeologically investigating mosques will also be discussed, including their recognition (along with the often-ignored ephemeral types of mosque) and where archaeologists could contribute to the study of the mosque, and thus to Muslim society in general. Finally, the implications for the archaeologist of the future confronted by the establishment of new Muslim communities in previously non-Muslim areas of the world will be examined through the analysis of the growth and development of the Cambridge Muslim community, and how it has adapted a pre-existing place of worship to its needs. Thus Islam will be placed firmly in context as a living religion, and the need for a socially aware Islamic archaeology will be re-emphasized.

Scales of Analysis: Structuring Principles and Cultural Diversity

The two scales of analysis were introduced briefly in the last chapter and it is not necessary to repeat what was said there. Nevertheless, a couple of points should be elaborated. Although a debt is owed to *Annales* theory, such approaches are not directly transferable for three reasons. First, because specifics such as the notion of 'fireflies' are largely irrelevant here; secondly, because it is not the purpose of this volume to provide anything so presumptuous as 'general laws', or to shoehorn the evidence into fitting such theoretical 'straitjackets'; and, thirdly, because it is easy, in the words of Bulliet (1992: 131), 'for appropriators of ideas and approaches originating in disciplines other than their own' not to understand them properly, or 'wilfully misunderstand them'. Rather, the concept of different scales of time or analysis can be borrowed, as was explained before, to allow a division to be made between the unchanging elements of being Muslim and, within this, the diversity which exists and which is apparent in all areas of human endeavour and its material remains.

The obligation of prayer, a Pillar of Islam, is a structuring principle in our 'Islamic structuring codes', an immutable element of being Muslim. The material manifestation of this is the mosque in all its many forms – with the many forms qualifying as the second scale of analysis, that of cultural diversity as comprising regional traditions, fashions and decorative and architectural trends. Thus, this second scale allows for the presence of diversity, which must always be recognized as existing within the broader structuring principle or code.

Structuring Principles: the Mosque

The criteria which define a mosque are 'forbiddingly simple: a wall correctly oriented towards the *qiblah*, namely the Black Stone within the Ka'bah in Mecca. No roof, no minimum size, no enclosing walls, no liturgical accessories are required' (Hillenbrand 1994: 31). Kuban (1974: 1) is even more minimalist when he mentions that, strictly speaking, a mosque is not needed at all, as a *hadith* records (al-Bukhari 7: 1) 'all the World is a *masjid*' (the place of prostrations). This statement would at first sight appear to be of little use in attempting to identify a Muslim community within the archaeological record. However, mosques of a form recognizable across the Islamic world developed rapidly after the establishment of Islam as structures for, and defined by, the requirements of prayer (*salat*). In part this was undoubtedly aided by sentiments recorded in another *hadith* (Muslim *b. al-Hajjaj: Book of Prayer*): 'prayer said in a congregation is twenty-five times more excellent than prayer said by a single person' (Brown and Palmer 1987: 90).

Prayer itself occurs at four levels: individually five times a day (*fajr*, morning prayer; *zuhr*, early afternoon prayer; *asr*, late afternoon prayer; *Maghrib*, sunset prayer; *isha*, night prayer); congregationally at noon on Friday; communally (village or town prayer) at festivals (discussed in chapter 4); and at the level of the entire Muslim world. Material manifestations of these prayer requirements are: first, the prayer rug and a simple *masjid* or prayer hall; secondly, the *jami'* or Friday (congregational) mosque; and thirdly, the *musalla* (place of prayer), a common term, but sometimes employed specifically to denote a place of prayer used at festivals. A physical embodiment of the fourth level of prayer does not exist, but pilgrimage to Mecca or *hajj* can perhaps be seen to be what Dickie terms 'a congregation of all the Muslims of the World' (1978: 35). The actual act of prayer is also reflected in the form of the mosque, with the rectangular shape of the mosque sanctuary, the *haram*, reflecting the need to pray in rows parallel to the *qiblah*, the wall facing Mecca. Prayer is led by an adult male, the Imam, at the front. Whether women are allowed to pray in a mosque depends on doctrines followed and regional variation. Where women do pray in mosques they pray behind the men, often in a special section. Lane (1883: 228) relates a saying attributed to the Prophet that 'the best rank of men [in a mosque] is the front; and the best rank of women is the rear', which is taken to mean those most distant from the men. Amongst the Shi'ah, Friday congregational prayer is of less importance, though they have other special prayers besides the obligatory ones for various occasions (Momen 1985: 181).

The origins of the mosque and its component parts have been, and still are, much debated. However, general consensus sees the prototype in the Prophet's house in Medina. Here, a *zulla*, or shelter of palm trunks and leaves was built on to one of the walls of the courtyard, initially on the side in the direction of Jerusalem (according to Creswell 1958: 4, perhaps due to the veneration Muhammad saw that the Jews, who formed the leading community in Medina, gave to Jerusalem). Following a revelation from God experienced by Muhammad, the direction of prayer was changed to the side facing Mecca (Kuban 1974: 1–2). This simple structure, the predecessor of the Arab hypostyle mosque, was also built to aid in the creation of the *ummah*, the Muslim community, by functioning not only as a place for religious ceremonies, but also where social gatherings were held, religious teaching was undertaken and public proclamations were made (Gibb and Kramers 1961; Nasr 1993). The functions encapsulated in the first mosque were to be replicated in mosques throughout the centuries, serving religious, social, communal, political and legal purposes. The Prophet's house was a place of both religious and political importance, emphasizing the lack of division between the sacred and secular in Islam, both being invested in the ruler. This duality is a theme which we will return to repeatedly in the following chapters.

Prayer axis

The one concern which can be isolated even in the first mosque, the Prophet's mosque, is the direction of prayer, which was ultimately fixed on Mecca and is perhaps the only universal which can be said to exist when considering the mosque as a structure (see figure 2.1). All mosques should be aligned in the direction of Mecca (allowing for

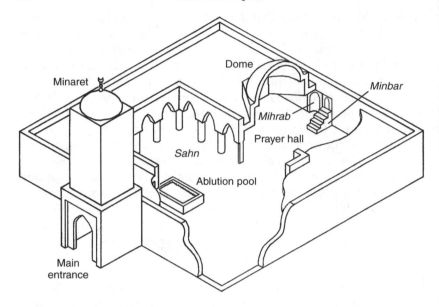

Figure 2.1 Stylized plan of mosque components in an 'ideal' mosque (after Chaudhri 1982: 36–7)

human error) and, as was noted above, all that is actually needed is a wall, built or even just marked out on the ground, and aligned in the correct direction before which the faithful can pray. Dickie has described this focus as 'spread out like a gigantic wheel with Mecca as the hub, with lines drawn from all the mosques in the world forming the spokes' (1978: 16). To the archaeologist this is of importance: given a compass and an understanding of the position of Mecca in relation to the area under study, theoretically at least, the archaeological recognition of a mosque should be straightforward (however, problems could arise when, for example, Mecca is due east, as churches are aligned in the same direction, or, as already mentioned, mosques are incorrectly aligned). Luckily, this task is facilitated by the fact that the vast majority of mosques do not only fulfil the simplest requirements of prayer, a correctly aligned *qiblah* wall, but incorporate various other features which in themselves form recognition criteria.

The mihrab

Related to the question of orientation is the physical marker of the direction of prayer, an almost universal feature which is built into, or salient from, the *qiblah* wall, and forms the focus of the prayer hall (see figure 2.1). From in front of the *mihrab* the prayers are led by the Imam, and, while almost always a niche in form, the *mihrab* can be decorated in many ways and is often surmounted by a dome, although this is not obligatory. Although Grabar suggests that the *mihrab* 'grew to commemorate the presence of the Prophet as the first imam' (1973: 121), it is extremely unlikely that Muhammad's mosque had such a permanent indicator of prayer direction: the earliest *mihrab* niche at Medina dates from 705, though does not survive in its original form (Gibb and Kramers 1961: 343; Hillenbrand 1994: 46). Flat plaque-like *mihrabs* were also occasionally used in the early Islamic period. The influences from which both the dome and the niche were drawn have been recognized: for the dome, Roman palatial architecture; and for the niche, the place for a statue in the Graeco-Roman temple or, on a larger scale, the apse in a church (Hillenbrand 1994: 45, 53). However, unlike a statue or an altar, the *mihrab* is not sacred in itself, but indicates the direction of prayer, which is sacred (Frishman 1994: 35). From the early eighth century the use of the *mihrab* spread, utilizing single or, less frequently, double or multiple niches. The *mihrab* is therefore a critical indicator of the presence of a mosque, as the symbol of prayer direction in what would otherwise be a blank wall.

Other features

A variety of other features exist which could be present in a mosque and which form further elements of the translation of the structuring principle of prayer into material culture. The *minbar*, introduced in the time of the Prophet, is a flight of sometimes moveable steps placed next to the *mihrab* (see figure 2.1) from which the Imam preaches a sermon (*khutbah*) at Friday prayers and, much less frequently today, makes public pronouncements (radio and television has made this function largely superfluous). This juxtaposition of *mihrab* and *minbar*, it has been argued, quite plausibly, is a reflection of the co-identity within the person of the Imam of both secular and spiritual power (Dickie 1978: 37). Orthodox definitions of the mosque usually classify the *minbar* as primarily a feature of the *jami'* mosque, and thus it could perhaps be seen as a material symbol of the obligation of Friday prayer upon every free Muslim male. Though perhaps valid in the past, such a definition has little validity today where the *minbar* is frequently found in the ordinary *masjid* (El-Rashedy 1997). The best-known visible feature of the mosque is the minaret, which has been called the 'symbol of Islam' (Bloom 1989).

Though common today, the original function, origins and introduction of the minaret in the eighth and ninth centuries have been the subject of debate – perhaps as a lighthouse, watch tower and so on (Gibb and Kramers 1961: 340–1; Bloom 1989; Hillenbrand 1994: 129–37). The importance of the minaret archaeologically is that in all its many forms it is a physical representation of the call to prayer (see figure 2.1). It is usually a tower, attached to or near the prayer hall containing a staircase leading to a balcony for the *muezzin*, who makes the call to prayer.

Further features of the mosque which might be found include an enclosed courtyard (*sahn*) attached to the sanctuary in which an ablutions area is situated, often centrally or near the entrance (see figure 2.1). Washing prior to prayer is obligatory, and thus a fountain, tap or pot of water should be provided for the use of worshippers. This would certainly be archaeologically recognizable, and theoretically may even allow doctrinal differentiation as, for example, the Hanafis disagree with washing in anything but running water, precluding the use of pots and pools of standing water (Kuban 1974: 9). The entrance to the courtyard and thence to the sanctuary should also be mentioned (see figure 2.1). Frequently imposing and ornate, it serves as a portal between the world outside and the 'tranquil atmosphere within' (Frishman 1994: 41). These two further elements of the prayer ritual might be archaeologically recognizable: the act of physical separation from worldly concerns by stepping over the threshold into the mosque courtyard, and ritual cleansing prior to entering the sanctuary. A number of other features may or may not be present: a screened area for women; a raised and screened enclosure (*maqsura*) for the ruler or Imam; Qur'an stands and chests; and a *dikka*, a platform formerly used by the *muezzin* to transmit responses to the prayers to the congregation before the advent of loudspeakers (Gibb and Kramers 1961; Kuban 1974; Dickie 1978); the *maqsura* and *dikka* are unlikely to be found in modern mosques.

It is therefore possible to isolate a number of features which show the structuring principle in action. Furthermore, although the basic archaeological recognition of the mosque is by orientation, the archaeologist can be helped by the existence of a number of other features. For example, perhaps 90 per cent of mosques found will have a *mihrab*, and a descending scale of features which might be present can be proposed below this: minaret, ablutions area, *minbar*, defined threshold, and a variety of less common items inside what is usually a clutter-free, clean prayer space lacking the paraphernalia associated with the places of worship of other world religions. Thus, the requirements of the structuring principle lead to the existence of a number of largely unchanging features, which will in turn allow (and have on numerous occasions allowed) the archaeological recognition of the mosque. It is at the second scale of analysis – cultural diversity – that great variation in the presence of these features, and how they are organized and constructed, is apparent.

Cultural Diversity: Regional Traditions

Cultural diversity is best exemplified by regional traditions, and these have been extensively covered elsewhere (see, for example, Hillenbrand 1994), but it is useful to draw upon Frishman and Khan's (1994: 13) five basic categories and seven regional styles of mosque design by way of illustration (see figure 2.2). Within them, numerous subtypes exist as defined by materials, decoration and differences in layout. With these must be considered the different types of mosque: Friday and ward mosques, collegiate, monastic, tomb and cemetery mosques, not forgetting temporary mosques and places of prayer used for festivals or laid out by travellers and nomads. But, looking at the mosques in figure 2.2, it can be seen that, though visually differing quite considerably, the structuring principle is in operation, with minarets, for example, along with defined thresholds visible. Although we cannot see inside the mosques, it is almost certain that a *mihrab* would be found set into the *qiblah* wall, used as they are in all these types of mosque, however well or badly aligned. Moreover, although Frishman and Khan (1994: 12) deliberately exclude the mosques of the 'Modern Movement' as these take many forms, it is probable that in the vast majority the structuring principle will be in operation, above and beyond the most important requirement of correct orientation. The actual recognition of these modern structures as mosques, however, will, as discussed below, offer further challenges to the archaeologist of the future, confronted by an ever-expanding range of cultural diversity. Cultural diversity, or regional tradition, can change, and the mosque can be adapted to suit context and fashion, but the structuring principle behind the mosque as a place of prayer, and the elements which result, cannot be altered beyond certain limits.

The Archaeological Study of the Mosque

What, then, of the mechanics of recognizing the mosque archaeologically? What are the practical issues involved? And how can

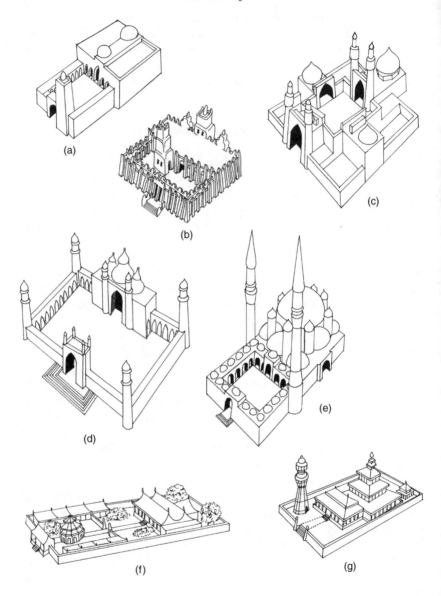

Figure 2.2　Simplified plan of types of mosque (not to scale). (a) Arabian heartland, Spain and North Africa; (b) Sub-Saharan West Africa; (c) Iran and Central Asia; (d) Indian subcontinent; (e) Anatolia; (f) China; (g) South-east Asia (after Frishman and Khan 1994: 13)

archaeology contribute to our understanding of the mosque and, in turn, Muslim society in general? To answer these questions, the following discussion has been divided into three areas: archaeological recognition, miscellany, and temporary mosques or 'ephemeral' structures.

Archaeological recognition

Churches to mosques   The one concern to be found in the mosque is orientation: prayer in the direction of Mecca. This is not only evident in the excavation of 'virgin' mosques, as at Madinat al-Zahra, a city founded in the tenth century by Abd al-Rahman III, a few kilometres from Cordoba in Al-Andalus (Islamic Spain), where the south-eastern orientation is quite striking in comparison to the other buildings (see figure 2.3), it is also visible archaeologically in the re-use of

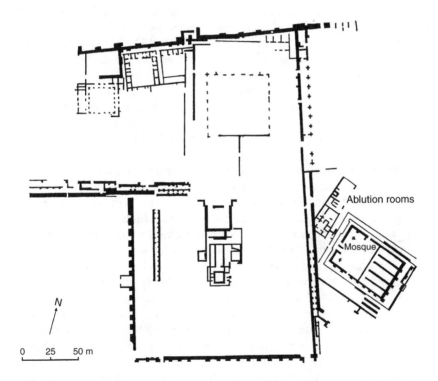

Figure 2.3   The position of the mosque in relation to the palace, Madinat al-Zahra, Spain (after Triano 1992: 28)

other places of worship, most noticeably converted churches. Rather than building anew, Muslims in many areas of the world, past and present, have converted churches into mosques, as with the Hagia Sophia in Istanbul, and this was a fairly common process through the simple expedient of altering the fabric to a greater or lesser degree. This process is often recognizable by archaeologists through the change in axis and direction of prayer. It may be seen in the wider context of 'conversion' practices, of adapting pre-existing holy places, and was by no means confined to Muslims alone.

Numerous examples exist. In Syria, where the *qiblah* had to be due south and churches faced east, Creswell (1958: 7) records that 'it was only necessary to close the western entrance (or three entrances), pierce new entrances in the north wall, and pray across the aisles.' In northern Jordan, the archaeological survey of two Byzantine churches found that various alterations had been undertaken, including destroying and walling off the apses, with the new walls functioning both to fill the gap and, 'perhaps more importantly, to negate the Christian direction of prayer that the apses indicated' (King 1983: 134). Interestingly, the church towers were not touched as they were designed as minarets 'from the first' (1983: 134). Church doorways once blocked could be utilized as *mihrabs* or, as in Jordan, constructed by removing a layer of stone from the church walls to create a simple niche. The paramountcy of the *qiblah* and its archaeological visibility are thus shown, and it appears that it is this process of '*qiblarization*' which is of fundamental importance. As will be discussed below, this process continues today in England.

Mosques to churches   The conversion of mosques to churches is perhaps less common, but is still archaeologically important. In former Islamic Spain, for example at Almeria, the principal port of the caliphate of Al-Andalus, the Great Mosque which was started in the late tenth century was converted into a church following the Christian reconquest in 1489. The *qiblah* wall forms the south wall of the present church, and both the *mihrab* and what appears to be the *minbar* niche survive to this day (Ewert 1971) (see plate 2.1). Similarly, on Gibraltar the congregational mosque was converted to a church in the fifteenth century, and recent excavations have clearly defined the mosque structure (Finlayson 1997). These actions of conversion and re-conversion of places of worship illustrate that in many areas we are not dealing with static processes. World religions such as Islam expand and contract, following conquests and defeats or other changes in circumstances, often on a large scale: witness the disappearance of Islam in Spain or of Christianity in North Africa,

Plate 2.1   Former mosque, now Church of St John, Almeria, Spain (*photo.* P. Mitchell)

for example. Archaeologists are well placed to investigate these phenomena through deciphering the legacy of material culture.

Buddhist and Hindu temples   These processes were by no means confined to a Muslim–Christian interchange. The vast extent of the Muslim world, and the fluid, changing boundaries, meant that other religions were encountered and diverse structures were converted into mosques. The Friday mosque at Istakhr, ancient Persepolis, was originally a palace hall of the Persian kings (Creswell 1958: 8); Zoroastrian fire temples, and Buddhist, Jain or Hindu places of worship in India were also converted. To quote Hillenbrand (1994: 35), 'its austerely simple liturgy meant Islam could appropriate almost any kind of building for worship.' Once again, the archaeologist is ideally placed to investigate this. The immutable requirements of being Muslim, the structuring principles, come into contact and mix with many different peoples and cultures which together form the great diversity of the Muslim world.

An interesting recent example of this comes from Kashmir, where archaeologists have investigated a syncretism of Buddhist, Hindu and Muslim traditions in mosque architecture. As well as building in the style of pre-Islamic Buddhist stupa-courts and Hindu temples, actual shrines were incorporated in mosques following Muslim domination of the region in the early fourteenth century. The mosque of Shah

Hamadan or Khanqah-i-Maulla, originally a shrine of the goddess Kali, contains within it a spring dedicated to the goddess, and 'the water flows down outside the structure where Hindus offer worship to Mother Kali' (Shali 1993: 247). At the mosque and tomb of Madin Sahib the steps taken to convert this Hindu temple into a mosque were minimal, the mosque being built on the temple plinth and the fluted stone columns re-used; 'only the superstructure of brick walls was raised over it so as to convert it into a mosque' (Shali 1993: 255).

Similar examples can be found across South Asia. Sir Alexander Cunningham describes the re-use of columns from Hindu temples in the mosques of Jaunpur (1880: 112), while in Ahmadabad (Gujarat) building materials from Hindu temples were employed along with Hindu craftsmen themselves who brought with them their artistic and architectural repertoire (Soundara Rajan 1980: 11). But perhaps one of the best-known examples of the re-use of a Hindu temple site, and some of the masonry, is provided by the Quwwut-ul-Islam mosque in Delhi. Here, plaster was used to cover 'offending' sculpture, much of which has come off over time revealing Hindu carvings of Vishnu, Indra, Siva and Brahma along with figures of the seated Buddha (Stephen 1876: 47) (see plate 2.2). Through appropriating a place of worship Muslim domination could be stamped upon an area: an assertion of religious superiority to non-Muslim populations which occurred often in an immediate post-contact or post-conquest situation, when the need for such a visible statement might be most necessary.

However, it should also be remembered that Christians, Jews and others were not persecuted as a matter of course but, on the contrary, enjoyed protected status under Islamic law, as *dhimmi*, or protected persons. Protection achieved through the payment of a poll-tax, *jizyah*, provided a status which, among other things, gave freedom to conduct their own religious practices. This can be attested archaeologically. An inscription found inside a Roman/ Byzantine *thermae* renovated in the early Islamic period at al-Hamma on the River Yarmuk in Jordan began with a cross, was in Greek and was dedicated to the Caliph Mu'awiya, a discovery which led Zeyadeh (1994: 124) to infer that 'a Greek inscription dedicated to the Muslim Caliph and with a cross suggests the degree of freedom which the Christian community at al-Hamma enjoyed in Mu'awiya's time.'

Mosque positioning   Much information can also be gained through the archaeological study of the context and position of the mosque

Plate 2.2 Decorated columns from a Hindu building re-used in the Quw-wut ul-Islam mosque, Delhi (*photo*. T. Insoll)

within a settlement. As well as a religious statement, the construction of a mosque can demonstrate secular concerns and statements serving as a unifier of communities which, as has already been stressed, was one of the primary aims of the Prophet's mosque. The mosque can also act as a symbol of authority and political power and, as will be discussed later (see chapter 7), as a medium for conveying individual secular status. Information on the growth of, and changes in, communities and settlements over time can also be gained through examining locational data; for example, it may be possible to examine changes in the composition of Muslim religious communities by identifying different Islamic schools and sects through inscriptions, mosque layout and other features.

In the early Islamic period sacred and secular power were usually invested in the same individual, and the mosque was frequently constructed alongside the palace, emphasizing the lack of differentiation between the two spheres as, for example, at Basra, Damascus and Fustat (Gibb and Kramers 1961: 347). The *jami'* was the focus of settlement, recognizable archaeologically, and the *minbar* a symbol of rule. However, quite quickly the separation of secular and sacred began, and the palace monopolized effective control and functioned both as the physical centre of the city and as the centre of true power, apparent, for instance, in Abbasid Baghdad (see chapter 7). Nevertheless, this did not necessarily mean that the close relationship between religion and the state dissolved, and material culture can again be informative in this respect. At Madinat al-Zahra, for example, it can be seen that the caliph went directly from the palace via a passage and bridge to the mosque, which he entered through a door adjacent to the *mihrab* in the double *qiblah* walls (Fernández-Puertas 1994: 103). Here mosque and palace were still physically connected in the tenth century.

The function of a mosque as a seat of power, an arbiter of communities or indeed as a vital component of a Muslim settlement is not, moreover, confined to sedentary communities. It is found throughout the Muslim world among sedentaries and nomads alike. In Timbuktu (Mali), for example, the available evidence suggests that mosque building was of fundamental importance in creating a unified community in this city. Initially, it appears that Timbuktu was founded in two parts, one animist and largely inhabited by blacks (Djinguereber), the other Muslim and largely occupied by white Saharan nomads (Sankore), following a common pattern of dual cities in the western Sahel and savannah in the eleventh to twelfth centuries (Insoll 1996a, b, 1997b). In the early fourteenth century mosques were built in each quarter (extant today), but the quarters seem to have remained divided, though this was to change in the mid-fifteenth century when a third mosque, also still standing, was built at their midpoint (Sidi Yahya). Thus, through the action of the mosque being built, these two quarters were both symbolically and physically unified (Saad 1983: 110; Insoll 1996a).

Context and condition   The presence or absence of certain categories of material might also be informative in aiding recognition of a mosque and elucidating possible phases of its use. A mosque could be expected to be a relatively sterile, clean environment, probably lacking the domestic or industrial debris and refuse often present in secular buildings, perhaps in close proximity in the surrounding area, and reflecting the sanctity and orderliness of the mosque setting, sustained through the conscious separation of the world outside, beginning with the defined entrance way or portal. The archaeological implications of this probable contrast in environment are obvious, and could well aid archaeological recognition.

The possible presence of various other key features must also be considered. An instance of the archaeological preservation of practically all the mosque features discussed earlier is provided by the congregational mosque at Siraf on the Iranian side of the Persian Gulf. As well as the *mihrab* foundations and an ablutions area which were recorded, the solid masonry base of a minaret, the shallow depression left by the base of a wooden *minbar*, and even a slot marking the position of a *maqsura* were all noted. If this were not enough, the presence of former abutments was interpreted as possibly indicating the existence of a *dikka* (Whitehouse 1980: 11, 23). These features variously date from phases of rebuilding between the mid-ninth and twelfth centuries and, of course, could not be expected to be encountered in every instance, but show the possibilities which could exist, above and beyond the minimum mosque requirements, and what can be achieved through careful excavation and interpretation.

Miscellany

It is also instructive to look beyond the primary features of the mosque to the details which could further aid our understanding of Muslim communities based on archaeological material. Yet here no universals will be found; instead, the information which archaeology might provide will tend to be contextually specific, both temporally and spatially. But this is obviously also of crucial importance, adding the culturally specific flesh to the bones of our structuring principle, so to speak. Furthermore, it is also necessary to re-emphasize the need to adopt a multi-disciplinary approach in developing a socially aware Islamic archaeology. For example, the significance of the materials and their contexts would often be difficult, if not impossible, to reconstruct without supporting evidence gained from ethnography, history and anthropology.

Other fields of archaeology have moved onwards and matured through the simple understanding that the wider the horizons enjoyed, the greater the possibilities for interpretation. For example, we might recognize a pot as a pot, but we would hope to know something more about its functions, possible social significance and who might have used it, aided perhaps by information gained from ethnography, practical studies and historical sources. Likewise, we might recognize a mosque as a mosque, and place it within a regional category, but it is probable that interpretation could be taken a stage further. Who used it? What makes it different? Is it individualized? Life can be breathed into description. For life, after all, surely equates with the social, of which we, as archaeologists, are certainly in pursuit. But while numerous examples illustrating the rich diversity and meaning of material culture associated with the mosque in the Muslim world could be provided, great selectivity has had to be exercised in this volume.

Materials   Ostrich eggshells, fig wood and pebbles are three examples of how the materials used within a mosque can be of significance beyond their obvious function. Ostrich eggshells are frequently displayed on the top of minarets in parts of West Africa and the Republic of Sudan (see plate 2.3). Purely decorative? Not wholly, the significance is deeper than this, for as well as having pre-Islamic ancestry (in the Sudan at least) within the Muslim context the shell acts as a symbol of the unity of Islam, and is of such cultural significance that now that the ostrich has largely vanished in the Sahel, ceramic copies are substituted (Laviolette 1994). Similarly, the very materials that a mosque could be built with can function above and beyond the decorative or utilitarian. Ahmed (1984: 314), for instance, relates how the Pukhtuns (Pathans) of Pakistan use the wood of the fig tree for beams in the mosque but never burn it, the reasoning behind this being that when the Prophet was a child, a fig tree lowered its branches and gave him a drink of milk.

Significant materials can be as mundane as flooring material. At Shanga on the coast of northern Kenya a mosque dating from between 750 and 850 was excavated (Horton 1991: 112) with a pebble floor. This type of floor, known to have been used in other areas in the early Islamic period, was laid as a convenient flooring material, but also as a dust-control measure. This is remarked upon elsewhere in the Muslim world as a means of stopping people clapping their hands to get rid of dust after prayers, an act which might be considered as part of the religious ceremony (Creswell 1958: 12, quoted in Horton 1991); hence a practical measure with immense importance. The significance of mosque floors can also be seen among the Shi'ah, where the only notable feature setting them apart from Sunnis during prayer is their insistence during the prostration phase of prayer that 'the forehead be placed on dust or the earth (preferably a

Plate 2.3 Ostrich eggshell displayed on the Sidi Yahya mosque, Timbuktu, Mali (*photo*. T. Insoll)

block of baked mud from the earth at Karbala)' (Momen 1985: 179). All these examples could at first glance appear to be minor details, but which when seen in their full context, through accompanying historical or ethnographic sources, are all of great importance in reconstructing the whole picture within specific local or regional contexts.

Mihrabs and minarets Details of minaret and *mihrab* form and use can also provide us with important culturally specific information

Plate 2.4   Sacrifice remains in a *mihrab*, Green Island, Massawa, Eritrea (*photo*. T. Insoll)

beyond the concerns of aesthetics, decoration and architecture. They can tell us about the specific nature of the Muslim community who worshipped in a particular mosque. The conversion of pre-existing places of worship and the structural incorporation of non-Muslim features has already been touched upon, yet the practice of Islam is much more diverse and can encompass a wide variety of non-Muslim practices. One of the richest veins of material which can be drawn upon to illustrate this is provided by sub-Saharan Africa where, over the centuries, dualistic ritual has developed in much of the continent (Insoll 1996c). On Green Island off Massawa in Eritrea, traces of sacrifices made by fishermen are to be found in the *mihrab* of a small mosque (see plate 2.4), all of which could survive in the archaeological record. These include a whole young goat and many pottery incense burners and braziers for 'burnt offerings' as well as the resultant ashes. Similar practices have been recorded on the East African coast (Serjeant 1959: 447). Examples such as these provide evidence for the existence of unorthodox ritual practices in local contexts but can also illustrate the development of syncretic Muslim traditions, a theme to which we will return.

Detailed information about more orthodox Islamic creeds can also be obtained from the archaeological study of minaret and *mihrab* form. In certain instances, it may prove possible to differentiate between the different sects of Islam based upon this evidence, though the existence of supporting documentation would make such reconstructions more precise. A wide-ranging study of the mosques of Zanzibar stone town (Sheriff 1992) has shown the various differences between the mosque architecture of the Sunni and Ibadi communities living there which could theoretically be archaeologically visible. The egalitarian ethos of the Ibadis was manifest in the absence of a *jami'* until recently, as none of the Omani rulers wanted to be elected to the Imamate; an elected Imam is a requirement of Friday prayers. This meant the absence of *minbars*. Secondly, their egalitarian and austere ethos (they have been described as 'the Calvinists of Islam' by Gellner 1981: 132) was further reflected in the shallow plain *mihrab* because 'their dogmas disapprove of their prayer leaders being isolated in the niche away from their followers' (Sheriff 1992: 13). Interior decoration was also lacking so that it did not distract the worshippers. Furthermore, the minority status of the Ibadis led to concealment which was achieved, for example, through the non-protrusion of the *mihrab* niche in direct contrast to the Sunni community, and by building a raised floor to the prayer hall so that their rituals could not be observed, and thus attention drawn to them. Finally, their mosques tended to be broad and shallow so that worshippers could obtain greater spiritual reward by being closer to the *qiblah*, and minarets were rare.

A further and related example of the difficulties of establishing doctrinal or sectarian recognition can be provided by examining the staircase minaret as a possible indicator of the Ibadi sect. The staircase minaret is described by Schacht (1961: 137) as the earliest type of minaret in Islam, and consists of a flight of steps built on the corner of the mosque which led up to the roof, where a sentry-box type structure was situated for use by the *muezzin* for the call to prayer. This type of minaret is found widely in East Africa, where its presence has been recorded in archaeological contexts at Shanga, and in West Africa, Anatolia, Iran, Tunisia and Egypt (Whitehouse 1972: 156; Horton 1991: 108). In certain areas there appears to be a correlation between the introduction of the staircase minaret and Ibadi influences, as in West Africa (Schacht 1954), or the presence of Ibadi communities, as in parts of Tunisia and in Zanzibar. But elsewhere no such correlations exist. The staircase minaret is common in Sunni mosques in East Africa (Bloom 1989: 191), and Whitehouse (1972: 156) mentions finding staircase minarets on both Shi'ah and Sunni mosques at Taheri in Iran. In general, it would appear that no universal translations of Ibadi tenets into mosque form exist, other than a vague emphasis upon simplicity, and how this is achieved depended upon local circumstances.

However, this is not necessarily discouraging for it has been shown that an Ibadi mosque can be recognized in certain contexts. This example serves to illustrate that fine-tuning of interpretations is possible, but that this will not always be the case. Once it has been established that the cruder structuring principles are in operation, that the structure being examined is in fact a mosque, then the other details can be examined more closely, with options considered and accepted or rejected. It is hoped (assuming that the recognition of presences and absences does not become an end in itself) that this will aid the detailed reconstruction of a more complete Islamic archaeology, mindful that much more can be made of archaeological evidence in all its many dimensions.

Impermanent and ephemeral structures

Temporary mosques   Many Muslim communities are nomadic. The requirement to pray exists, the structuring principle still operates, but 'temporary' or 'ephemeral' mosques have been ignored through being perceived as lesser structures. As Islamic history neglects the 'productive activities and material life' (Keddie 1992: 49) of nomads, so Islamic archaeology is guilty of the same omission. This presents a distorted picture of the nature of the Muslim community, past and present, usually in favour of the sedentary population. Ethnographic, historical and archaeological sources tell us that many mosques and prayer areas are not made from durable materials, but could still be archaeologically visible. Depending upon doctrine, the requirement for a building is not even a necessity: a marked-out space will suffice (Gibb and Kramers 1961: 338). The first mosques of Islam were sometimes more ephemeral in nature; at Basra in Iraq, for example, the first mosque founded c.635 was, depending on the source followed, either simply a marked-out prayer area on the ground, or an area enclosed with a reed fence (Creswell 1958: 9). By visualizing a place of prayer as not necessarily only a 'well-finished' structure as represented by the five types of mosque in figure 2.2, we expand our possible interpretative horizons, even if they might be difficult or impossible to recognize archaeologically in many instances.

An example of the great diversity which exists is provided by Schimmel (1980: 107), who describes a variety of ephemeral places of prayer which are found in the Indian subcontinent: huts of acacia twigs in the Thar Desert of Rajasthan, places of prayer built of multi-coloured blocks of salt in the Khewra salt mines in the Punjab, rectangular stone enclosures with semi-circular *mihrab* niches in Baluchistan and Sind, bamboo oars bound together with fishing nets and palates of swordfish used to mark out places of prayer in the Makran. To these can be added many more among nomads in Africa and Central Asia, for example. To many nomads, the ease of worship which Islam offered may have been an attraction (Insoll 1996b); the outline of a mosque could be scratched out on the ground, or a crude enclosure built of stone or other readily available material. Scratched mosque outlines were used among the Bedouin, both while on the move in the Rub' al-Khali (Empty Quarter) of Saudi Arabia, and in their camps, where 'nothing more than a place drawn in the earth just to the east of the tent' (Cole 1975: 127) was used by men for prayer. More tangible was a stone 'outline' mosque recorded at Ancient ar-Risha (Jordan) (Helms 1990: 73), dating perhaps from as early as the second half of the seventh century. This, it was suggested, was once roofed at its southern end with fabric supported on wooden rafters, the evidence being several 'Y'-shaped worked flints found near the *qiblah* wall, whose recovery in nomadic contexts elsewhere allows the suggestion to be made that they might have been used to attach guy-ropes, or some similar function (Betts 1990: 165).

To enumerate individually the probabilities of archaeological survival of other types of temporary or ephemeral mosques is unnecessary. However, undoubtedly some will form part of the archaeological record, but which will survive is as much down to chance as particular local circumstances such as environment and soil conditions. Nomad prayer enclosures and mosques, for example, have been recorded in various areas of the Muslim world, predominantly in areas, perhaps not surprisingly, which are little visited by people other than nomads. Throughout the western Sahara dry-stone crescentic prayer walls are found, with similar structures built by the Tuareg of the Hoggar in the central Sahara (Reygasse 1950; Mercer 1976: 144) (see figure 2.4). These structures are somewhat difficult to date being devoid of any associated dating evidence, but in the Negev desert in Palestine, Rosen and Avni (1993: 198) have dated similar dry-stone nomad mosques 'to the earliest stages of the rise of Islam' and, of even more interest, have suggested that 'the juxtaposition of the mosques and non-Islamic shrines reflects the transition from paganism to Islam' (1993: 198).

Portable 'mosques' Similarly transient, though permanently manifest places of prayer, are prayer rugs, which can be used to provide a clean place to pray almost anywhere. The literature on prayer rugs

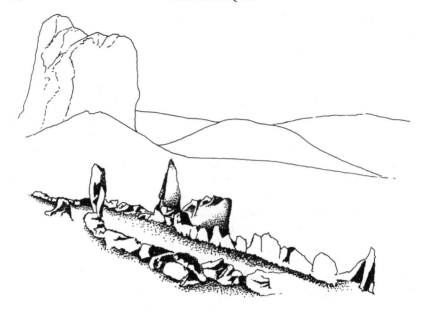

Figure 2.4 Simple dry-stone mosque, Hoggar, central Sahara (after Rey-gasse 1950: 43)

and carpets is vast, almost wholly because of their desirability to Western collectors, but reduced to their barest essentials the prayer rug acts as a personal place of prayer, easily moved and stored. Almost always a *mihrab* design is incorporated into the rug which can be oriented in the correct direction. They are common in Central Asia, India, Iran and Turkey (Gassong 1987: 83), but are found in all areas of the Muslim world. Prayer rugs are generally made for a single person, but can also incorporate multiple *mihrabs* for the family or, on an even larger scale, as a mosque carpet (Denny 1990: Sakhai 1991). Rugs and carpets can survive archaeologically, both as scraps of material on archaeological sites, as at Fustat (Old Cairo), Quseir al-Qadim (Egypt) and in Sinkiang (eastern Turkestan) (Thompson 1993: 67; Vogelsang-Eastwood 1993: 86), and also in the form of strata on mosque floors, where (uniquely) in Turkey, the rugs and carpets given to mosques by weavers have sometimes built up in such a fashion that 'from the layers accumulated over the centuries, it is possible to reconstruct a fairly complete history of Turkish carpets' (Thompson 1993: 66).

Archaeology can contribute to the study of the mosque in many different ways, and thus in turn to that of Muslim society. It is an archaeologically recognizable structure manifest in various forms and materials, both more and less permanent, but the information which can be gained from its study goes beyond mere recognition criteria. It can attest to the contraction and expansion of the Muslim world, the interplay with pre- and non-Muslim elements and the development of syncretic traditions, enable the recognition of sects and doctrines, and chart changes in power structures and community relations.

It is now pertinent to move on to examine material culture 'in action' through three case studies, considering how Muslim religious identity can be stated through the mosque in different ways: as a symbol of religious dominance, in difficult or challenging circumstances, and in new environments. Our three examples will illustrate the diversity evident in mosque form, the operation of the 'structuring principle' and the meaning which can underlie the mosque, but which could elude the archaeologist hampered perhaps by a much less complete set of data.

Places of Prayer and Muslim Religious Identity

The Dome of the Rock

The Dome of the Rock in Jerusalem is both the third holiest shrine in Islam after the Ka'bah in Mecca and the Prophet's mosque in Medina, and the earliest building in Islam to survive in its original form (see plate 2.5). It is not a mosque but is both a place of prayer and of pilgrimage, and is included here because of its significance in the creation of Muslim religious identity. The Dome of the Rock is built on a large flat open area in the Old City, the *Haram al-Sharif*, the 'noble sanctuary', which is also known as the Temple Mount, being the site of the three Jewish temples. The Dome enshrines the tip of Mount Moriah, and is a site holy to Muslims, Christians and Jews alike. Its significance to Muslims lies in the tradition that it was from here that Muhammad made his Night Journey and ascended to Heaven. However, it has been argued that this tradition was not the reasoning behind the original construction (Grabar 1959: 38), but that the building served a variety of purposes, 'a mixture of religion and politics' (Nuseibeh and Grabar 1996: 49). The Dome was commissioned by Caliph Abd-Al-Malik and is dated 691–2; it comprises an octagonal building capped with the famous golden (alloy) dome which encloses a double ambulatory with the rock at the centre, in which there is a small cave. It is richly decorated inside and out with coloured marble tiles and mosaics, forming both textual, pictorial and

Plate 2.5   The Dome of the Rock, Jerusalem (*photo*. T. Insoll)

abstract decoration. It is, to quote Nuseibeh and Grabar (1996: 27), 'a building of powerfully palpable substance that contains hidden and unexpected meanings, a building that is not quite what it at first appears to be'.

Grabar (1959), and to a lesser extent other scholars (see, for example, Kessler 1970), have reconstructed something of the meaning and significance which underlay the construction of the Dome of the Rock. First, the position of the Dome of the Rock is of importance, built upon a site sacred to both Christianity and Judaism, and thus symbolizing through its setting a victory monument, with Islam 'as the continuation and final statement of the faith of the People of the Book' and 'of setting up a symbol of the conquering power or faith within the conquered land' (Grabar 1959: 57). The power of Islam and its position as the revealed truth is further emphasized in the inscriptions and imagery inside the Dome of the Rock. Several bands of inscription run around the interior, one of which is 240 m in length, with the majority of the text religious in nature and composed of carefully and deliberately selected Qur'anic passages, utilized in a unique form. Three basic points are emphasized, according to Grabar (1959: 54): the fundamental principles of Islam are forcefully asserted, the special position of Muhammad and the importance of his mission are underlined, and, thirdly, the position of Jesus and other prophets is defined in the theology of the new faith. These inscriptions are interpreted by Kessler (1970: 11) as 'declaring for all to read – Muslims or People of the Book – that Islam had superseded both Christianity in its doctrine of Jesus and Judaism in its inheritance from David'. A further concrete statement of the power and identity of the new faith.

The pictorial imagery inside the Dome of the Rock is also significant in this respect. Again, Grabar suggests an interpretative option which is highly convincing in explaining why Byzantine and Sasanian royal symbols were utilized, as these symbols 'demonstrated that the unbelievers had been defeated and brought into the fold of the true faith' (1959: 52). The fact that the Dome of the Rock is also influenced by Byzantine ecclesiastical architectural traditions has similarly been interpreted as of importance: 'this first monumental building of Islam, planted in the heart of the supreme Christian city, modelled after Christian churches and intended to surpass them in splendour' (Kessler 1970: 12). The Dome of the Rock, though a unique building, illustrates both the degree of interpretation which can sometimes be achieved, and how material culture can be used to signal religious identity. The theology, vitality and power of the new faith of Islam are writ large in the Dome of the Rock, a new place of worship, which through considered use of position, form and decoration lays claim to, and supersedes, the pre-existing religious traditions.

Hui mosques

In contrast to the Dome of the Rock, which acts as a supremely powerful statement of Muslim conquest and the superimposition of a new religious identity, the following example shows how this same religious identity, encapsulated within the mosque, can be adapted without breaking the structuring principle, while at the same time taking 'cultural diversity' to new limits. The Hui Muslim communities of coastal China provide an example of the adaptation and evolution of Muslim material culture. This is because they have had to adapt their identity as a Muslim minority within a non-Muslim country, where 'otherness' and 'belonging' have to be accommodated and 'juggled' in an ongoing relationship with their often hostile neighbours. Hui is the name given to Chinese Muslims who do not have a language of their own (in contrast with the Turkic-Altaic languages spoken by the Muslim groups of Central Asia), but speak that of the surrounding people (Gladney 1991: 20). The Hui are in part descended from merchant communities (Arabs, Persians) who settled on the coast of China from as early as the ninth century, and in 1990 they numbered about 8,500,000.

The ambivalent relationship between the Hui and the majority of the Chinese population is eloquently attested in the mosque architecture which has been developed. The core features of the mosque are present, but the outward appearance of many of these structures displays little or nothing to set them apart from traditional Chinese architecture, helping to distract unwanted attention. Minarets could be built in a pagoda shape as in the Great Mosque in Xian built in 1392, which is laid out in Chinese courtyard fashion, and where dragon figures, a traditional Chinese decorative form with supernatural and celestial associations, were used as decoration on the minaret, in a further fusion of Chinese and Muslim elements (Xiaowie 1994: 214, 222) (see figure 2.5). Xiaowie describes how this syncretism is apparent in many other outward characteristics, including the capping of the *mihrab* not with a dome but with a wooden roof, which

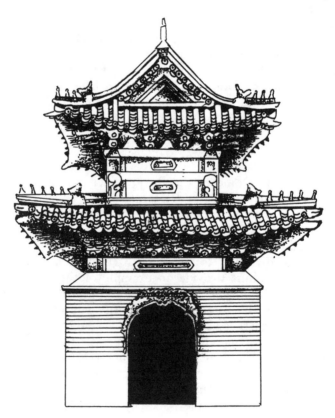

Figure 2.5   Minaret built in pagoda style, Niu Jie mosque, Beijing, China (after Xiaowie 1994: 216)

was not only a response to climate but 'one of the essential formal characteristics of indigenous Chinese architecture' (1994: 211). Minarets, it seems, could have a triple function: for the call to prayer, to serve as the portal or entrance way, both obvious Muslim requirements, but also as a 'moon pavilion' for observing the moon, a Chinese tradition.

Yet it would be simplistic and incorrect to say that the Hui were merely subservient in their relationship with the majority non-Muslim population, and that they sacrificed the structuring principle for an easier life. On the contrary, although the exterior of the mosque might be Chinese in appearance, the interior, the inward face, was recognizably Muslim, a fact noted by commentators. 'Our second thought is, this place is clean. Those who know what a Chinese temple is like, will appreciate this remark. Our third thought is, here there are no hideous idols. The whole of the west end, the Mecca side, is adorned with Arabesque in gold, blue and black, some sentences from the Qu'ran being most conspicuous' (Broomhall 1910: 185). Prayer halls were correctly oriented and *mihrabs* were built. The Emperor's tablets, which were kept in a prominent position inside, and whose presence placed the Hui Muslim congregation under imperial sanction, an important consideration, were the only example of Chinese script to be found within the mosque. From every external angle the Hui mosques might look Chinese – pagoda or pavilion minarets, courtyard gardens, traditional wooden roofs – but this was surface dressing to suit the social and political context. It was part of the 'double standard of behaviour' described by Israeli (1979: 169). Where it mattered, the mosque was a mosque, orientation was unaltered, and other features, though adapted, were present – the minaret, *mihrab*, portal and so on. The structuring principle was thus left intact.

The Hui mosque also provides an instructive example of how the mosque can be read as a 'social document', imbued with a significance to archaeologists far beyond its functioning as a place of prayer. It is not solely a 'dead' structure of architectural or art-historical interest, but imbued with a wealth of information on Hui society and identity, its creation and maintenance over time. Similarly with the Dome of the Rock, understanding of the significance of this edifice has extended far beyond recording the structure and extolling the virtues of its decoration; we understand its purpose and importance within its social context. But too often interpretative opportunities have been lost or passed over in Islamic, medieval or historical archaeology in favour of the easier typological or cataloguing option. These two examples might be unusual, but are not overly so; mosques as places of prayer are social constructs built by, and filled with, individuals. Even what might appear to be the most mundane of mosques can tell us something about the community which used it and thus provide valuable social information. This, after all, is what we should be seeking to obtain, rather than only being preoccupied with building plans and architectural styles, which even a quick perusal of much of the literature shows to be still a continuing fascination.

The Cambridge mosque

A third example of how Muslim religious identity can be manifest through the mosque is provided by the Cambridge mosque. As with many of the subjects discussed in this volume, it is important to draw in modern examples to reinforce the point that Islam is not static, but a vibrant living religion. Furthermore, by considering contemporary examples, the privileged position of the Islamic archaeologist as an observer of a living religion is re-emphasized. Although the core tenets of the religion remain unaltered, fresh challenges are faced by many recently established Muslim communities in North America and Western Europe. An obvious part of these challenges is how to adapt the situation to Muslim requirements, perhaps in the face of financial and other constraints, such as planning laws. The mosque as a symbol of a Muslim community and a place to pray is usually one of the first priorities, and many ingenious solutions have been adopted in creating places of prayer and community.

The Muslim community in Cambridge, England, can be used as an example. This community numbers some 2,000 individuals, having grown rapidly from about 70 in 1973 (CEN 1973). The ethnic origins and social backgrounds of the community are diverse, with the majority from Pakistan and Bangladesh, and others from India, Turkey, Morocco, East Africa, and Saudi Arabia, for example. Some 20 converted European families also form part of the community. Shopkeepers, restaurateurs, engineers and many other occupations are represented (CEN 1990) and, not surprisingly, considering that Cambridge is a university town, university students and staff, visiting scholars and researchers are well represented. The presence of the university and a large sector of high-technology industry does in fact mean that the Cambridge Muslim community is probably more mixed than in other medium-sized cities in Britain. However, although it might be convenient for the sake of academic procedure to break the community down into its component parts, it should be noted that the mosque authorities prefer to regard the community as one unit, superseding ethnic identities, and thus, it could be said, acting in the true spirit of the Muslim community, is how it should be conceived.

As well as growing in numbers over the past 25 years, the community has also grown in strength and in actions, mirroring processes apparent across the whole of Britain where the number of registered mosques has grown from 16 in 1966 to 452 in 1990, the latest figures found (Nielsen 1995: 45). Originally, in Cambridge, the incipient community used a room in the City Guildhall for prayers (CEN 1973), which was obviously not ideal, but which could be adapted, albeit temporally, as requirements dictated. In 1972, an ordinary terraced house of a type found all over Britain, dating from the late Victorian period, was bought as a more permanent place of community and prayer, number 175 Chesterton Road, where the two small downstairs rooms were used as a mosque (see plate 2.6). Unfortunately, this was found to be unsatisfactory, as the house was obviously built without the direction of Mecca as a primary concern, a fact commented upon by a reporter from the local newspaper, the *Cambridge Evening News*: 'those praying are in lines at an angle across the room, facing the south-east corner' (CEN 1976). A further problem was that planning permission to use the house as a mosque had not been obtained; the City Council therefore served an enforcement notice, which was given a stay of execution while another property was sought (CEN 1981a, b).

The third, and current, location which was chosen as a place of prayer was originally a gospel hall, then a meeting house of the Plymouth Brethren and, finally, a social centre for the Co-operative Society. It began to be used as a mosque in September 1982 (CEN 1982, 1988). Although still not ideal, in many ways the new location, which became the Abu Bakr Siddiq Islamic Centre in Mawson Road, was much more suitable, primarily because the orientation is right; prayer can be said, by chance, on exactly the right alignment by making use of the original layout of the building, which is also, being a hall, relatively open and spacious. Secondly, the former choir or stalls area upstairs serves as a ready-made area for women. The necessary alterations have been minimal: 'those who look for minarets or listen for the distant sound of the imam ... will, however, be disappointed. The church hall-like building has mundane sloping roofs, while any sounds from the imam would be lost in the roar of nearby traffic' (CEN 1985). The process of converting pre-existing places of worship to mosques, which was discussed earlier, is here being continued.

Plate 2.6　Former mosque, Chesterton Road, Cambridge (*photo*. T. Insoll)

As figure 2.6 shows, the interior of the mosque is plain and uncluttered. It is divided into two parts. The former church meeting hall contains the cloakroom, women's area and one prayer hall where a *minbar* and copies of the Qur'an and other religious texts are stored. Adjacent to this a second prayer hall has been added in which the Imam stands to lead Friday prayers, directed via a microphone relay throughout the building. Due east of the *qiblah* wall are the ablutions area and a kitchen. Entrance is through the main western doorway or via a passage which leads into the second prayer hall. Noticeably, a *mihrab* is absent. At normal daily prayers between 30 and 50 people

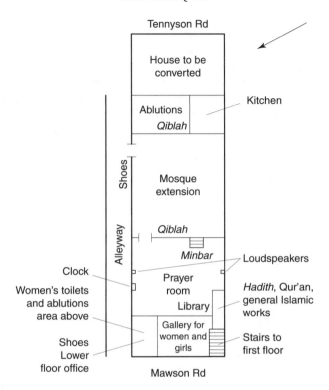

Figure 2.6 Plan of the interior of the Mawson Road mosque, Cambridge (not to scale)

are usually present, but for Friday prayers and at festivals these numbers increase dramatically, highlighting the lack of space. The primary disadvantages of the mosque are the general lack of space and the inconvenient position of the ablutions area, as well as a preference for a building aligned so that more worshippers can be accommodated parallel to the *qiblah* (Ali 1996). A programme of rebuilding is planned to solve these difficulties, and ideally the sentiments expressed in 1981 still hold true – to build a mosque, 'in the classical style with a gold-decorated dome and a minaret' (CEN 1981b) – but finances are unlikely to allow this option, even if the planning authorities were amenable to such a suggestion.

The development of the Cambridge Muslim community over the past 25 years, and the resulting material culture, are important to the themes discussed in this volume in a variety of ways. First, and fundamentally, is the fact that this example shows that a Muslim sacred space, no different in ethos to that encountered in the perceived Islamic heartlands, is now to be found in a new environment. Although the material culture translation of the church hall to the requirements of a mosque are minimal, this structure is unmistakably a mosque when one sets foot inside. Its function as the centre of worship remains the same as that evident in Jerusalem or on the coast of China. But how would the archaeologist define this structure in the form it is today 200 years hence? If the contents were complete, the identification would be immediate, but divest of these and levelled to its foundations it would be much more difficult: only an empty space with an east–west orientation would remain, no traces of *mihrab*, minaret or *minbar*, thus differentiating it little from any other hall. In this respect, it provides a sobering reminder of what can elude the archaeologist.

Summary and Conclusions

The mosque is the material culture embodiment of one of the fundamental components of Muslim life, the obligation of prayer, an immutable pillar of belief and of being Muslim. The origins of the mosque can be traced directly back to the Prophet, as regards both its religious and social significance. The latter element is of crucial importance: the mosque, as well as its religious role, also serves as a perpetuator of the Muslim community, through acting as its centre and, as is apparent in so many areas of Muslim life, as a unifier of the secular and sacred domains. The mosque is found in a similar form throughout the Muslim world, and should be recognizable for what it is in the archaeological record. Yet diversity is great, and numerous types of mosque exist, from the most ephemeral to vast edifices, but all are subject to the structuring principle, even if this is only represented in its simplest form through a concern for correct orientation. This in turn is one of the most pertinent points which can be drawn for the archaeology of religion in general: that a place of worship can encompass such a vast range of forms within a set of prescribed limits, and that pre-existing structures can be absorbed and adapted with minimal effort to suit the requirements of a different religious tradition, leaving recognizable material culture residue for the archaeologist to interpret. Churches and temples to mosques, mosques to churches and temples, the targeting of other holy places as the pre-eminent place to stamp religious identity would appear obvious, but perhaps a pre-existing religious structure also appeals for other reasons, questions which remain largely unexplored in terms of archaeology and world religions.

It is also obvious that many challenges undoubtedly await the archaeologist of the future as the modern movement takes hold, and regional diversity disappears under the spread of a uniform concrete mosque in a vaguely 'oriental' style. Such architecture has been recorded as far afield as Albania and Uganda (Vickers 1995; Insoll 1997a), and is built with the best of intentions, but creates what has been termed, a 'pan-Islamic style' employing a universal 'kit of standard parts', elements such as the dome and minaret, 'as a result of pressures to become more "normative" and international, as well as of a conscious desire on the part of Muslim communities to be seen as Muslim' (Khan 1994: 267). However, such developments offer far from insurmountable challenges for the archaeologist, and, on the contrary, present exciting possibilities for future research in the archaeology of Islam.

3

The Domestic Environment

Believers, do not enter the dwellings of other men until you have asked
their owner's permission and wished them peace.

Qur'an. The Light 24: 27

While the mosque could perhaps be expected to accord with a fairly
standard form (and therefore be archaeologically recognizable), what
of the domestic environment which is not imbued with any overt
religious importance? Does this form a significant component of
Muslim life, or is it somehow neutral and merely confined to the
secular domain? Before examining specific 'Muslim' examples of the
use and creation of domestic space, it is as well to draw in certain
strands of current thinking on the social role of the domestic environment.

Archaeologists appear to have come rather late in comparison with
other related disciplines to realize that a structure used for domestic
purposes does more than just provide shelter. It is an environment
which is thought out prior to construction and becomes the 'physical
embodiment of an ideal environment' (Rapoport 1969: 48, 1980). It
has been referred to as a 'structuring structure', both a medium for,
and the outcome of, social practices (Bourdieu 1977; Giddens 1979).
It is the home of the family unit, 'the foremost and fundamental
institution of human society' (Mawdudi 1986: 39), and the one
which forms the primary sphere in the Islamic social order. Thus,
the domestic environment can tell us much about society, beyond
merely illustrating the technological choices available to the builder,
and the architecture preferred by a society. It is also the environment
for family life within which children are raised, and in which social
codes and gender roles are defined, taught and transferred. In these

events, the house itself (here meant in its broadest definition) need not be a passive player, but can be utilized, consciously or unconsciously, in teaching processes and in perpetuating social codes and values.

Thus space can be used to reproduce the social or cosmological order (Moore 1986), and the very structure and layout of the house can be a metaphor for society (see Cunningham 1964; Humphrey 1974; Hugh-Jones 1985). To quote Carsten and Hugh-Jones (1995: 2), 'house, body and mind are in continuous interaction, the physical structure, furnishing, social conventions and mental images of the house at once enabling, moulding, informing and constraining the activities and ideas which unfold within its bounds.' Archaeologists have similarly become interested in viewing domestic architecture as imbued with a greater social significance than previously acknowledged (see, for example, Kent 1990; Samson 1990; Parker Pearson and Richards 1994). This is of great significance as domestic structures are one of the categories of archaeological evidence most frequently encountered by archaeologists, and within Islamic archaeology this is no exception.

Having stressed that the domestic environment is far from neutral, is it possible to define a type of domestic architecture as specifically Islamic? Can it be said to be distinctive, even with an idealized generalized form? Although culturally diverse, there is a definable Islamic domestic architecture, and this has been studied in some detail both by architects and archaeologists (see, for example, Petherbridge 1978; Fentress 1987, Campo 1991). However, one of the primary concerns of this study has rarely, if at all, been considered, namely, the archaeological analysis and recognition of Islamic domestic structures. For example, if the archaeological recognition of nomads, including their architecture, is considered (as by Cribb 1991), then Islam is not considered as a structuring principle, even though the majority of the groups used as examples are Muslim, and in many cases their religion could have been of fundamental importance in structuring their domestic space.

In contrast, where Islamic domestic structures have been considered, there has often been a tendency to focus upon the grander monuments, a further instance of 'top-heavy' Islamic archaeology and architectural studies. As has been generally voiced elsewhere (Petherbridge 1978: 193–5; Rudofsky 1981: 1), study of the vernacular is usually neglected in favour of largely non-representative palatial architecture which, when the full corpus of domestic architecture is considered, forms a numerically insignificant part. Archaeological site plans might portray a central cluster of buildings perceived as important, a citadel perhaps, but the periphery, perhaps of less permanent, and thus more archaeologically ephemeral, structures, is given short shrift or left unstudied. This imbalance in the study of the archaeology of the Muslim domestic environment is unfortunate, as again the archaeologist interested in Islam is privileged in the sources of information available in pursuing this field of study (textual, ethnographic, iconographic). Thus, this chapter will be concerned with defining what constitutes Muslim domestic architecture, exploring the criteria for its recognition archaeologically, and placing it within its social context.

An Ideal Islamic Domestic Environment

The model for the Muslim household can be regarded as that of the Prophet, and the courtyard house built by the Prophet in the first year of the *hijrah* (622) in Medina as the first Muslim domestic structure. Although often seen as the progenitor of Muslim domestic space, it was in fact based on existing west Arabian architectural traditions, and the pre-Islamic architectural heritage must be acknowledged. The Prophet's house itself, as far as it has been reconstructed historically, consisted of a rectangular walled courtyard, in which livestock were kept, and on one or more sides of which were rooms for sleeping, storing goods, and for each wife and her children. The house functioned as both a dwelling and a meeting place for believers (Cresswell 1932: 7; Marcais 1965: 113; Fentress 1987: 63). The terminology applied to the Muslim house varies, but the most frequently encountered Arabic names are *dar*, for the enclosed compound, and *beit* or *bayt*, for smaller dwellings, and a name which can also be applied to a tent as in *bayt sha'ar* (Campo 1991; Petersen 1996).

Obviously, the concept of privacy was not invented by Muslims, but domestic space is referred to in both the Qur'an and the *hadith*, where the sanctity of the house is indicated, and strict rules to maintain domestic privacy are outlined (see Petherbridge 1978; Campo 1991). The primary and over-riding concern is with privacy and the protection and seclusion of women (in certain cultural contexts referred to as purdah) and the sanctity of the family. Both wife and domestic space are to be protected, and domestic life is linked to ideas of purity. Indeed, Campo (1991: 21) suggests that Muslim 'rules governing access to domestic space are regarded as similar to rules governing exposure of and access to the human body'. To achieve this, physical space is often segregated into two spheres, whether two halves of a tent, within a single or double courtyard or spread over

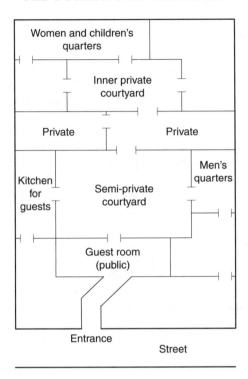

Figure 3.1 Stereotypical layout of an idealized Muslim courtyard house

several palatial complexes. The private area is for family life, including the harem or women's quarters, which is the arena for domestic activities and from which all men except immediate male relatives (husbands, sons, brothers) are usually excluded. The second area forms a male–communal sphere, usually referred to within the literature as 'public' or 'semi-public', and which can include a reception room or rooms, or area where guests (usually male) are entertained, and possibly separate men's living quarters (see figure 3.1). Numerous permutations are possible, and many devices can be used to ensure privacy.

Within the traditional courtyard house, the dominant permanent type which might be encountered archaeologically, privacy can be further maintained through a deliberate inward orientation of space. Exterior windows, which are usually few, are above street level to avoid views inward, and the exterior walls are usually austere and undecorated and entered by a single door; a second (women's) door is sometimes present. Angled entrance ways are employed to deny the passer-by a view into the interior of the house, and guest rooms are placed close to the entrance so that the family quarters are left undisturbed (Al-Azzawi 1969). It should be noted, however, that Muslim houses do not have a monopoly of features developed to promote privacy. These predate Islam in many areas, as in Ancient Greece, examples from which Nevett (1994) discusses and compares with Islamic houses, and also in Assyria, and equally with many non-Muslim Byzantine period houses, including those described by Woolley and Lawrence in southern Palestine (1936: 92–3). Similarly, domestic features promoting privacy can also be found today among adherents of different religions, Jews, Christians and others.

Allied with the social requirements which Muslim domestic architecture might aim to satisfy, cultural and environmental factors must also be considered. It is perhaps best to define traditional Muslim domestic architecture as a *mélange* of varying local cultural, religious, social and environmental factors, and Rapoport (1969: 17) raises the need to differentiate between the primary forces acting on house form and those which he terms secondary or modifying. As regards the Muslim domestic environment, the relative dominance of various factors will vary, and it is the innumerable secondary or modifying forces which serve to create the diversity found. But it is apparent that to attribute the development of Muslim domestic architecture to purely economic or environmental factors would be wrong. As will be discussed in greater detail below, what might at first glance appear as solely utilitarian, need not be so; the *mashrabiyya* or boxed wooden lattice-work window screens, which were commonly used in many regions of the Muslim world, provide a case in point (see plate 3.1). They both reduce glare and allow the entry of cooling breezes, but at the same time can provide privacy for women to observe the world beyond the domestic unit without being seen (Oliver 1987: 120–3).

Regional diversity has to be acknowledged, but a common concern can be seen to run through the entire spectrum of Muslim domestic architecture, from the palaces of the rich to the tents of the pastoralists. This (where observed, and this is, and even more so, was frequent) is a preoccupation with maintaining privacy through gender segregation and the separation of the domains of public and private life. Yet this explicit spatial division into public equals male, and private equals female, can be criticized for being too rigid in its definition (see figure 3.2). It has been argued that, through the terminology used, the fact that women also visit each other is denied, and in reality there is a constant but less visible round of public life in the female sphere, which renders it not really private at all (Webster

Plate 3.1   *Mashrabiyya*, Massawa, Eritrea (*photo*. T. Insoll)

1984; Maclean 1996), with women exercising 'veiled power' (Webster 1984: 256). Male 'public' space is thus pushed to the fore at the expense of a de-valued 'domestic' female space. This is a valid criticism of somewhat restrictive terminology and in many ways the category of 'male communal sphere' is preferable to 'public', as is 'female communal sphere' to 'private'.

To the archaeologist, who for interpretative simplicity likes the existence of common codes or rules, the existence of these separate domains, however termed, is reassuring. But as with all the other categories of material culture discussed, exceptions do occur, and how space is demarcated can vary and need not necessarily be fixed. As Carsten and Hugh-Jones note, 'we should then be wary about describing the house as a structure of unchanging gendered oppositions' (1995: 41). Yet, the existence of these public/private spatial domains means that a definable Muslim domestic space exists. However, we can recognize a Muslim domestic space not merely

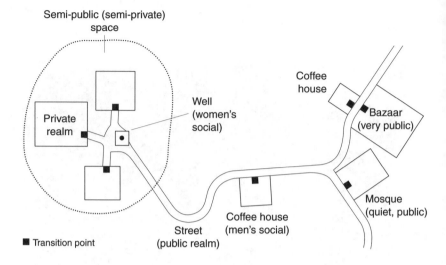

Figure 3.2   Spatial domains in Isfahan (after Rapoport 1969: fig. 3.14)

because of a spatial divide; furnishings, inscriptions, individuals all create the image. But it is when we come to try to recognize a domestic space archaeologically, basing this identification solely upon the existence of these separate domains, that difficulties arise. A terraced house in Leicester, England, for example, reduced to a ground plan or standing as an empty structure, though perhaps inhabited by a Muslim family for many years, and perhaps formerly curtained or partitioned into separate areas, would defy identification. It is not possible to define a Muslim domestic space utilizing plan alone; in this manner it could not be set apart from a Christian, Hindu or secular domestic structure which shows privacy concerns. Not all Muslim domestic structures do or have maintained a public/private divide, and Muslims do not and have never maintained a monopoly on privacy. The only way in which the Muslim domestic structure can be archaeologically identified is if it is found in company with other categories of archaeological evidence.

Archaeological Recognition

Assuming that we are investigating the Muslim domestic environment as part of a complete package, the practical issues which might be of interest to the archaeologist can best be summarized as the axes of investigation: how can Muslim domestic space be visualized both horizontally and vertically in buildings, and how can the essential structuring principles be recognized in more ephemeral materials.

Permanent structures in stone and brick

The horizontal axis   The most frequent level of archaeological investigation of domestic architecture will be upon the horizontal axis, for two main reasons. First, single-storey dwellings are much more common than multi-storey ones: probably over 70 per cent of the world's total today according to Oliver (1987: 136), and the figure was almost certainly even higher in the past. Secondly, very rarely will standing structures be preserved in the archaeological record. No hard and fast rules exist, but within the rural environment it is probable that single-storey Muslim dwellings will be more frequently encountered. While pressures of space in the urban environment, certain defensive situations and specific environmental conditions (for example, taller houses can capture breezes, as on the Red Sea coast) will facilitate the use of multi-storey houses (Petherbridge 1978). In many cases only the strength or depth of foundations will suggest upper storeys.

Although numerous regional traditions exist which dictate differences in how this space is structured (see, for example, Marcais 1965 for a summary of regional variations in domestic architecture, their development and spread), archaeological excavation of the horizontal axis in many areas of the Muslim world has provided data which supports the existence of public and private spaces, as argued for above, but this could only be defined as 'Muslim specific' because it was found in association with other categories of evidence, or identification was achieved by using other sources of evidence such as historical documents. Examples include Siraf (Iran) where courtyard houses dated to *c.*1000 were found. These were originally multi-storey buildings, but the walls only survived to a maximum height of 3.5 m (Whitehouse 1970, 1971). Similar courtyard houses were recorded at Sétif (Algeria), where Fentress (1987: 65–6) charted changes between the tenth and eleventh centuries, with a greater emphasis on the seclusion of women becoming apparent. In the later phase, the courtyard was divided into two sections, in one case by a suite of rooms, in another by a wall ensuring that male visitors did not have to pass through the women's quarters to reach the reception rooms. Likewise, in what has been termed the 'Abbasid popular quarter' at Samarra (Iraq), houses were often linked by secondary doorways, perhaps, as al-Janabi has suggested (1983:

308), 'reflecting the extension of families by marriage, or possibly even an earlier Mesopotamian combination of separate public and domestic quarters'. A further variant of the courtyard house is the *iwan*, which differs from the previously discussed Maghrebi and Persian examples in its layout, and is defined as 'a room enclosed by three walls, opening out in the whole width of the fourth side', and open to the courtyard space (Marcais 1965: 113), examples were recorded at Fustat, the initial Muslim settlement in the vicinity of Cairo (see Scanlon 1970a; Kubiak 1982; see chapter 7). This type of house is extensively found throughout Central Asia, Iran and the Middle East.

Similar spatial concerns can be seen within palatial complexes, and Hillenbrand (1994: 377, 381) makes the point that, although palaces are something of a problematical category, they meet all the private and official requirements of Islamic decorum. They replicate and amplify the smaller everyday domestic environment on a much larger scale, with their public audience quarters, private rooms, strongly fortified entrance and storerooms, magnifications of features found in smaller houses. Some palaces were even in part composed of multiples of courtyard houses, as in the eleventh-century *Palais de la Salut* at Qal'a (Algeria) (Fentress 1987: 60), and certain of the Umayyad 'desert palaces' of Syria and Palestine were comprised of a number of *bayts*, each housing a tribal or family unit (Petersen 1996: 296), with some of the latter inhabited by Muslims but built by Byzantine architects. Yet, obviously, we should not take the analogy between palaces and more humble domestic environments too far, as most houses do not contain features such as mosques and baths.

Examples on the horizontal dimension can also be found at the very base of the domestic architectural spectrum. In the village of Ti'innik (Palestine) during the sixteenth to mid-eighteenth centuries, up to seven or eight single-room houses (*bayt*) were clustered together within walled courtyards (*hawsh*). Though built like this for defence, Muslim requirements regarding social relations were not relaxed, and thus dictated that the occupiers of each *hawsh* were members of the same extended family (Ziadeh 1995: 1004–5).

The existence of structured Muslim domestic space is also found within military installations. In the garrison fortress of Qasr Ibrim, 220 km south of Aswan (Egypt), characteristic double courtyard houses were built in stone during the Ottoman occupation (late sixteenth to early nineteenth centuries), with a clear subdivision into distinct male and female areas (Adams 1990: 4–7), forming recognizable public and private domains. These certainly indicated a changed social pattern from that of the previous Christian and pre-Christian settlements, and the arrival of a Turkish military garrison (Alexander 1988: 86, 1994). Far to the west in Al-Andalus similar spatial concerns were also evident in Granada. Within the Alcazaba, the fort attached to, but preceding, the Alhambra, the capital of the Nasrid kingdom in Granada dating from the thirteenth and fourteenth centuries, 17 houses for guard families were found, 'laid out in the characteristic Islamic urban pattern' (Lopez 1992: 154), with angled entrance ways, and attention focused inwards on the courtyards.

The vertical axis Spatial structuring according to Muslim social requirements need not only be projected in the horizontal dimension, but vertically as well. It is perhaps too easily forgotten that a multi-storey building could equally be structured spatially into male and female, family and guest areas, a factor of great importance where space might be restricted for many reasons, especially in the urban environment. At the Ottoman fortress on Sai Island in the Sudan, a roughly contemporary southern companion to Qasr Ibrim, mentioned previously, mud-brick houses of up to three storeys were recorded still standing (Alexander 1997b; see also Vercoutter 1958; Alexander 1997a). These structures could have been similar to the so-called 'castle' houses found along the same stretch of the Nile (Adams 1987: 334–8; Insoll 1996c: 453), but at Sai were perhaps less overtly defensive in character, surrounded as they were by a substantial wall. This fact is indicated by the surviving slots for the now-missing *mashrabiyyas* which were recorded, a feature which parallels the houses of the Red Sea coast, such as those in the abandoned town of Suakin where numerous multi-storey houses survive (Greenlaw 1995).

Possibly the best-known examples of multi-storey housing in the Muslim world are the 'tower houses' of Yemen, clustered in the mountainous central plateau and San'a, the capital (Kirkman 1976; Serjeant and Lewcock 1983). These extraordinary structures provide us with an example of how the public and private domains, most frequently encountered horizontally, can also be articulated through vertical space (see figure 3.3). Beginning at the ground floor, interior space is highly structured, fulfilling both practical and social requirements, through between five and nine storeys. Of importance within this context is the relationship between the *mafraj*, the principal reception room for men, and the private quarters of the women (including the kitchen). The former is usually located on the topmost floor, while the latter are situated just below. Practicality and social requirements are combined. For example, chance encounters on the staircase can be avoided through the presence of strategically placed

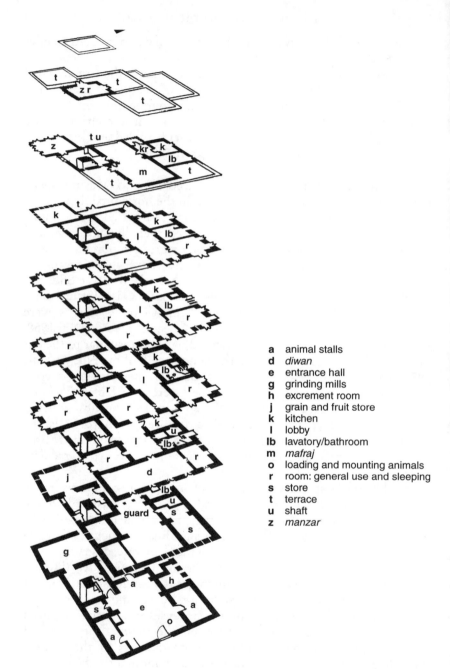

a   animal stalls
d   *diwan*
e   entrance hall
g   grinding mills
h   excrement room
j   grain and fruit store
k   kitchen
l   lobby
lb lavatory/bathroom
m   *mafraj*
o   loading and mounting animals
r   room: general use and sleeping
s   store
t   terrace
u   shaft
z   *manzar*

Figure 3.3 Vertical utilization of space in a San'a tower house (not to scale) (from Lewcock and Serjeant 1983: 458)

wooden grilles which allow women to observe who is on the stairs. Similarly, the open-work wooden box windows, already referred to, have an aperture in their base to 'allow women to see down to the street and control access to the house' (Kirkman 1976: 54).

What might be of cultural importance here is what Gerholm (1977: 163) terms Yemeni 'sensitivities to height difference'. This is certainly not a Yemeni Muslim prerogative, but perhaps status was also involved in reaching such heights in construction (perhaps as well as something as mundane as wanting a pleasant view!), while at the same time not infringing upon social codes. Another factor which should be considered is that being a Muslim gave, as is universally found in the Muslim world, superior status. Jewish houses in San'a and elsewhere could not overlook Muslim ones, in case Muslim women were observed and Muslims should similarly not be able to overlook their neighbours. Jewish houses were thus restricted to two storeys, and differed architecturally from Muslim houses in many other ways (Lewcock and Serjeant 1983: 497; see also Rathjens 1957). These are factors which could be archaeologically discernible, and might facilitate the identification of different religious communities.

Another example of the vertical utilization of domestic space is provided by contemporary African-American Muslim communities who live in blocks of flats. Here, choice is restricted as these communities do not live in a Muslim society; however, at the same time, they attempt to differentiate themselves and demarcate their domestic space from the outside world (McCloud 1995: 105–6). To achieve this a variety of mechanisms are utilized. Where feasible, complete blocks of flats are bought; failing this, emphasis is placed upon signalling the existence of a Muslim domestic space at the entrance to the home, through calligraphy, stickers and similar mechanisms. Inside, space is 'gender neutral' unless visitors are present, then the public–private divide becomes apparent, as does gender segregation, the living room for men, the kitchen for women. To quote McCloud, 'in their domestic spaces, African American Muslims have thus taken small portions of various Muslim cultures and woven an interesting tapestry that transcends (without denying) both their American nationality and their ethnicity. They have, in short, created a space for Islam inside the boundaries of Western architecture and culture' (1995: 110). Just how this would be recognizable to the archaeologist of the future presents great problems: the fabric of the home does not set it apart from those occupied by non-Muslim neighbours, other than that the windows are covered.

Impermanent and ephemeral structures

Both nomadic pastoralists and sedentary agriculturists living in structures built of less durable materials have obviously been attracted to Islam since the beginnings of the religion (see plate 3.2). The fact that such people frequently live in shelters constructed of ephemeral materials, cloth, skin or reeds for example, does not mean that they were excluded from structuring their domestic space according to Islamic custom.

Tents This incorporates a huge range of structures utilized by numerous ethnic groups over a vast region and time period. Four examples drawn from the substantial literature which exists will be discussed to illustrate to what degree the tented domestic environment can be structured to fulfil Muslim requirements where they are followed.

Among the Bedouin of the Arabian peninsula, the customary shelter, the textile 'black tent', is divided into men's and women's spaces (see Feilberg 1944; Faegre 1979). This separation is maintained through a dividing curtain, the *qata*. The men's side, usually the smaller, is covered with carpets and cushions for guests. Here also

Plate 3.2 Kazakh family in front of tent, early twentieth century (Haddon Collection, Cambridge)

will be a hearth for preparing coffee and all the accompanying accoutrements. The larger women's side is the main living and working area, which will not usually be seen by any other man except the tent owner. Therefore, in this example it can be seen that spatial use is the same as that found in more permanent domestic structures. Other tent users can maintain a similar spatial divide. The Hassaniya Moors of north-west Africa utilize a curtain-divider which can seclude women when visitors are present (Andrews 1971, 1995), and among the Kababish of the Sudan internal space (within the Sheikh's tent at least) is firmly demarcated into public and private areas, with each wife having her own tent positioned so no wife would have precedence over another (Verity 1971: 31). Also of interest, though obviously without wide archaeological significance, is Andrews (1987: 151) mention of a historical source which records that private tented rooms were created for queens in the great Mughal tented courts of early seventeenth-century India, so they could see but not be seen.

In other areas and with other ethnic groups explicit domestic spatial separation is not so clear. The Qashqa'i of the Zagros Mountains in Iran do not divide the tent structurally into male and female sections, though in practice such a division, of tasks and entertaining, does occur (Beck 1978: 356–8). Similarly, the Tuareg and Tedu of the central Saharan regions, who utilize a type of free-standing frame, non-tensile, mat and skin tent, do not generally maintain a spatial division (Nicolaisen 1963; Faegre 1979). However, although internal physical boundaries might not be created, manifestations of a concern with privacy may be present. One such feature can be the orientation of the tent or indeed of the whole camp. With the Qashqa'i, for example, although they might not subdivide the tent, the tents themselves are positioned so that no tent entrance faces another (Beck 1978: 357).

Although we cannot directly transfer from the past into the present, it is also reasonable to suggest that information gained from ethnography has some bearing upon the tented domestic environment of the past. It can be seen that variety is found, and the degree to which space is structured into public and private domains, male and female spaces, varies greatly, and in many instances no such demarcation exists at all. Once again we are largely concerned with an ideal, but where such a spatial separation exists could it be archaeologically recognizable? Matters are complicated by the very nature of the tent which allows great flexibility of space. Cribb (1991: 101) notes that the tent is rarely a self-contained spatial unit; activity areas can be extended, as can the tent itself to cope with feasts and similar occasions. Furthermore, within the basic unit, space can change function: a domestic space can become a guest area, for example. This complicates things, as does the ephemeral nature of the structure, and the transient lifestyle of its occupants. The archaeological recognition of a tented domestic space which has been structured by possible Muslim requirements is difficult, yet this is not an impossible undertaking. Whereas nomads are frequently attested archaeologically, as with Garlake's (1978) survey and excavation of a temporary tented camp at Ras Abaruk (Qatar) re-used from the seventeenth to the nineteenth centuries, evidence which might allow the recognition of a division of domestic space is more elusive. Recent research in southern Jordan isolated a number of features which could attest to this (Banning and Köhler-Rollefson 1992: 195). In recently occupied nomadic encampments near Beidha there were two hearths within the tents, the larger one placed in the centre of (or just outside) the tent (itself represented by an area cleared of stones and blanketed by sheep and goat dung) which was used by the women for cooking, and a smaller one used by men for coffee-making. Faegre (1979: 25) claims that 'the size and depth of the coffee hearth tells the observer whether the host was a generous man and even what tribe camped there.' Numerous other features testified to the former tents: stone bed platforms, stone storage platforms, ditches for water run-off, stone bases for poles, and stone cord weights or trailing weights.

The existence of such features could illustrate that an internal division had existed within a tent, possibly reinforced by the patterning of domestic items and faunal remains within the demarcated area. To make such an identification more secure, physical evidence for the partition would be needed, such as lines of stones to hold a curtain in place. Avni (1992: 245) found that just such an arrangement was used to strengthen tents externally in pre-Islamic contexts in the Negev desert. Thus, it can be argued that in certain cases it could be possible to recognize archaeologically the former presence of a tented domestic space which had been structured according to different spatial domains, but to take this identification one stage further, to say it was structured by Muslim social codes, requires more than an outline of stones on the ground. Other categories of archaeological evidence are required as well (see figure 3.4).

Reed, grass and palm architecture   A second example which can be drawn from the repertoire of domestic structures made from more ephemeral materials, and which can show a spatial division, are houses built of reeds which, as with the tent and the courtyard house, significantly predate Islam. The split-reed houses of the Shi'ah

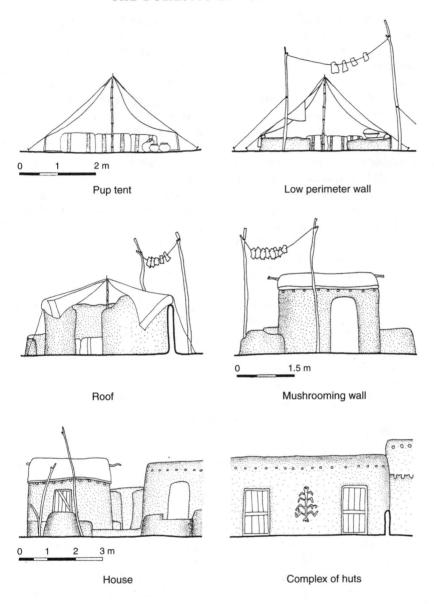

0   1   2 m

Pup tent   Low perimeter wall

0   1.5 m

Roof   Mushrooming wall

0   1   2   3 m

House   Complex of huts

Figure 3.4 Although we are not told whether the initial tent is structured according to possible Muslim social codes, this evolutionary sequence from pup tent to mud-hut compound in Afghanistan provides an example of how privacy gradually increased over time through various stages of construction (from Hallet and Samizay 1980: 56–7) 'marsh Arabs' (Madan) of southern Iraq are built on reed platforms or natural islands and are usually occupied by a family unit (Thesiger 1954, 1980; Salim 1962: 55; Young and Wheeler 1977). Although little attempt is made to keep women apart from visitors, a raised reed platform divides the family quarters from the area used to entertain male visitors in the absence of a separate guest house, the *mudhif*, often an elaborate barrel-vaulted structure. In contrast, a stricter division of space into the usual public and private spheres is found in the palm-branch houses built in the Muscat region of Oman. Here a *soubla* or *maglis*, a guest room made of branches for the reception of males, is incorporated into the courtyard house. This is entered from outside the house and is adjacent to the main entrance (Abdulak 1977: 20). Similarly, a spatial demarcation is maintained by the Hamar Arabs (Kordofan province, Sudan). A grass or cane compound is built surrounding three inner compounds, one for men, one for women (and children) and the other for animals, and a guest hut of grass on a wooden framework is incorporated within the men's compound (Asher 1986: 54).

Although all these examples of domestic structure – tents, and reed, grass and palm houses – are made from less durable materials, it has been shown how they too can be spatially structured into different domains, and how in certain instances it might be possible to identify these as structured according to Muslim social requirements, if other categories of evidence are found. It is this latter point which is of critical importance as all of the recognition criteria outlined for the recognition of Muslim domestic space could be exhibited by non-Muslim groups, including the ground plan with the existence of internal partitions, division of internal space and angled entrance ways. Secondly, there is the question of orientation, with a focus on the interior not the exterior (decoration, windows and so on), and the orientation of structures so as not to face each other; and, thirdly, the artifacts present, the positioning of features such as hearths, and the patterning of artifacts which might allow the recognition of a gender division. A satisfactory identification of Muslim domestic space based on these criteria alone cannot be achieved: it is necessary to strengthen this identification by examining the other evidence which might be present within (coins, personal possessions, inscriptions, furnishings, dietary remains) and around (burials, other structures) the domestic structure. Fortunately, we do not, or should not, study the domestic environment in a vacuum, as devoid of all contextual information, and thus the above criteria are valid when a more holistic examination is being undertaken.

Archaeology, Domestic Space and Social Use

Once domestic space has been identified as being formerly occupied by Muslims, can more be made of its study? Of course it is possible, and indeed necessary, to move beyond building materials and the actual physical dimensions of domestic structures to a broader, more socially aware, Islamic archaeology. A variety of further information may be retrieved: the composition of the society and the family, gender and status concerns (and possible links with purdah), spatial use and the way physical and spiritual thresholds or boundaries are created.

Society and the family

To see what might be learnt about Muslim society at a larger scale, and the Muslim family at a smaller scale, from a study of domestic architecture, three examples will be considered here: orientation; house form in sub-Saharan Africa; and the in-built expansive mechanisms of the Muslim domestic structure.

Orientation House orientation is in fact an area of research with very little general applicability; there is no one fixed orientation for Muslim houses. Instances occur where the domestic structure is oriented to Mecca, but this is by no means uniform, though latrines may deliberately face away from Mecca. Often orientation is primarily for climatic reasons, to encourage cooling breezes and prevent the entrance of dust (Petherbridge 1978: 201–2). Unfortunately, this absence of a dominant domestic orientation removes from the archaeologist an avenue of interpretation, which is usually exploited to the full.

House form However, one interesting and broadly inter-related example of a link between orientation and possible social change can be provided. In many areas of sub-Saharan Africa there appears to be a correlation between round houses and local religions, and square or rectangular houses and Islam. While some Islamized groups live in round houses and vice versa (Insoll 1996b; see also Engestrom 1959: 65; Sanogo 1991: 152), the correlation occurs frequently enough in the archaeological record to suggest that it is of some significance, and that there can be a switch in how space becomes ordered following conversion to Islam in certain areas.

Rapoport (1969: 41) has suggested that in general round houses cannot be easily oriented, a statement that would not appear to make sense. Rather, it is perhaps possible that it was easier to fulfil privacy requirements, perhaps newly introduced with Islam, or, as is more likely, increased in significance following conversion through the use of rectangular or square house plans. Moore (1986: 191) has suggested that there is a link between a prestige system with positive 'modern' values (Western ones in her example) and the replacement of round houses by those of rectangular plan. Similar thinking appears to have in part underlain the recent use of rectangular architecture in favour of round houses in the northern Cameroons, and where the government pushed 'modernization' policies (Lyons 1996). Perhaps a similar interpretation can be projected further back in time. Thus, along with the new religion come elements of different material culture, not necessarily better or improved, but part of the package proclaiming Muslim identity. In turn, it also brings us back, though without any direct connection whatsoever, to the sentiments underlying the inscriptions in the Dome of the Rock and its very construction (see chapter 2) – making a statement of the new faith, in this instance by utilizing the domestic environment as one of the signalling mechanisms.

Communality and individuality   Although studies of house orientation might be largely unprofitable, it could be possible to reconstruct something of Muslim family structure from an archaeological study, taking as our starting point the fact that we know from both historical sources and modern observation that Muslim society has been based around the extended family comprising the father, his wife or wives (up to four), their children, and sometimes including married sons and their households. Physically, this is best exemplified by what has been termed the 'accretive nature' of the Muslim house (Petherbridge 1978: 198); as the extended family grows so does the house, which is often left unfinished to allow further quarters to be built on. An example of this process in action is provided by Talib (1984: 55), who describes how the roof timbers of courtyard houses in Saudi Arabia were often left uncut to allow new beams to be connected to the old. Such a process could even be archaeologically recognizable through a careful evaluation of structural phasing.

Indeed, Fentress (1987: 66) has gone as far as to draw parallels between the structure of the house plans excavated at Sétif and the Muslim families who occupied them, with the individuals of the family standing as subordinate to the patriarch 'as the single rooms do to the courtyard'. Here also additional wings could be added to the house as a son got married. This process was facilitated by co-operation between the inhabitants of the quarter and, according to

Fentress (1987: 67), reminiscent of the development of the Prophet's house itself. Yet to reconstruct how a particular Muslim domestic complex of one or more natural families was conceptualized in the past is difficult for it could vary regionally and according to gender. This is the case with the Qashqa'i, for example: their camp was viewed by men as a number of different households, while women saw it as a single community (Beck 1978: 357). Such differences in conception serve to reinforce the point that, when dealing with the archaeological record, with the legacy of different groups and individuals with different conceptions, to stress too firmly that a single interpretation of events is the only possible answer is flawed. If a multiplicity of options can exist regarding something as prosaic as how a settlement is conceived, what does this infer for more complex entities?

The division of house types into two categories correlating with 'collectivistic' and 'individualistic' societies (Parker Pearson and Richards 1994: 60–1) is of importance with regard to Muslim households. Collectivistic societies are defined as possessing a shared value system and having an emphasis on restricting and 'containing' women. Features relevant to their domestic structures include gender separation inside and outside houses, separate men's accommodation and dwellings largely functional and similar in appearance. In contrast, in individualistic societies, mobility is high, kinship is weakened and competing value systems and fashions develop. Here identity (personal status) is affirmed through the house, which in itself is more public, although domestic life may be private. These categories can be seen to equate with what Rapoport (1969: 5–6) terms the 'additive quality', characteristic of vernacular architecture as compared to the 'closed, final form of high-style design'.

It is obvious that, while elements of the 'collectivistic' social definition apply to Muslim society, elements of the 'individualistic' definition also apply, and it would certainly be wrong to say that the Muslim domestic environment is somehow egalitarian and thus devoid of any competitive tendencies as elaborately decorated house interiors testify. But, on the whole, collectivist values dominate, although increasingly coming into conflict with 'individualistic' ones. Collectivistic attributes are having to be shoehorned, and not through force, into domestic structures associated with individualistic design as outlined above. Al-Azzawi (1969: 98–9) has studied this and describes how 'Western', 'European' or 'closed' houses have been introduced into Iraq and in many cases replaced the traditional 'collectivistic' courtyard house. These new structures did not fulfil any of the social, environmental or religious requirements discussed. Simple yet obvious shortcomings were apparent: ventilation was poor, air-conditioning needed, and courtyards which were built over and turned into the main living room, failed to fulfil privacy requirements being frequently over-looked by neighbouring houses.

However, this apparent incompatibility with the 'modern' does not mean that Muslim societies have lived in a form of stasis for 1,400 years; merely that the process of change has accelerated much more rapidly recently. Ziadeh's (1995: 1005–7) study of the village of Ti'in-nik provides a case in point. Altered social and political conditions since the 1950s could be plotted through changes in architecture and residence patterns. The collective houses (*ahwash*) were largely abandoned in favour of separate multi-room concrete buildings which reflected the shift from an economic system based on self-sufficiency and collective free labour by members of the extended family to one based on waged labour and the nuclear family. At the same time, an economy which had been dependent on animals disappeared, indicated by the absence of the internal stalling of animals within the courtyard.

These examples show how house form can reflect familial and social structure within Islam, the domestic environment being an active rather than passive aspect of material culture. But, regardless of change, it is still possible that the existence of the structuring principle, even if only reduced to an emphasis upon privacy, will be seen to continue, as it has done for so long. This element, a concern with privacy and its resulting manifestation in many different forms, is thus presented as a generality, where utilized, and is the structuring principle of the Muslim domestic environment and the possible key to its archaeological recognition (bearing in mind the points already made to make such an identification more certain).

Public and private faces

But what of other factors which might be investigated once the initial identification is certain? The pursuit of status and how this is manifest is one factor. To display one's finest possessions within the area where one receives guests is a universal characteristic; such a room or rooms, courtyard, open area or tent can become an arena for signalling status and wealth. The primary means of achieving this is simply by displaying the choicest possessions within the space used to entertain guests. Kirkman (1976) mentions that in the guest room (*mafraj*) of the San'a (Yemen) tower house, for example, ornate copper trays, candlesticks and other expensive items were displayed alongside a concentration of equipment ancillary to entertaining guests:

water-pipes, tobacco boxes, braziers, spittoons for the ubiquitous *qat* chewing sessions, and cushions and rugs, often richly patterned and finished, for the guests to sit and recline on. Similar processes are apparent in traditional houses in the Ghadames oasis (Libya) where the room used to receive guests was also the focus of decoration; painted motifs, mirrors, brass utensils and wall hangings were all used to create an impression of wealth (Evans 1975–6: 35; Shawesh 1995: 43). Likewise, such notions of display are present in the sitting rooms where guests are received in modern apartments of the Egyptian middle and upper classes in Cairo, which Campo describes as a 'blend of Euramerican and Islamic material culture' (1991: 127).

More complex was the pursuit of status by the ruling class within the Lebanese village discussed by Michael Gilsenan (1982). Here space itself was transformed for status purposes. Foremost in this process was the house itself, described as a Franco-Italian *château*, which was built in direct contrast to the traditional inward-looking castle of the ruling class. The *château* was all 'facade, appearance, show' (Gilsenan 1982: 169), used to enhance status and distinguish the owners from the other members of the village, and the *maglis* or reception room was also transformed into a 'salon'. Whereas the traditional *maglis*, the 'social heart of the house' (1982: 182), had been furnished in a conventional and austere manner with mats and cushions, coffee-making equipment and water-pipes, the salon was the absolute opposite, furnished with polished marble tables, plastic chandeliers, high gilt chairs and gilt mirrors, all for show, and to express wealth and status. Emulation, again for status purposes, was pursued lower down the social scale; even the peasants occasionally replicated in cheap materials the 'salon' or aspects of it in order that they might 'pretend to a minute but crucial economic advance over the others' (Gilsenan 1982: 186). In fact, the only group who resisted this process of emptying social space of any traditional value in the blatant pursuit of status were religious men, concerned as they were, as Gilsenan notes, with inner rather than outer meanings. Such processes of display and of emulation might well be archaeologically visible. Furthermore, a preoccupation with gaining status advantage, no matter how small, is not confined to the upper echelons of society, but is something that can be found through all levels of society and across the Muslim world, and in other societies. But a concern for status need not solely be concerned with inanimate material possessions. Status is also a factor which must be considered with regard to the seclusion of women, with once again the domestic environment functioning as one of the primary mechanisms by which this can be achieved, which in turn has certain archaeological implications.

Status, society, culture and purdah

Yet to propose status as the sole reason for the existence of an emphasis upon secluding women in parts of the Muslim world would be incorrect. Three dominant factors influence the extent to which the seclusion of women is practised: social concerns, status considerations and cultural context. Equally, the existence of seclusion practices (sometimes referred to as 'purdah', meaning literally screen or curtain) should not be taken to mean that women in Muslim societies are weak and devoid of any power; this too is wholly incorrect. Gender relations and social 'power' can be negotiated in many ways.

But if we consider social concerns, a link between these and purdah appears to be directly connected with religious considerations through the existence of a conscious effort to restrict female social interaction as outlined in the Qur'an, where this subject is considered in some detail. For example, it is stated that one should 'Enjoin believing women to turn their eyes away from temptation and to preserve their chastity; to cover their adornments (except such as are normally displayed); to draw their veils over their bosoms and not to reveal their finery except to their husbands, their fathers, their husbands' fathers, their sons, their step-sons, their brothers, their brothers' sons, their sisters' sons, their women-servants, and their slave-girls; male attendants lacking in natural vigour, and children who have no carnal knowledge of women' (The Light 24: 31). What can perhaps be seen as being intimately linked with this are concerns over purity and pollution, not in the manner that Douglas (1966) discusses them, that is, the physical concern with polluting substances, but more with social matters; namely, the physical power of women, and the protection of the purity of the family through the seclusion and protection of women, who are potent as the agents of reproduction, and who have, according to Khan (1976: 100), 'the power to defile the pure blood of the group'. Khan defines purdah as a 'control mechanism', ensuring acceptable and orderly relationships between the sexes (1976: 106).

The second major factor linked with secluding women can be manifest as a concern with status. The degree to which women can be segregated depends much on social and economic position, and 'social prestige is associated with strict observance' of segregation (Khan 1976: 101). Cosar (1978) discusses how, in Turkey, peasant women could not wear the veil due to its impracticability for working in the fields, whereas women working in towns were veiled and segregated. Similarly, Gilsenan (1982: 172–3) relates that peasant women in Lebanese villages are 'seen to work', which is crucial within an environment where 'seeing someone is a socially determined act and not a question merely of images on the retina and physiological process'. The reverse of this, not seeing someone, is thus also of importance, and status is gained through the absence of a family's female members, thereby implying that their work is being done by someone else.

The third dominant factor is cultural, and the importance of this should not be underestimated. Although the seclusion of women is found in Muslim societies from Morocco to Indonesia, the status of women can and does differ markedly (Papanek 1973: 305; see also Stowasser 1984; Webster 1984): in certain areas, a concern with secluding women is particularly manifest; in others, it is of no importance. An example of commonplace close purdah is provided by the Muslim communities of South Asia. Here seclusion has been explained as a cultural response to the patriarchal society which already existed, rather than being 'a reflection of Islam' (Raza 1993: 60). It might in part have been influenced by the existence of a caste system, although, strictly speaking, caste should not be accepted by Muslims as it goes against the notions of the universality of the Muslim community; in practice it has deeply influenced Muslim groups in the region. This can in turn affect the domestic environment. Ahuja (1979: 33) records that among certain Indian Muslim groups, the kitchen, considered the purest part of the house, is carefully positioned according to place in the caste hierarchy. This ranges from being exposed at the front of the houses of lower-caste families to being situated on the top floor, and away from the entrance as far as is possible, in high-caste, two-storey dwellings. Otherwise, Indian Muslim houses often manifest the usual spatial pattern of public and private domains, frequently based around a courtyard (Mujeeb 1967).

Of particular interest in this context are studies of the Muslim communities of South Asian origin in the United Kingdom (Khan 1976; Barton 1986; Raza 1993; Lewis 1994). Along with the physical movement of these people from South Asia have come their cultural concerns, including those relating to purdah. However, the translation of purdah concepts into practice in Britain is not the same as in Bangladesh or Pakistan; as we saw with the Cambridge mosque adaptation in chapter 2, compromises have had to be reached. An example of this is provided by the Bengali community from the Sylhet region of Bangladesh who, since the 1960s, have settled in large numbers in the city of Bradford in the north of England. This group has been studied by Barton (1986), who found that in the village environment in Sylhet purdah was maintained in many ways, through, for example, erecting screens around houses. In Bradford this is more difficult, but purdah is both considered customary and attached to status connotations, making its abandonment improbable; likewise, among Muslims of Pakistani origin who have also settled in Bradford. In many cases, they came direct from villages where purdah concerns were strong, especially among those from Mirpur district (who number some 15,000, out of a total community of 25,000 Pakistanis in the city) (Khan 1976: 102). In certain instances, women are now isolated more than they ever were in Pakistan or Bangladesh.

In both of these communities the domestic environment is considered the female domain and a public/private spatial division is maintained, yet many of the houses occupied are small terraced houses built during the Victorian era which do not always suit the social requirements of Muslim families, often of the extended type (even though a public/private spatial division was frequently maintained during the Victorian period, as evidenced by the parlour; Petersen 1997). As Nielsen notes, constraints of climate and traditional domestic architecture in northern Europe have 'forced domestic family activities indoors into accommodation designed for small nuclear families' (1995: 102). Existing space has to be adapted to suit cultural, religious and social requirements through, for example, utilizing back rooms as female quarters, with the front for men, and by erecting curtains and other partitions to maintain divisions (Barton 1986). Yet although purdah is practised, perhaps even to a greater degree than was ever the case in South Asia, the archaeological visibility of this would be nil if these houses were reduced to their foundations and studied on the basis of ground plan alone. However, it assumes relevance to the archaeologist interested in Islam because it again shows that rigorously defined boundaries do not exist; what constitutes the Muslim world and the non-Muslim world has in fact a great degree of fluidity, as in all probability it always had. Although Bradford is patently not within the *dar al-Islam*, a large Muslim community lives there which will offer future challenges to the archaeologist.

Space, gender and its archaeological recognition

Within archaeology in general there has been a move towards rectifying the imbalance in gender studies (see, for example, Conkey and Spector 1984; Ehrenberg 1989; Conkey and Gero 1991). In Islamic archaeology a similar imbalance exists, which may in part be due to neglect, but also because of the difficulty in recognizing and defining both gender-specific items and space archaeologically. Yet having said this, there often appears to be an emphasis, albeit in all probability subconscious, on male space and activities. This is expanded upon by Chatty (1978: 399), who argues that the women's sphere, private, domestic and informal, is often regarded as secondary to the extra-domestic, public and formal 'universe of men'. In fact, one could be forgiven for thinking that the Muslim world through much of its history, as presented in many sources, was populated solely by caliphs and soldiers, with women (if considered) subordinated to concubines and servant girls.

Recognizing gender relations is a necessity in understanding the 'social' content of Islamic archaeology. Conkey and Gero (1991: 9) discuss gender as 'a structuring principle – setting certain guiding rules for the enactment of daily life'; and, with reference to social structure in many parts of the Muslim world, to propose such guiding criteria would certainly be valid. The domestic environment is more than just a shelter offering physical protection from the elements, but the arena in which gender roles are 'taught', making its study much more significant than merely charting a succession of architectural styles, decorative finishes or ground plans. Yet at the same time it should be acknowledged that 'engendering archaeology' is no easy process.

In the archaeological study of a domestic environment structured according to Muslim social requirements, various possibilities to study gender exist. By, for example, examining the patterning and typology of personal artifacts, and the contextual examination of features such as hearths, it might be possible to begin to recognize the division and interplay between male and female space. Allied with this, the privileged position of the archaeologist interested in Islam is again a factor of some significance, for he or she has recourse to observing a living faith and numerous cultures influenced by it, and can supplement his or her archaeological data from an extensive body of ethnographic, anthropological and historical evidence. To emphasize this point, recourse will be made to two studies, one of which is drawn from ethnography, and which it is argued could not be reconstructed archaeologically (Bourdieu 1973), and the other which is archaeological, but which the author, Linda Donley-Reid (1990: 115), admits would have been difficult to reconstruct from archaeological evidence alone. Both have direct reference to the domestic environment, but at the same time illustrate the range of interpretative possibilities which can exist, but which equally could elude us.

The Berber house   Bourdieu's (1973) analysis of a contemporary Berber (Kabyle) house in Algeria shows strict male/female opposition through the existence of demarcated public and private domains. The rectangular house interior is divided into two parts: a 'dark and nocturnal' lower part of the house, of moist, green or raw objects, natural beings (animals), natural activities (sleep, sex, death, birth), and tasks such as fetching water, wood and manure. The second is a light-filled, noble, upper part, which is defined as a place of human beings, fire and objects created by fire, including the rifle, the symbol of male honour, and the protector of female honour (see figure 3.5). Various spatial oppositions were recorded, with the low, dark part opposed to the higher, as female is to male. Gender oppositions were also extended from the internal to the external world, and evident in how the very physical structure of the house is visualized, with, for example, the main beam being identified with the master of the house, and the supporting pillar with the wife, interlocked in a representational act of physical union (1973: 99–102).

The existence of genderized space is of great significance and the fundamental structuring mechanism of the Berber domestic environment. However, this example is in its details particular to the specific context in a part of Algeria, it is not Islamic, but is within the Muslim

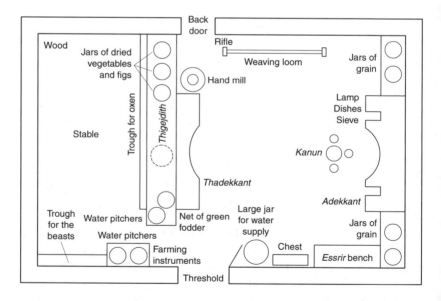

Figure 3.5   Interior of a Berber house, Algeria (from Bourdieu 1973: 107)

world; moreover, it could even be suggested that how one person, male or female, might visualize the domestic environment in terms of gender need not necessarily be the same as another. Thus we can draw no general conclusions from such an example. Rather, it serves to illustrate that the seemingly innocuous material we encounter in the archaeological record, such as a house plan, can be the residue of complex or perhaps even unexpected meaning or process. The application of such concepts within Islamic archaeology is rare, although it must be recognized that drawing this kind of anthropological explanation from archaeological data is at present difficult, and frequently, impossible.

The Swahili house   This second example attempts to combine just these sources of evidence, archaeological and ethnographic, in the examination of several Swahili coral and clay houses in the Lamu Archipelago and on the adjacent mainland of Kenya, all dating from after the early eighteenth century (Donley-Reid 1990; see also Donley 1982, 1987). The Swahili conceptualized people as falling into five basic groups: *Waungwana* (freeborn men and women), *Madada* (female domestic slaves), *Wazalia* (locally born slaves), *Watumwa* (plantation slaves) and, finally, *Washenzi* (all other Africans). Within the inter-relationships between these groups the domestic structure took on a great importance. To quote Donley-Reid (1990: 119), 'the hierarchical relationships among groups of individuals and the inter-actions between each of these groups centre on the types of houses and where houses were built.' Space and location were paramount. Who built what, where and when was decided by the *Waungwana*, and social progression into and through Swahili society was repre-sented by the progression from the grass round hut into the lower levels of the multi-storey coral house, and finally into the upper levels, and the inner sanctum, the *ndani*. Non-*Waungwana* men were excluded from the process of upward mobility altogether, but it was possible for the female descendants of a slave girl taken as a concubine to have a coral house built after a couple of generations. Thus here it can be seen that both social mobility and specific gender exclusions are manifest with the domestic structure as the key to both.

Donley-Reid records that, with the Swahili, status was linked with purdah, and women were secluded both through the use of the veil (discussed in chapter 4) and through the house. Women were excluded from the mosque, and in turn the *ndani*, the room at the very centre of the top of the house, though reserved both for the woman who owned the house and her husband, became the ritual centre for women, and associated with their polluting and shameful aspects, such as childbirth. Women were also regarded as a highly valued commodity, similar to the correlation between status and purdah evident in the South Asian examples discussed above. In this context, a point made by Donley-Reid is of great relevance: 'the most valued objects, *including the highest status women*, were located in the innermost room, the *ndani*, of the house' (1990: 124; emphasis added to stress the explicit link between women, the domestic environment and status).

In this instance genderized space was again created, and material culture actively utilized within gender relationships. Furthermore, within this example it can be seen that the links with Islam are more explicit than was apparent in the Berber house. This is evident in the interplay between the pure mosque, the male space, and the *ndani*, the female and impure space, as one level of meaning which can be discerned in the complex interplay of factors, indigenous and foreign, Muslim and non-Muslim, which characterize Swahili society itself. The challenge herein lies in attempting to reconstruct such rich tapestries of detail (remembering that this example also relates to the vertical axis of reconstruction, making the archaeologist's job even harder) in other contexts, where perhaps the accompanying ethnographic and historical evidence is not so abundant.

Thresholds, boundaries and entrances

A final area of study is how boundaries and thresholds between the different domains can be created. Frequently, for them to be effective they must be demarcated, and three primary categories can be isolated of how a threshold or boundary can be created. The first comprises physical boundaries, such as angled entrance ways, blind walls and similar features. According to Parker Pearson and Richards these 'can serve to mark differences in domains and thus restrict and control access between them' (1994: 24). The second category are thresholds with lesser degrees of physical visibility, perhaps evident within the domestic environment as charms and amulets buried under entrance ways, for example. They might not be visible, and thus are not known to the individual crossing the threshold, but to the house owner they exist and can protect both from the *djinn*, 'a race of supernatural beings created before man' (Westermarck 1933: 5), and more manifest threats such as people harbouring bad intentions. They constitute a further way of creating a boundary or threshold beyond the use of bricks, mud or concrete. A third means of creating a threshold or boundary is through visible decoration and calligraphy, plastic or painted, which can serve to signal a 'transition zone' (Parker Pearson and Richards 1994: 27), as with the stickers in the Afro-American Muslim apartments discussed earlier.

All three of these categories could be archaeologically visible, and the frequent emphasis upon creating, defining and protecting spatial domains within Islam means that they might also be widely found. Angled entrance ways could survive in ground plans, and although often regarded as unorthodox, charms and amulets can likewise survive. Examples could include items placed in the house foundations, as in Egypt where Campo records that a variety of objects were buried: grain, salt, dates or small items in gold or silver (1991: 101). Qur'anic or magical texts could be buried in a pot or a similar container, or a sacrifice interred. In al-Rabadha (Saudi Arabia), one of the centres on the *hajj* route, the Darb Zubayda (discussed in chapter 4), a skeleton of a baby camel was found in a building of apparently Abbasid origin. This, King argues, 'was certainly a sacrifice, pointing to a continuation of a pre-Islamic threshold-laying ritual associated with a building's foundation' (1994b: 198). While far removed in both time and space, Donley-Reid mentions that the remains of a goat were found buried in the floor of an *ndani* excavated in an eighteenth-century Swahili coral house (1990: 121), which might have served the same purpose. Other protective charms found included cowry shells and an owl bone, and imported Chinese porcelain which, especially if blue, was considered effective protection against the 'evil eye' (Donley 1987: 187–8). Again, context would have to be examined to state categorically that the charms were Muslim, as their use has a long pre-Islamic background, but their importance lies in the fact that such concerns can be materially manifest, and frequently still are today in various protective threshold rituals in Palestine, Syria and Turkey for example (Petersen 1997).

Numerous other examples of the use and/or archaeological survival of protective devices could be cited. In nineteenth-century Egypt, aloe was hung over the door of a house to give both the house and its occupants a long life (Lane 1895: 259), while in the Mzab area of Algeria, an Ibadi stronghold, amulets and other prophylactic objects could be hung above the door lintel for protection (Mercier 1922: 162–3; Roche 1970). Visible decoration might also survive, such as protective religious inscriptions. The presence of a pilgrim returned from *hajj* or pilgrimage to Mecca (discussed in chapter 4) can also be proudly signalled around or on the door or on house exteriors in various areas of the Muslim world (see, for example, Wenzel 1972: 60–1; Michot 1978; Campo 1991: 149–58).

But besides the threshold having significance as a device which serves to demarcate and protect at a practical level, it can also be invested with a more overt religious significance. Members of the Bektashi Sufi order, for example, showed reverence to the threshold, and would not step on one, because of its powerful religious symbolism, which is described by Birge (1937: 174): '[as] Ali is the Gateway or Door of the city of knowledge any doorway is symbolic of Ali's spiritual significance in life. One side of the door is said to represent Hasan, the other Huseyin (Hussein); the top stands for Muhammed and the bottom threshold for Fatma.' Thus in this instance the threshold, whether in the domestic environment, a mosque or Sufi lodge, is explicitly linked with religious considerations. However, this would appear to be the exception rather than the rule; the threshold in general functions as (within the context of the domestic environment) the defining marker between the domestic, private, public, natural and even supernatural worlds, and for this fact it is the key link between many of the themes discussed in the chapter.

Summary and Conclusions

The preceding discussion has shown that the Muslim domestic environment is remarkably diverse in form, and in underlying meaning, which could lead us to determine that few general conclusions could be drawn. Yet although great variety is apparent in layout, architecture and materials, the existence of demarcated public and private domains, and a concern with gender segregation, can be seen to be manifest through almost the entire spectrum of Muslim domestic architecture, from nomads carrying their religious and social codes and transiently fixing them with skin or cloth tents, to others who more permanently anchor them in mud, brick and stone, ranging from one-room structures to vast palatial complexes, and projected through space both horizontally and vertically. Aspects of this might be archaeologically visible; others will not. Religion can be of fundamental importance in structuring the Muslim domestic environment but, importantly, need not be. Explicit links between Islam and the domestic environment do not exist in the same way as we saw with the form of the mosque, structured as it was by the fundamental obligation of prayer. The traditional domestic environment is the result of the fusion of cultural and environmental factors, and social and religious requirements, and owes a major debt to a substantial pre-Islamic heritage. A religious element is present, but it is indirect, though links can be seen to stretch back to the Prophet's house, and thus the domestic environment can be imbued with what Campo (1991) terms a degree of 'sacrality'.

A domestic environment structured according to traditional Muslim requirements might be archaeologically recognizable through a variety of defining features, but to base our identification of the former presence of a Muslim community upon house plans alone is insufficient. It forms one element of a possible package which could indicate the existence of a Muslim community archaeologically. To be certain, various categories of material would need to be found in association with each other. At the same time, it should be noted that not all Muslims live in courtyard houses structured according to a 'traditional' model. Muslims have never all lived in such houses and, as we have seen, certainly do not today. But the existence of a domestic environment which can be structured according to a Muslim ethos is undeniable, and we should be aware that this can be manifest in many different ways. Beyond questions of identification, various other types of information might be retrieved: these included changes in the structure of the family and of society over time, perhaps with a shift from a communal to a more individualistic ethos; status and display considerations as manifest in material culture patterning; gender differentiation as a structuring agent for domestic space; and how thresholds, boundaries and entrances might be created, protected and maintained.

Consequently, having considered the implications of the domestic environment for the archaeology of Islam, are there any further implications for a more general 'archaeology of religion'? Essentially, it can be seen that another facet of material culture, not necessarily considered by archaeologists within the rubric of religion, can in fact be placed under this heading in certain instances. Although the connection need not be direct, and can range along a proverbial sliding scale from overt to nothing at all, it is obvious that to reduce the domestic structure *per se* to a mere shelter is banal and inaccurate. It can and, in most instances, does structure, act upon and intimately involve social life. Social life and religion are difficult to separate, with the latter influencing the former to a greater or lesser degree. Therefore, religion has to be considered as more than just a set of conveniently pigeonholed beliefs, but rather it should be seen as an agency which can act upon the whole of life and which can influence many, if not all, aspects of material culture. Finally, it is also apparent, as we saw with the mosque, and as we will see in future chapters, that we are also dealing with dynamic ongoing processes. Unsuitable house types might be introduced, and subsequently rejected, but many new forms of domestic structure, ideally suited to traditional

Muslim social requirements, are also being designed and built in the Muslim world, and wherever Muslim communities are found. Thus, as with the mosque, evolution of material culture will again provide further challenges for the archaeologist of the future.

4

Muslim Life

Children of Adam, dress well when you attend your mosques. Eat and
drink, but avoid excess. He does not love the intemperate.

Qur'an. The Heights 7: 31

It may be difficult to recognize archaeologically the religious element
in many everyday activities, but the archaeologist must be aware of
the possibility of its existence if we are ever to begin to achieve the
'social archaeology' sought in the past two decades. Many other
aspects of life can also be influenced by Islam, as the above epigraph
indicates, and being a Muslim supposes more than mosques and
domestic structures. These are not always considered by archaeologists as being within the domain of the archaeology of religion,
whose interest often lies with the evidence of the 'big issues' of ritual,
death, the household and the rural or urban environment. However,
within a study such as this, which attempts to assess the possible
archaeological study of Islam in its totality, attention must be paid to
all areas of life in which complete or partial obedience to Islamic
precepts might be recognized, especially feasts and festivals, food and
drink, education and health, pilgrimage and travel, personal possessions and dress, magic and, finally, war. Each of these can be used in
many different ways to create the overall religious, and in turn social,
identities. As diverse as each of these categories may appear to be at
first glance, there are in fact many ways in which they are interlinked. Besides the more obvious connections, the most important
link is that none of these categories can be classed as purely secular
activities for each is, or can be, influenced by Islam to a large extent.
Their importance (to the archaeologist) cannot be overemphasized, as
their existence again disturbs the notion that religion or 'ritual' can be

conveniently pigeonholed, with a neat dividing line from those classified as secular.

Furthermore, once we begin to consider each of these aspects in life, and as many of them show they can be used 'actively' to create and maintain group identity, negotiate social position, establish gender relations, and legitimize political authority. All these areas will be examined through a series of examples, both to illustrate how the apparently secular can be imbued with an element of the sacred, and to assess their archaeological implications. Thus although it must be acknowledged that the lives of many Muslims are not and were never structured by such considerations, the following examples serve to illustrate the possibilities which can exist.

Food and Drink

Diet and cuisine

Food and drink, as 'the fuel of life', make a convenient starting point, yet almost simultaneously a distinction needs to be made between diet and cuisine. It will be argued that there is no such thing as a 'Muslim cuisine', whereas there is a Muslim diet, structured by dietary laws, as set out in the Qur'an and *hadith*.

Cuisine Within the vast geographical area which is the Muslim world great culinary variety exists, which renders the idea of a uniform Muslim cuisine absurd. Certain similarities might be found, in the use of spices or the preparation of similar breads in many regions, or the common use of certain items of equipment, but there is no 'Islamic kitchen' or 'Islamic dish'. Perhaps a common inheritance might be evident in different regions. As Waines (1991: 807) notes, the Muslim world inherited the chemistry and technology of cooking from the ancient centres of the Middle East, an area where there might be an element of 'coherency' in culinary cultures for whatever reasons (see Tapper and Zubaida 1994). Yet how applicable is this concept to Indonesia or West Africa where the culinary heritage differs? It is not, and where conversion to Islam occurred, regional cuisine was merely modified to the taboos of the new faith.

Diet More profitable for the archaeologist is the identification of the Muslim diet, which is structured by religious law and provides a further category of evidence which might allow the archaeological recognition of a Muslim community. Issues of non-observance must be acknowledged, and differences between the Islamic schools of law recognized, but in general terms a number of binding rules exist. There are three categories of food: *halal*, that which is lawful; *haram*, that which is prohibited; and *makruh*, that which is reprehensible, but which is not subject to the degree of prohibition as *haram*. Alcohol, spilt blood, pork, dogs, excrement, carrion, and milk of animals whose flesh is not eaten are forbidden, and a complex body of laws regulates in great detail which food is considered lawful and when exceptions concerning consumption can be made. Similarly, slaughter is subject to religious law, and an animal must be killed facing the *qiblah*, the name of God invoked and its throat cut (see Gibb and Kramers 1961: 431–2, 556; Pellat 1971a: 304–9). Rules concerning hunting wild animals vary, but often saying a prayer or muttering a *basmala* before dispatching the arrow or bullet will suffice.

To the archaeologist studying a faunal assemblage it might theoretically be possible to identify the remains generated by a diet structured according to these Muslim dietary laws. Pertinent questions which might be asked include:

1 Are certain species absent in faunal assemblages, pigs and dogs for example, and is this a result of dietary avoidance?
2 Is a *halal* diet noticeable, for example through special butchery patterns, cut marks on bones, body parts and offal left over?
3 Are slaughter patterns different among herds owned by Muslims, as opposed to those of other religious groups?
4 Is the composition of a 'Muslim herd' different, and can this be recognized archaeologically?

Often subtle differences exist in what may or may not be eaten between the different legal schools, and an 'ideal' faunal assemblage could theoretically allow not only differentiation between the various religious groups, Jews, Muslims and Christians, for instance, but perhaps also within the Muslim community itself on the basis of these differences. Three examples have been chosen which suggest exciting, but as yet solely theoretical, interpretative possibilities. Among adherents of the Hanafi school all marine creatures which are not shaped like fish are unlawful, whereas the other legal schools are not so strict; the Maliki school pronounce the hyena *makruh*, yet they can eat birds of prey, which adherents of the other legal schools do not, as all carnivores, whether birds or mammals, are forbidden (Pellat 1971a: 306–7). Dietary differences are also evident between the Sunni and Shi'ah creeds. For example, Thesiger relates how in Iraq Sunni Muslims would eat hares while Shi'ahs would not (1980: 81).

These are patterns which might theoretically be evident in a faunal assemblage; they also illustrate that diversity is again evident, and that entities such as dietary laws can be differently interpreted depending on context and circumstances.

Archaeological reality: a case study from Jordan

Having outlined some of the theoretical possibilities which could be considered when analysing faunal assemblages from Islamic sites, it is worthwhile testing them against archaeological data from Jordan. The sites which will be considered are Gadara, where occupation of a major Roman and Byzantine city has been approximately continuous up to the present; Pella, with specific emphasis upon the Umayyad and Abbasid levels above and adjacent to the Byzantine city; Aqaba, a Umayyad and Abbasid city; the Ayyubid and later occupation of the village of Khirbet Faris; and, finally, the late Muslim occupation of the three Crusader castles of Kerak, Shobak and el-Wueira. The information in the following section is primarily drawn from the detailed answers to my questions kindly provided by Louise Martin on general issues (1996) and Kevin Rielly on the specific Jordanian material (1996).

Absence of species   The absence of certain species in faunal assemblages can be meaningful, as long as consideration is given to other factors (Martin 1996). These include excavation bias, differential disposal, and the possible local environmental constraints involved in keeping species such as pigs. A possible approach is offered through examining patterns across a series of sites, or changes through various sequences. In Muslim period deposits few pig bones were found, 'but most of these could be interpreted as residual, i.e. mixed in from earlier levels' (Rielly 1996). An exception to this pattern was provided by the small number of pig bones recovered from Pella, where context, according to Rielly, 'strongly suggests the continued use of pig (albeit as a minor food resource) well into the Muslim period', perhaps the result of toleration towards a small Christian or recently converted Muslim population. Certainly, in other instances, the presence or absence of specific species can be very informative. At Qsar es-Seghir in Morocco the appearance of pig remains in Christian Portuguese levels helped serve to differentiate this assemblage from the preceding Islamic one, where cattle, sheep and goats predominate (Redman 1986: 229–30). Similarly at Qasr Ibrim (Egypt), pig bones were completely absent from the Ottoman levels (Alexander 1997).

The other animal whose presence or absence might be informative in differentiating a Muslim faunal assemblage is the dog. But this is again by no means uniform. As regards the Jordanian sites, dog remains are fairly common in Muslim period levels, where they were not used as a food resource, but rather for herding, guarding and hunting. Two factors indicate this: the absence of butchery marks, which are 'a fairly clear indicator of a food use, in particular if the cut marks are found on the meat rich part of the carcass' (Rielly 1996), and the fact that most of the dogs found were represented by partial or complete skeletons, clearly showing no post-mortem use. Thus, it is not necessarily assured that certain species, notably pigs and dogs, will be absent in faunal assemblages from Islamic sites. Factors other than adherence to dietary law must be considered, but, as the examples illustrate, in certain instances relevant patterning can be found.

Halal diet   *Halal* slaughter 'involves a clean cut to the throat', and it is 'highly unlikely that a skilled practitioner will cut down to the bone (most likely the hyoid), thus leaving no trace' (Rielly 1996) (see plate 4.1). Even if this were done, the hyoid of a sheep or goat, for example, is usually small in size and prone to fragmentation, which further complicates the recognition process. Where hyoids were found on Islamic period sites in Jordan, no cut marks were evident, but in any case these could also have been made after death, for example, while removing the head. In general, little differentiation was evident between pre-Muslim and Muslim butchery methods, while the practice of not eating certain offal would not be apparent in the archaeological record 'short of extremely good preservation' (Reilly 1996). Although it can be seen that this example relates only to Jordan, it is applicable elsewhere, and therefore it is unlikely that *halal* diet would be recognizable archaeologically.

Muslim animal husbandry   The third and fourth of our questions above can be considered together as both are related to animal herds, their slaughter and composition. As regards the former, Martin (1996) suggests that a conceivable approach would be linking 'slaughter patterns to particular feasting times, for example, Ramadan'. However, since Ramadan is movable rather than seasonal, 'one would need very good ageing data from animals', and zoo-archaeology cannot get anywhere near the resolution of ageing needed to address this issue at present, though cementum banding may eventually help. However, *id al-adha* perhaps offers better possibilities for recognition on account of a 'special' lamb being preferred for the sacrifice: male, neither too

Plate 4.1 *Halal* butchers, Kom Ombo, Egypt (© Hutchison Picture Library)

young nor too old, healthy and without broken horns (El-Rashedy 1997).

The composition of a Muslim herd as an aid to its recognition is likewise complicated. The imprecise nature of the archaeological record obscures things, and the archaeological assemblage can be best described as a death assemblage, and rarely an accurate reflection of the herd structure pertaining to the period under study (Rielly 1996). Certainly, with regard to the Jordanian sites, Rielly notes that 'it would appear that the major food animals, i.e. sheep, goat and cattle, suffered very little change in either their relative importance as food items or their major uses, as this area shifted from a Christian to a Muslim state.' However, he continues, 'one species is worth commenting on with respect to a possible change in diet, i.e. the camel.

There would appear to be more camel bones (many with clear butchery marks) on Muslim sites relative to those of an earlier date. In fact the finding of a camel bone can almost be used as a marker for a Muslim period context.'

Therefore, we appear to have one animal, the camel, which can act as the sort of 'marker' which we require, an archaeological indicator of Jordanian Muslim diet. (Its wider applicability as an indicator of Muslim diet will be considered below.) In general, however, it appears that in many ways an 'ideal' faunal assemblage would be required to answer the questions outlined. However, several possible useful lines of enquiry have been suggested which at a practical level might begin to allow Muslim diet to be recognized and investigated archaeologically in a regional study. Moreover, such questions need to be asked because, as will be discussed later, diet, and therefore the archaeological remains, are not solely the residue of logical economic decisions; they too can be strongly affected by religious reasoning.

Alcohol and vegetable crops

Can other elements of Muslim diet, drink and vegetable foodstuffs, for example, be archaeologically associated or indeed identified with Muslims? The ban on alcohol within Islam is well known, and this might in certain instances be archaeologically visible. Sadan (1991: 721), for example, notes that the use of certain receptacles is forbidden to Muslims 'for ease with which they might be used to ferment liquids'. However, observance of this proscription is by no means uniform, as is frequently attested in *The Rubaiyat of Omar Khayyam*: 'and David's lips are lock't; but in divine high-piping Péhlevi, with "Wine! Wine! Wine! Red Wine!" – the Nightingale cries to the Rose, That yellow cheek of hers t' incarnadine. Come fill the cup, and in the fire of Spring the Winter garment of repentance fling' (Fitzgerald 1970). Physical evidence for the infringement of the prohibition on alcohol was found at Samarra in Iraq, where several tall pottery vessels painted with Christian imagery and dating from the mid-ninth century were found which were interpreted as wine flasks, and which led to the inference 'that there was a wine hall near the Caliph's harem at Samarra' (Talbot Rice 1971: 37).

More complex even is the recognition of the vegetable component of the Muslim diet. This is not subject to dietary law as is flesh and associated products, and thus cannot begin to be an archaeological indicator of a Muslim community in the same way; staple food crops often remained unchanged in regions to which Islam spread. Botanical remains might, however, indicate the spread of crops associated with the Muslim world. Crops such as rice, sugar cane and wheat were widely diffused, but obviously they do not take on a Muslim identity! Rather, at a precise point in time they can be said to be culturally associated with Islam, as Al-Hassan and Hill (1992: 212–13) discuss. For example, wheat was a staple food in Islamic agriculture in the medieval period, as compared to rye bread common in northern Europe, and sugar is a basic commodity which 'owes much of its development and spread to the Islamic civilisation' (1992: 220). The significance of wheat was also reinforced by taboos, as in Turkey where Leach and Leach make the point that, 'though lacking prominence in the Qur'an...wheat is considered a blessing from God and offences against it are open to divine retribution' (1977: 64). Various prohibitions exist about what one can or cannot do in a wheat field, with wheat, and when eating bread in Turkey. Similarly, certain fruits are especially esteemed through their being favourites of the Prophet Muhammad; these include water melon, banana and pomegranate, each of which is said to contain 'a fecundating seed from Paradise' (Lane 1883: 161).

But greater use of archaeobotany needs to be made in Islamic archaeology before we can even begin to approach these issues. As King notes, 'very little has been done in the way of paleobotanical research for the Islamic period as a whole, and it is hoped that more attention will be given in the future to this subject by archaeologists' (1994a: 6). One instance of its application is at Qasr Ibrim (Egypt), a site already mentioned in the context of the domestic environment and which will be referred to again on account of the exceptional preservation conditions found there. This meant that abundant botanical remains survived, and when sampled indicated that the crops grown varied over time. Significantly, one of these changes occurred at the interface of the late Christian and early Islamic periods (c.1500), when the bicolor variety of sorghum ceased to be cultivated, though the cultivation of the durra variety continued. This has been interpreted as due to the fact that bicolor was more suited to the making of beer and 'so the Islamic prohibition of the consumption of alcohol may be one possible reason for this ' (Rowley-Conwy 1989: 135).

Although only a cursory treatment of Muslim dietary law has been provided here, the importance of this fundamental area of Muslim life to the archaeologist interested in Islam has been emphasized, and is one in which numerous possibilities for research exist.

Food and society

Equally important as the practical recognition of Muslim diet from archaeological remains is the manner in which the whole spectrum of food and drink can function socially, both in the creation of Muslim identity and within Muslim life. Grant (1991: 109) makes the important point that too often the preoccupation of the archaeologist dealing with animal bones is with economic matters, herd management, animal improvement and the like, with ritual and symbolic elements separated out; however, she adds 'the religious, the symbolic and the economic are all inextricably combined' (1991: 110). Faunal assemblages need not be the residue of solely economic decisions, and this is particularly true of pastoral communities of all kinds, including Muslim ones. Abu-Rabia (1994: 90), for example, records that among the Bedouin of the Negev desert (Palestine), the significance of the flocks of animals kept is much more than merely economic. 'The flock is the connecting link not only between men but also between men and God, prophets, saints and pious people.' The faunal assemblage, the residue of this 'significant flock' and of the subsequent 'significant meals', would not indicate that the animals had been taken to saints' tombs, or that they were perceived of as any more than wealth on the hoof, but as archaeologists we should consider such possibilities, otherwise we might again run the risk of losing something of the rich tapestry of meaning which could underlie the archaeological evidence. The following examples show that food, drink and their raw materials can be of significance beyond being palatable or even apparently logically chosen.

Pigs in China   The Muslim Hui communities of China have already been mentioned (see chapter 2), and it was noted that the creation and maintenance of Hui identity was not straightforward. As with the utilization and adaptation of mosque architecture in the relationship between the Hui and the majority non-Muslim Chinese, so pork avoidance is significant. This forms part of the concept of *qingzhen*, 'pure and true', which is described by Gladney as more than an expression for the absence of lard or pork but a sacred symbol 'marking Hui identity' (1991: 9). China is one of the most important pig-breeding nations in the world, and pork is a major source of protein. Thus, to avoid it serves as a distinguishing sign from the mass of the population. However, the degree to which pork is avoided varies greatly. In areas where the Hui are less visibly Muslim, the pork taboo 'becomes the most distinguishing marker of identity', separating them from their Han neighbours. In the north-west of China the word for pig is even avoided, and euphemisms such as 'black bug' and 'black bastard' are used instead (Gladney 1991: 25, 185). Porcine euphemism, however, would appear to be highly flexible, as Simoons (1981: 27) notes that pork is often eaten if it is called mutton, a more pragmatic response. In contrast, other Hui groups, such as the Chendai Hui, who are virtually culturally indistinct from their neighbours, are not at all scrupulous in maintaining pork avoidance, openly or otherwise. But this is more easily understood if the overall cultural context of this Hui lineage is considered, among whose practices Gladney describes the lighting of 'incense to ancestors in their lineage temple', some going as far as not believing in Islam (1991: 264).

Even within one ethnic group the range of behavioural variability, religious observance and non-observance is immense. In this example, it can be seen that, although pork avoidance is one of the fundamental Muslim dietary laws, the degree to which it is upheld depends upon the perceived degree of social need and how practical it is to maintain; thus a pragmatic attitude exists. Although the prohibition on eating pork is scrupulously observed by many Muslims and the circumstances affecting this case study are somewhat exceptional, this behaviour is far from confined merely to the Hui. Such general issues as the perception and practice of religion by its adherents, and how the accompanying social laws or requirements are followed, are subject to both individual or group choice and external pressures, a fact which has direct material culture implications as a primary structuring agent for cultural diversity. Furthermore, supposed economic rationality as a structuring factor can often be exposed as false. There is no connection in this instance between pig prohibition and, as Simoons points out, 'rational explanations' of health (1981: 111). Here, food avoidance is used as a sign of separate cultural and ethnic identity, which concurs with a point made by Farb and Armelagos (1980: 118) about Mosaic and Qur'anic dietary laws in general. Namely, the emphasis put upon them was 'in part because foods can serve as badges that distinguish one people from another'. With regard to the Hui this is true, but is obviously divorced from economic and rational concerns, almost to the point of disadvantage, it can be suggested, in China, the land of the pig.

The camel   The camel is perhaps synonymous in many people's minds with Arabia and the heartlands of Islam. Although such associations are clichéd, they do, however, contain a kernel of truth, and it is useful to consider the camel as a 'cultural symbol' within Muslim society. The camel is mentioned several times in the Qur'an; for example, The Heights 7: 40. The Prophet is also seen as 'the Camel Rider', and the camel as the beast ridden by the Messianic Redeemer (Bashear 1991: 74). Bulliet (1975) has also charted the near total disappearance of wheeled vehicles in much of western Asia and North Africa following the Arab conquests, with dominance passing to a camel-riding elite. The camel also played an important role in pre-Islamic sacrifice, and Pellat (1971b: 666) makes the point that it was 'one of the animals endued with *baraka*, and to eat its flesh amounted to an act of faith'. Simoons (1981: 87) argues that the slaughter and consumption of camels 'has come to be regarded in the Middle East as almost an Islamic rite, and a sort of profession of faith'. Thus to many Muslims the camel has important associations, possibly owing to its spiritual connotations (but this is far from clear), but certainly to its 'multi-functional' nature in many geographical regions as a source of meat and a beast of burden (see Bulliet 1975; Wilson 1984). Owing to these strong Muslim–camel cultural associations, non-Muslims in many areas avoid consuming camel meat; Ethiopian Christians, for example, because 'they regard this as a Muslim habit' (Simoons 1981: 42).

Archaeological research in Spain and Hungary, both areas once occupied by Muslims, has provided unequivocal evidence for the perception of the camel as a cultural symbol identified with Muslims by non-Muslims. Only seven dromedary (one-humped camel) bones have been found in Spain in Muslim contexts, two from caliphate period levels of the tenth–eleventh centuries in Granada, and five from Almohad period levels in Guadix dating from the twelfth century. Some of these bones exhibited saw and cut marks, as well as traces of having been exposed to fire, which contrasted with camel remains recovered from Roman levels suggesting that 'the consumption of dromedary meat in Iberia could have had ritual connotations in affirming the Muslim condition of Andalusians... in this way, eating dromedary became a sign of cultural identity' (Muniz et al. 1995: 373). The dromedary is not found in Iberia today; this would not appear to be due to ecological reasons (the absence of suitable habitat, and the existence of viable alternatives such as oxen and horses), but because they had been introduced as 'signs of cultural identity' and were rejected once their importers left the peninsula (1995: 374). Following the re-conquest, the Christians could neither eat nor even ride camels, as animals too closely associated with the previous Muslim residents. In Hungary, camels were introduced during the Ottoman occupation (fifteenth to seventeenth centuries), and their absence today, according to the excavator of various Ottoman period sites, is partly due to the same variety of reasons, including the factor of 'cultural resentment' (Bartosiewicz 1996: 453) against a beast associated with conquering peoples (both Roman and Muslim). These examples show how it is possible for an animal, its by-products such as meat, even its tractional advantages, to be rejected because of its perceived cultural associations. Economic logic, though playing a part, is not the dominant factor.

Patterns of communal and private consumption   This offers a further factor for the archaeologist to consider when interpreting archaeological material relating to Muslim food use. What is present need not only reflect availability; more often than not a process of conscious choice is behind what is consumed and, as with many of the areas of material culture discussed in this volume, food can also be actively used for a variety of purposes (Douglas 1984). Food can be used as an active agent of communal inclusion or exclusion; perhaps, it can be suggested, of special importance within Islam, the religion of community (*ummah*), where the communal consumption of food is a recommended activity according to a *hadith*, which records that the Prophet remarked 'eat together and do not eat separately, for the blessed is with the company' (Ali 1951: 356, quoted in Goody 1982: 206).

Communal purposes to which food can be put are many. In Old Delhi (India), Murphy (1986: 111) describes how Muslims manipulated feasting foods for social purposes, to emphasize Muslim identity by excluding others and to improve relations with different religious groups, especially the Hindu community by 'making special provisions for their food'. Obviously related to this is the issue of the cow in Muslim–Hindu relations in India. The Muslim ruler Akbar, for instance, banned the slaughter of the cow, not through reverence for the animal but as a political gesture, as a means of building better relations with the Hindus. Conversely, Hindus could be actively encouraged to eat beef 'so that they would thereby become outcast from Hindu society and turn to the religion of Allah', of greatest effect in the lower strata of Hindu society where the cow was less revered (Lodrick 1981: 65).

Food can also be used at an individual level for social purposes; for example, in the relationship between the sexes, as Hastorf stresses: 'food can express political, social, and economic relations as well as nutrition, it also expresses the development and maintenance of gender relations in the past' (1991: 132). Unfortunately, this is an area of study which has been much neglected by archaeologists, as has the whole area of food preparation and related technical systems in

Plate 4.2   Songhai women cooking in Gao, Mali (*photo*. R. Maclean)

general (Maclean 1997), possibly, as Hastorf notes, because it is popularly perceived as a woman's activity (see plate 4.2). Suitable illustrative case studies based upon archaeological material are thus few and far between, and it is anthropology and popular fiction that provide the most interesting examples.

Maclagan's (1994) research in the western highlands of Yemen illustrates just how gender relations and food can be intertwined. She describes how male and female obligations and relations were negotiated in this area in terms of food, and how 'women's relation to food is defined by their relation to men' (1994: 159). Food could be utilized as a means of female protest, by being withheld or badly prepared. It could also be used in the forming of friendships between women, and foods associated with men, such as meat, were usually not eaten by women, unless there were men in the household. Food was thus the very medium of discourse in this area of Yemen, and a similar scenario is described in the *Buddha of Suburbia*, a novel depicting the life of a half-English, half-Indian young man in 1970s London. When, for example, the relationship between the main character's Muslim uncle and aunt breaks down, his auntie Jeeta uses food subtly, as one means of expressing her anger with her husband. She 'cooked for him as before, but provided only plain food, the same every day, and long after the expected time, bringing it to him when he was asleep or about to pray' (Kureishi 1990: 208). She served food designed to cause constipation, and when he complained, she served the opposite, on a monumental scale. In both these unconnected examples, far removed in every context, food can be seen as truly socially significant and as actively used. It is not merely a fuel for the body, but functions within the social arena, within an Islamic context, yet at the same time without being specifically Muslim.

Stimulants   A further dimension of food use in a social context in the Muslim world is provided by the consumption of stimulants. There has been much learned debate among Muslim scholars about their use, but many are used in different communities. Qat, an evergreen shrub whose leaves and shoots are chewed to produce a mild stimulating effect, and coffee have been the subject of recent studies (Weir 1985; Hattox 1991). Initially both substances, which originated in Ethiopia and spread to Yemen in the fourteenth to fifteenth centuries (though a recent find of three coffee bean fragments at Kush in the United Arab Emirates in contexts dated to the twelfth to thirteenth centuries will probably mean that the date of their introduction to Arabia will need revising; British Museum 1998), were associated with some religious men and Sufi orders as the effects were thought to bring 'them closer to God and enhanced meditation capacity' (Weir 1985: 76). However, over the course of time both coffee and qat underwent a definite change in status, they lost any religious overtones, although they were never religious substances in themselves. The public coffee house and the private qat party became, as they are today, social outlets, places to meet, gossip, and even compete socially. Tea, coffee, tobacco, qat, hashish, opium, pan – although substances which effect the mind might be forbidden, and the substances themselves might vary, the Muslim world can hardly be said to be free of the consumption of stimulants, each of which can generate its own peculiar and recognizable material culture, and provide a further dimension of life which could be visible archaeologically.

Feasts and festivals   Directly related to the subject of the social use of food and drink are feasts, fasts and festivals which form an important element in Muslim religious and social life, and are thus of relevance within a consideration of the possible archaeology of Islam. Huge local variety exists, but four pre-eminent examples can be isolated: the Fourth Pillar of Islam, *sawm* or daytime fasting and nightly feasting, which takes place in Ramadan, the ninth month of the Muslim calendar; *id al-fitr*, the feast and festival to celebrate the end of the fast of Ramadan; *id al-adha*, the feast to celebrate the day when *hajj* pilgrims sacrifice in the Valley of Mina near Mecca, which is an obligation on every free Muslim who can afford to buy a sacrificial animal, usually a sheep, camel or cow; and, finally, the tenth of Muharram, of special importance to the Shi'ah, and also significant to the Sunni as Ashura. This is an emotionally intense culmination of a ten-day mourning process to commemorate the death of Hussein at Karbala in 680 (Gibb and Kramers 1961: 47, 156, 409, 469; Von Grunebaum 1976).

These four examples differ immensely both in character and emotional tone, and it is difficult to assess what general implications feasts and fasts hold for the archaeologist. Although certain categories of specific material culture are utilized, such as special foods and dishes, or certain specific relics might be generated (faunal remains resulting from sacrifices or various types of artifact), it is extremely unlikely that a particular festival, feast or fast could be recognized archaeologically. The one exception to this might be Muharram, with its own specific material culture such as the *tazia*, the replica of Hussein's coffin carried in procession, and the *Karbala*, the building in which these replicas are sometimes buried, as well as the *Imambara*, a large religious structure also used during Muharram (see Asher 1984: 89–90 for Bengali examples). Yet within the sum total of elements which constitutes the archaeology of Islam this is of little importance. It is the awareness of such events which is significant, as a further possible (and probable) component of Muslim life, past and present.

Food and drink within the context of Muslim society can therefore be seen to be more than just fuel for the body, and thus should be of greater interest to the archaeologist than merely a source of economic data. Food in itself was not explicitly religious, but through dietary laws has been influenced by a religious component. At a practical level, the existence of these dietary laws could allow the archaeological recognition of a Muslim diet, a further category of evidence in the possible identification of a Muslim community. Furthermore, we have seen that food, here meant in its broadest definition, can be used in myriad ways – manipulated, avoided, associated with – and can also serve a variety of purposes: as a cultural symbol, or a means of communication or protest, for example. These are all things for us to consider when examining faunal remains, pottery forms, botanical samples, all the residue of food use. And once again the privileged position of the archaeologist interested in Islam is apparent. We are able to see, from diverse historical, ethnographic and anthropological evidence, the many dimensions of food use in Muslim life.

Education and Health

Education and health present further dimensions of life which can be visible archaeologically. Education, for example, could be represented materially by a wide range of evidence. The importance of education, particularly religious education, in the Muslim world, both today and in the past should be stressed (secular education is discussed in chapter 5): 'from its inception, indeed from the very first word of the first revelation to Muhammad, Islam had the character of a literary and, therefore, learned civilisation; in such a context the acquisition of knowledge and its transmission were paramount' (Dickie 1978: 38). The material manifestations of education could range from a Qur'anic school set up in an open area, where boys learnt to memorize the Qur'an from wooden boards, as described by Lane (1895) in nineteenth-century Cairo (see plate 4.3), to purpose-built *madrasahs* (religious colleges), which grew in importance from

Plate 4.3 Qur'an school, Rakai District, Uganda (*photo.* T. Insoll)

the tenth to eleventh centuries, to the great mosque universities such as al-Azhar in Cairo or Zeitouna (Kairouan) in Tunisia, where Qur'anic sciences (commentaries), *hadith*, law and theology were all taught (Gardet 1970: 588). Lane also describes the form of the al-Azhar, a large building surrounding a central court with a place of prayer on the side facing Mecca, and 'on each of the three sides are smaller porticoes, divided into a number of apartments called *riwaks*, each of which is destined for the use of natives of a particular country, or of a particular province of Egypt' (1895: 213).

Madrasahs could frequently have a similar plan, though on a much smaller scale, and which in their developed form combined the functions of the mosque (*masjid*) and hostel (*khan*) (Hillenbrand 1986: 1123). They are by no means universally found but were built in many areas of the Muslim world. For a summary of their origins, development and spread, see Pedersen (1986) and Hillenbrand (1986). The *külliye* or building complexes constructed by the Ottomans provide an example of what could be built incorporating a *madrasah*. These structural complexes began to be built in a fairly simple form in the fourteenth and fifteenth centuries, combining a mosque and *madrasah*, and perhaps a soup kitchen. One hundred years later these could be much more elaborate, exemplified by the Yilderim *külliye*, which combined a mosque, *madrasah*, bath, soup kitchen and hospital, all fortified and with two entrance gates (Kuran 1987: 134). Although this example is obviously exceptional, it gives an idea of the types of integrated structures which could be built. Furthermore, health was represented in this instance by the hospital (*maristan*), which could equally be found as a single structure, as could more simple hospices (Dunlop 1958). The study of such buildings might also allow the archaeological recognition of *waqf* or charitable endowments. A hospital, hostel for travellers, religious college, complex such as the *külliye*, possibly even a bridge, could be supported from *waqf* foundations, and indicated through inscriptions (see Rogers 1976, for example), perhaps in certain instances along with the architect's name (see Mayer 1956: 21–2).

Pilgrimage and Travel

Yet another element of Muslim life which has definite and recognizable archaeological implications is provided by travel in all its many forms. *Hajj*, pilgrimage to Mecca, is possibly the best-known example, but many other manifestations exist. Travel for other types of pilgrimage, migration, journeying for curiosity or trade, all have been an important element of Muslim life since the very beginnings of Islam, both for men, and with the first two at least, for women. Muslim travel is, according to Netton (1993: x), 'old as the religion itself', a process which began with the Prophet's migration, the *hijrah*, from Mecca to Medina, year one of the Muslim calendar. In its broadest sense, 'travel' can be said to be imbued with a spiritual significance, expressed thus by Gellens (1990: 53): 'embedded deep in Muslim consciousness is an identification of travel with pious activity, an appreciation that achievement in such endeavour is a sign of divine approval and munificence.' The direct implication of such sentiments means that it is often difficult, or impossible, to separate one activity from another. As will be discussed in greater detail below, trade could, and did, accompany pilgrimage; once again leading to a blurring between the secular and sacred as is apparent in so many other aspects of Muslim life.

All these types of travel can leave, to a greater or lesser degree, material culture traces (the archaeology of pilgrimage at least has recently been considered; see Graham-Campbell 1994). These can be plotted diagrammatically in a simplified form, providing what can be termed 'circles of visibility' and allowing the recognition of different aspects of this journeying. This ranges from greater observational clarity of *hajj*-related activities the closer one is to the Holy Places, with correspondingly a blurring of definition with distance, when local pilgrimage trails and centres become more easily recognizable. Each of these should be considered individually, beginning with *hajj*.

Hajj *and* umrah

Pre-eminent among Muslim travels is *hajj*, or pilgrimage to Mecca, one of the Five Pillars of the Faith, and an obligation (with certain exceptions) on every adult Muslim with the requisite means. Ideally, *hajj*, with all its attendant ceremonies, should coincide with the Festival of Sacrifice, *id al-adha*. Otherwise, lesser pilgrimage to Mecca, *umrah*, can be undertaken at any time, with the same ceremonies, but minus the sacrifice, and with less religious benefit accruing (Gibb and Kramers 1961: 121,159; Petrushevsky 1985: 64–6). Besides bringing individual religious merit, *hajj* is also significant in strengthening the *ummah*, by acting as a unifying force bringing together all Muslim ethnic groups, classes and cultures. Equality between these often disparate groups is obtained by various means, through, for example, the mandatory wearing by men of a simple white robe, the *ihram*, made up of two seamless pieces of white cloth which are wound around the body leaving one shoulder exposed. This garment must be worn during *hajj* or *umrah* in the sacred territory as a symbolic gesture of the erasure of class and race distinctions.

Alongside the creation of a feeling of community, the intermingling of people during pilgrimage can lead to the spread of new ideas, and have much political significance. Control of the Ka'bah, the sacred sanctuary in Mecca, could aid secular power (Hawting 1993: 31–2), and prestige accrue from the ownership of relics associated with it, as the collection in the Topkapi Palace in Istanbul (the former Ottoman court), attests. Here keys to the Holy Ka'bah, a fragment of its door, the gilt waterspout of mercy from the Ka'bah, and the golden cover of the black stone itself (probably a meteorite, and recorded as given by the Angel Gabriel to Abraham, who is believed to have built the Ka'bah) are all displayed. The possession of these items, along with relics of the Prophet and his family, invested the Ottoman Sultan with a certain legitimacy to rule, and were the 'emblems of Islam' (Wheatcroft 1995: 52), reinforcing the claim to be caliph (where used), the highest political and religious authority in Islam, and the Prophet's successor as leader of the Muslims.

It is not necessary to repeat here the origins of, and ceremonies involved in, *hajj*, which have been well covered elsewhere (Burton 1898; Peters 1994), but the centrality of Mecca and Medina as the hub of a web of routes leading from all corners of the Muslim world should be emphasized. The three major routes before the modern era and the dominance of air transport were the Syrian route via Damascus, which also carried Anatolian, Balkan and some Central Asian pilgrims; an Egyptian route from Cairo which also catered for pilgrims from the Maghrib and West Africa; and an Iraqi route which carried pilgrims from Iraq, Iran and the East (see figure 4.1). Further, less important, sea routes were followed by pilgrims from the East African Coast, India and beyond (Petersen 1994: 48–9).

The archaeology of the *hajj* routes has been the subject of recent interest (Petersen 1994). Archaeological studies of the Darb Zubayda, which flourished under the patronage of the Abbasids, linking Kufa in Iraq to Mecca, with a further trail to Medina, have shown that a variety of installations exist. Thirteen hundred wells, 54 guard stations and halting places, a hundred reservoirs, numerous cisterns, mosques and milestones and in places a delimited trackway cleared of stones, were recorded (al-Rashid 1980, 1986). Archaeology has also provided information on the *hijrah* route between Mecca and Medina. A paved roadway, up to 4 m wide, made of flat stones and cobbles filled with gravel, was found, protected in the Ottoman period by fortified

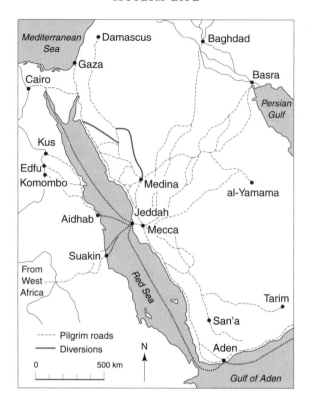

Figure 4.1   Pilgrimage routes in Arabia (after Peters 1994: xxv)

posts (Whalen et al. 1981: 53). Parts of another *hajj* route from Tarim
in the Wadi Hadhramaut through the mountains to Aden have been
recorded, as at Andar near Hureidhah (Whitcomb 1988: 182).

Away from the Arabian Peninsula, further archaeological evidence
of the *hajj* pilgrim traffic has been found, as at the former Red Sea port
of Aidhab (Sudan) opposite Jeddah, the port for Mecca. This port was
connected to the Egyptian route, and grew in importance after the
land route through Sinai was closed by the Crusaders in the twelfth
century (Peters 1994: 90–1). Visited by Ibn Battuta in the mid-fourteenth century, it appears to have been a pretty miserable place, but
extensive precautions were taken to ensure adequate supplies of water
by digging cisterns and wells (see figure 4.2) (Elisséeff and el Hakim
1981: 14). Extensive cemeteries were 'ample reminder of the appalling
death rate among the pilgrims' (Paul 1955: 67), and included a non-
Muslim zone of burial, recognizable through grave orientation (see
chapter 6), and interpreted as the burial place of Jews or Coptic

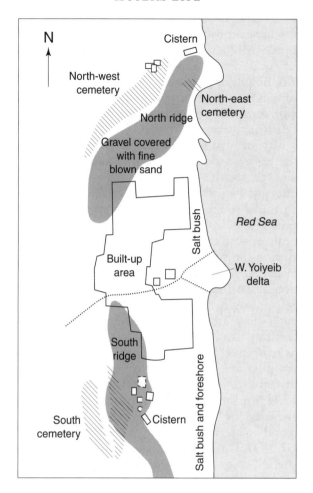

Figure 4.2 Plan of Aidhab, Sudan (not to scale) (after Paul 1955: 65)

Christians (Elisséeff and el Hakim 1981: 41). A living legacy of *hajj* traffic has also been left in the Sudan, with the significant numbers of people of West African origin who have stayed there.

Ziyara, rihlah *and* hijrah

Pilgrimage to Mecca is not the only form of religious journeying undertaken in the Muslim world (Eickelman and Piscatori 1990; Netton 1993). Myriad shrines and holy places are visited continually, in the process of *ziyara*. These range from major centres, such as the Shi'ah foci of pilgrimage, the tombs of Hussein at Karbala and Ali at Najaf, where almost parallel rituals of visitation to those of *hajj* have developed (Momen 1985: 182), to individual saints' tombs, important in local contexts. Criss-crossing the Muslim world are vast networks of pilgrimage trails, as Ibn Battuta recorded during his extended wanderings in the mid-fourteenth century (Gibb 1993).

As with *hajj*, local pilgrimage is archaeologically recognizable on a lesser scale. Instructive examples can be drawn from Central Asia, where local pilgrimage to tombs is still of great importance. This was especially the case, as Bennigsen and Enders Wimbush (1986: 23) discuss, during the Soviet era, when they served as substitutes for closed mosques and *hajj* was impossible. In this region the deep-seated tradition of 'parallel Islam' (1986: 23) is better described as syncretism with traditional beliefs. Among the semi-nomadic Uzbeks, for instance, local pilgrimage was incorporated within the seasonal cycle, and during the summer drive of the animals to new pastures various shrines and holy places were visited by Uzbek herders. At these, sacrifices and offerings would be made, and 'thus, Islam and the ancient belief in magic, were united' (Emeljanenko 1994: 49). This again illustrates how apparently secular activities, such as seasonal transhumance, can also be placed within the overall religious framework. This is reinforced by an example from Sinai, where Marx (1977) discusses how pilgrimage to saints' shrines is an important feature of social life through helping to create local community, as *hajj* serves to create the world Muslim community. It also offers material advantages to transact business for 'they [the Bedouin] do not conceive of purely spiritual or purely material occasions, as found in specialised industrial societies' (1977: 41). Thus, the inter-connectedness of many elements – spiritual, material, cultural – is again apparent.

Many journeys were also made purely in the search of knowledge, or *rihlah*, and promoted by the Prophet who, according to a *hadith*, counselled his followers 'that they should seek knowledge as far as China' (Netton 1993: x). There is also *hijrah* (migration), defined by Eickelman and Piscatori as 'the obligation to migrate from lands where the practice of Islam is constrained to those where in principle no such constraint exists' (1990: 5). This is certainly something which could be archaeologically visible as with the Andalusian Muslim refugees who settled in Morocco, Tunisia and Algeria after the Christian re-conquest.

Commerce and travel

The final category of travel which will be considered here as having archaeological implications is that which has an overtly commercial character. Although 'trade' itself is examined in greater detail in chapter 5, the mechanics of land-based caravan travel will be discussed here because of its intimate relationship with pilgrimage. The relevant categories of archaeological evidence will be broadly the same as those already outlined for pilgrimage, with caravan trails differing little from pilgrimage routes. An example of the mapping of a major trade route is provided by the results of archaeological survey in the Seistan region of Iran, through which a route ran linking the Persian Gulf ports in Iran to Herat in Afghanistan, and on to Pakistan and India. Exceptional preservation has allowed the study of a variety of features indicating the former roads and tracks, dwelling or watch towers between towns and forts, orange brick dust stains, the residue of former way-markers, wells and bridges (Tate 1910; Fischer 1973). Milestones may also be found. Welch describes a milestone dating from 685–705 from Palestine which bore the inscription: 'the highway... Abdullah 'Abd al-Malik, amir of the Faithful, Allah's mercy be upon him, this mile is eight miles (from Jerusalem)' (1979: 44). A similar inscription from close to Aqaba (Jordan) is described by Woolley and Lawrence (1936). Erected between 1500 and 1516, it reads: 'the cutting of this blessed road was ordered by our master the Sultan al-Malik al-Ashraf Kansuh al-Ghuri, may his help be strong, who also erected in this blessed *khan* towers for the deposits of the pilgrims' (1936: 161).

A further category of structure, specifically associated with Muslim travellers of all types, which would be of great importance to the archaeologist attempting to identify trade and pilgrimage routes, is provided by the 'caravanserai' or *khan*, which has been likened in its modern equivalent to a petrol station, 'occurring at regular intervals, ubiquitous, unremarkable and unremarked' (Sims 1978: 98). The usual architectural form was of a central walled courtyard, surrounded by lodgings for men and beasts, facilities for storing goods, and perhaps a prayer area, baths, water-storage facilities, and a few small shops or kiosks. Caravanserais could also be provided with defences, and varied both in size and according to region (Sauvaget 1940: 1–4; Petersen 1994: 51). Numerous examples have been recorded and investigated archaeologically all over the Muslim world: from Central Asia, as at Talaihan-Ata in the Kara-Kum desert, where a caravanserai dating from the eleventh to fourteenth centuries was excavated on the trade route leading to Bukhara and Samarkand (Fedorov-Davydov 1983: 401), to the Jaulan (Golan) in Syria, where Schumacher (1888) recorded caravanserais ranging from the humble to the well appointed. But among the most unexpected, though clearly archaeologically visible, examples yet found (Insoll 1996c:

486) was a structure recorded at Yendi Dabari in Ghana, deep in the tropical forest zone of West Africa, where the remains of a two-storey structure interpreted as the remains of 'a strangers' complex of warehouses and paddocks for pack animals' (Ozanne 1971: 55–6) were investigated.

Thus, as with the other aspects of life discussed so far, it can be seen that pilgrimage and travel are further important dimensions of Muslim life; specific material culture is associated with these activities which can be recognized by the archaeologist. Once again, direct connections between the sacred and the secular exist, through actions such as combining trade with pilgrimage, either in the local context or on *hajj*. This inter-connectedness, apparent with many areas of Muslim life, is a theme running throughout this chapter and throughout this book. Further possible markers of Muslim identity, and potentially important components of Muslim life, are provided by personal possessions and dress.

Personal Possessions and Dress

Both personal possessions and dress are intimate items which are often invested with a meaning beyond their surface appearance, and can convey a variety of socially important information, state Muslim identity, and could be encountered archaeologically. Though perhaps conceived of as 'lesser items' of life, they should not be ignored by the archaeologist for this reason. However, it should be noted that the examples chosen do not imply the existence of universals: that all women were veiled, or that all Muslims wore seal rings and used prayer beads, for instance. These are obviously interchangeable with many other items, and though present in one area could well be absent in another. Similarly, many of the items discussed are of little relevance today. Rather, the chosen examples function as an illustration that the archaeology of Islam is equally composed of large and small alike, and favouring one at the expense of the other is to bias the picture we present.

Personal possessions

The seal ring   The seal ring can be seen to be an object combining both secular and sacred significance, and certainly of utilitarian and aesthetic value. Functioning both as a sign of individual identity, but also of Muslim identity, and an item connected through tradition with the Prophet, it served a variety of purposes on a variety of levels. Although rare today, seal rings were common and, through their function as a form of signature, were used to seal goods and documents. Inscriptions frequently consist of the name of the wearer and a pious inscription engraved on a semi-precious stone, which was set in a silver band, following the example of the Prophet. The quality obviously varied, but the choice of materials was often deliberate, as the Prophet did not approve of gold, although it was sometimes employed, while 'brass savoured of idolatry' and iron was 'emblematic of souls condemned to the eternal fire' (Allan 1978: 1103–4; and see also Juynboll 1986: 110–11). Carnelian was frequently used for the seal (for examples, see Content 1987: 35–6), and Jenkins and Keane suggest that among the qualities which recommended its use were 'availability, toughness, and resistance to abrasion' (1982: 20). Its popular use might also be connected with the tradition that the Prophet advised everyone to wear an agate, a material which, according to Donaldson, was primary in the magical hierarchy (1939: 152). Such an interpretation could in turn help in explaining the trade in carnelian which took place across vast distances in the Muslim world during the medieval period.

Examples have been found archaeologically. A seal ring, inlaid with a disc of black jasper on which was cut an Arabic inscription in reverse, was found at the site of Shanga on the Kenyan coast (Horton 1996: 357). This find, along with a variety of other evidence, allowed the suggestion that a Muslim community was present at this site from its foundation in the late eighth century. Engraved seal stones of carnelian, turquoise, lapis lazuli and hematite were recovered from Nishapur in Iran (if the provenance is correct) and dated from the tenth to eleventh centuries (Jenkins and Keane 1982: 19–21), while at Ras al'Hadd in Oman a reverse-cut carnelian seal was found at this Indian Ocean trade centre (Petersen 1997).

The rosary or prayer beads   More overtly religious in character is the rosary (*subha*), which has been described as a 'visible example of the passion for the words of God' (Bravmann 1983: 21), and which is also a comparatively rare example of Muslim religious paraphernalia, as in many ways Islam lacks the trappings associated with other world religions. The simplicity of worship in Islam precludes a large body of ritual material culture. The rosary is a set of prayer beads usually made up of 99 beads indicating the 99 beautiful names of Allah, which are used in prayer or meditation. They can be made of many materials: wood, semi-precious stones, ivory and, more recently, plastic. Although they are not universally used, they can be both generally associated with Muslims, and more specifically with certain movements, such as the Sufi orders where their use is very widespread. Indeed, Gellner (1981: 143) makes the point that they are, 'so characteristic of the religious fraternities that one can refer to a fraternity, or its distinguishing spiritual technique, as a *wird* (rosary)'. Prayer beads thus provide another example of an object that is both intimate and yet specifically Muslim in character, individual in association, durable in nature and with definite archaeological implications. At Gao (Mali), for example, the recovery of a large turned-wood central bead from a rosary dated to between the early eleventh and late fourteenth centuries helped prove that Muslims lived in a particular area of the city.

Miscellany   Other items could help to denote the former presence of a Muslim in the archaeological record, yet to define them as categorically Muslim would be misleading, even though they might be intimately linked with Islam, Muslim culture or the Muslim world. The direct religious association, as with prayer beads, or indirect, as with the Arabic inscribed seal ring, is missing. Within this category could be placed the *miswak* or *siwak*, a toothbrush or toothpick made from fragrant wood, valued by the Prophet Muhammad for hygiene purposes, and recommended for cleaning the mouth prior to prayer (Gibb and Kramers 1961: 388–9). Owing to associations with the Prophet, it could take on a significance for which it was never intended; Kalesi relates, for example, that pilgrims returning from Mecca used to bring *miswak* back to the Balkans with them owing to this association (1978: 374).

Similar are various female items such as *kuhl* or *kohl* pots and applicators. The applicators, decorated or plain, were small probes of wood, ivory or silver, and their containers were of glass or metal. *Kohl* is still commonly applied as an eye cosmetic in many areas of the Islamic world, especially the Arab lands; its use is described in detail by Lane (1895: 44–5, see also Wiedemann 1986). Such applicators were found in Islamic period levels at Qsar es-Seghir in Morocco, along with a variety of other personal items which clearly differentiated the Muslim community from the subsequent Portuguese Christian one (see chapter 7; Redman 1986: 129). Likewise at Nishapur in Iran, *kohl* applicators were found and, although they have a pre-Islamic background, Allan records how decorated and undecorated *kohl* sticks 'were common throughout the Islamic world in the early Islamic period' (1982: 38). Other find spots he lists include Fustat (Egypt), Hama (Syria), Rayy and Siraf (Iran) and Samarra (Iraq). Unfortunately, an item such as a *kohl* container or a *siwak* cannot obviously be said *per se* to be an object which belonged to a Muslim, yet a clear association with Muslim culture exists. Such objects might, however, be of value depending on the context in which they are found, as at Qsar es-Seghir.

A further illustrative example of the possible usefulness of personal possessions in recognizing Muslim communities is provided by material recovered from the Ottoman fortress at Qasr Ibrim in Egyptian Nubia. Exceptional conditions meant that many of the personal possessions associated with the garrison were preserved. Distinctive male possessions included reed pens, wooden combs, keys and spoons, iron razors, leather shoes, amulets, horse trappings, musket parts and smoking pipes (see plate 4.4). None of these items could be said to be specifically Muslim, but all are of types which can be identified as coming from the Muslim world, though similar items were found in late Christian levels (see Adams 1996). The same is true of the female possessions found: multi-coloured glass bangles, *kohl* accessories, sandals, jewellery and perfume containers. However, in both instances the association with Islam is still indirect. The importance lies in the fact that such a diverse range of materials was found in association with each other, and that these were found in conjunction with other categories of evidence which directly indicated that the

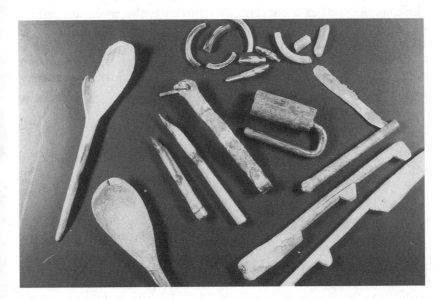

Plate 4.4   Various personal items from Ottoman period levels at Qasr Ibrim, Egypt (*photo*. T. Insoll, courtesy of the Egypt Exploration Society)

former owners of these items were Muslim. Therefore, a wealth of information on often neglected aspects of life was obtained through archaeological evidence, details which begin to allow Muslim life in total to be reconstructed.

Dress

A second category of personal objects which might be of use to the archaeologist in pursuing such issues are items of dress. Dress is a medium which can be used to convey a variety of information, and thus constitutes a further 'actively used' area of material culture (see, for example, Cordwell and Schwarz 1979). Dress, like the domestic environment, is an area of material culture which can be used to uphold Muslim social codes, but can, like food, be used for a variety of different social purposes: to signal status, gender, religious and political affiliation, and class or caste. Within Islam, clothing has a special significance; Watson (1983: 41) mentions how, 'in practice if not in doctrine...the faithful should be clothed, preferably from the neck to the ankles, with only the face, neck, hands and feet showing'. Obviously, great variety in types of dress is found, but at the same time an underlying and recurrent concern with modesty is often apparent across the Muslim world, especially as regards women's clothing. As well as a concern with modesty, the speed and extent of the Arab conquests frequently led to the widespread adoption of their fashions, and these could replace local costume or be amalgamated with it. Thus, quite apart from religious demands, elements of a recognizable Muslim *couture* existed and could be identified archaeologically from textile fragments.

Status and affiliation   Although ideally it should not occur, as all believers are meant to be equal, clothing can obviously be used to emphasize status distinctions, and it would be foolhardy to deny the often great divergence which exists between theory and practice in many areas of Muslim life. In the Yemen, for example, Kirkman (1976: 67) describes how clothing could serve 'as a chosen marker of social identity'. Religious scholars could set themselves apart through their dress, affirming their position in society. Similarly, female dress in the Yemen could also exhibit social distinctions, but in a different form from that of men, reflecting not public role but isolation from public life (though this in itself is an often-debated point, and is discussed further below). Besides indicating status, clothing could also set a Muslim apart from his or her neighbours. In parts of India, Schimmel relates how tailored (sewn) clothing was closely connected with Muslims as they 'could barely perform their prayers in draped or tied clothing, as the women needed a decent covering from ankles to neck' (1980: 109).

Certainly one of the most elaborate examples of the use of dress to convey information concerning status in the Muslim world was provided by the Ottoman court where, according to Wheatcroft, 'colour and form had their own eloquence, and costume possessed a subtle grammar' (1995: 39). For men, beard length, turbans, colour of robes and shoes and the cut of the sleeves all defined social status according to intricate codes (see, for example, Rogers and Ward 1988: 164–85). Although women lacked public roles, Turkish dress styles were still widely worn throughout the Ottoman provinces, and were 'emulated in the towns by any of the subject population who had aspirations towards status and wealth' (Scarce 1987: 14). Over the centuries, until reforms in the early nineteenth century swept them away, this language of dress, though maintained, came to be somewhat less well understood and was, as Wheatcroft puts it, 'imperfectly spoken but still eloquent' (1995: 39). Dress codes were kept because they were traditional (though they were also subject to fashion), even though their symbolic meaning had ceased to be completely understood. This raises the question of how much more material culture functions in this way, and how much interpretative meaning in turn is lost, removed as we are from the events themselves.

The turban and the veil Besides the more culturally specific instances of the social role of clothing within Muslim society, other factors must also be considered. A particularly instructive example is provided by the turban, as the Prophet Muhammad is said to have encouraged Muslims to wear a turban 'as a badge of their faith' (Miles 1952: 170). A *hadith* states that turbans are a mark of Islam and divide believers from unbelievers, and wearing one, though not a religious duty, is recommended for men (Gibb and Kramers 1961: 596). The use of a turban representation on some Ottoman tombstones as a means of stating religious affiliation will be discussed later (see chapter 6); the turban could serve a similar role in life. Turbans, through their material, style and colour, could also be used to differentiate between different religious groups within society. In nineteenth-century Cairo, for example, Lane (1895) describes how a Muslim was distinguished from the Coptic and Jewish populations by the colour of his turban, as well as through other aspects of dress. Green turbans were reserved for the descendants of the Prophet, while Copts and Jews were restricted to black, light-brown, blue and grey turbans and 'generally dull-coloured dresses' (1895: 43). Although the turban, as the seal ring, was by no means universal, it serves to illustrate that items of clothing exist which can serve as markers of religious identity.

For women, the headgear denoting Muslim identity is the veil and headscarf. Many items can be subsumed within this category, from the all-concealing *chador* to the more modest Western style headscarf. The veil is of significance for two main reasons: it is intimately connected with women, the 'hidden' 50 per cent of the population (archaeologically at least); and it can be used to enforce Muslim social codes concerning the privacy of females and of modesty in general. But, again, universals should not be promoted; the extent to which the veil was or can be used, if at all, varies greatly, and, as with the turban, need not be restricted to Muslims. Scarce (1987), for example, describes how Orthodox Christian women in the Balkans could be heavily influenced by Turkish traditions of dress, even as far as wearing a veil, and makes the important point that 'it would be a naive simplification to assume that sartorial difference could be neatly divided between Christian and Muslim women' (1987: 99). The veil could also take on an exaggerated significance. Remedius Prutky, a Franciscan missionary, recorded that, at Jeddah (Saudi Arabia) in the mid-eighteenth century:

> although the women guard their faces solicitously, that they may not be seen, yet they pay little attention to the other parts of the body, especially the poor: for it often happens, when they leave the house to wash their shifts and ribbons, that, having no others save those they are wearing, they stay at the river washing as naked as God made them, with only their faces covered, and sit their while their washing dries in the sun. (Arrowsmith-Brown 1991: 33)

The degree to which veiling has been practised, and thus the seclusion of females maintained, has often depended on social class. In the Middle East, for instance, Keddie (1992: 48) makes the point that 'except among the recent, modernised elite, veiling has been widely regarded as a sign of status, showing that the husband and wife can afford for her not to work.' It can be seen that in many ways the use of the veil is linked with the structuring notions which can underlie the form of the traditional Muslim domestic environment, namely, to protect the purity of the female members of the household (see chapter 3). By the veil being worn outside, these concerns are extended into the public domain. It is a further example of how material culture can be used to convey the traditional norms and requirements of a Muslim society. But, equally, the role of the veil is subject to many different interpretations as to the degree to which it actually excludes women from society at large, or alternatively includes them, though in a less obvious manner (see, for example, Webster 1984). The veil can, in conditions where textiles survive, be encountered archaeologically. At Quseir al-Qadim, for example, the earliest known surviving woman's face veil was recovered from Mamluk period levels dated to between the mid-thirteenth and mid-fourteenth centuries in this Red Sea port (Vogelsang-Eastwood 1993: 87).

Colour Another dimension of clothing and its possible significance within Muslim life is colour. Colour as a medium of information display has already been touched upon in the context of the turban; green is the colour connected with the Prophet's descendants and has been widely used in flags and banners. Athamina (1989) also describes how colour in dress and banners was used by the Abbasid regime as a means of manipulating and legitimizing power, a process which began in the mid-eighth century when Caliph al-Mansur introduced black garments for his courtiers and entourage. A deliberate background with religious associations was created for this uniform with reputed links back to the Prophet, who was said to have had a black banner the day Mecca was conquered, and who foresaw salvation for his family after his death coming from the east with people bearing black flags. The black uniform became the official uniform of the Abbasid regime, and symbolic of social class and power. Hence, according to Athamina, 'persons striving to improve their social standing sought permission to appear in the black uniform' (1989: 320). Likewise, as it became a symbol of loyalty to the regime, traitors could be stripped of it, and on occasion made to wear white, a colour adopted by the opposition 'deliberately in contrast to those of the Abbasids' (1989: 322). But the meaning of colour is not static; as with the seal ring, the veil or any other element of material culture, it can be subject to the developmental process, to fads and fashion, and meanings can change. The significance of the colour black turned full circle in nineteenth-century Cairo, for Edward Lane mentions how black dress and turbans were 'characteristic, almost solely, of Christian and Jewish tributaries to the 'Osmánlee, or Turkish, Sultan' (1895: 43).

In summary, the few examples which have been discussed have been chosen from a vast range of possibilities, and are not meant to be exhaustive; rather, they serve to show that even what could be termed the 'small items' or ephemera of life – the seal ring, the turban, the veil – can also help in serving to create or denote overall Muslim identity. They are objects associated with the individual, and illustrate that the archaeology of Islam is more than mosques, palaces and elaborate funerary monuments. It is the sum total of all these elements, both large and small. Yet, at the same time, it should also be realized that diversity must be acknowledged. Though seal rings might have been popular in one area, they might be unheard of elsewhere, and black uniforms, for example, were certainly not universal. To enumerate individually all the objects which could signify a Muslim, geographically and temporally, would run to several volumes and exhaustive cataloguing was not the point of this exercise. The chosen objects are readily interchangeable with many others; they are not in some way defining items of 'Muslim culture', but equally these 'lesser items' of Muslim life, in all their many forms, should not be neglected. They provide a possible source of much useful social information for archaeologists, perhaps blinkered through the pursuit of the so-called 'big issues'.

Magic and Talismanic Protection

A further area of Muslim life which could be of significance to the archaeologist is that of magic in general, and personal talismanic protection in particular. A deep concern with magic is apparent in many areas of the Muslim world, especially magic for protection, fulfilling desires, health, potency in love or war. This can sometimes be approached by the archaeologist through the artifacts involved. 'Orthodox Islam denies the efficacy of amulets and other magico-religious devices, but these traditions have always been a vital aspect of popular Islam, just as they have played a significant role in the belief systems of many people throughout history' (Silverman 1991: 19). Usually, a distinction is drawn between good magic, which could aid Islam, and bad magic or sorcery. Numerous media can be employed to protect, curse or destroy – paper, metals, water, textiles, leather – but a common element is the efficacy of the Qur'an, as a supremely powerful agent. This is due to the fact that 'the Qur'an differs from the other major scriptures of the World in that it contains not reports about God by a Prophet or his disciples, but his direct speech, the syllables, words and sentences of Allah' (Geertz 1976: 1489–90, cited in Bravmann 1983: 16). Besides verses from the Qur'an, notably the *basmala* and the *Fatihah*, cabbalistic signs, magical formulas, the beautiful names of God, numerical representations and various substances can all be used for magical and protective purposes. The actual material forms of protective or destructive magical items can be many, and a universal type certainly does not exist, but generic categories which might be encountered archaeologically may be briefly considered.

Magic bowls

One such group of items, the so-called 'magic bowls', appear to encompass not merely bowls, but plates and cups as well. These are always made of metal, silver and copper most commonly, though iron is infrequently used, and they date from the later medieval period into the present. Formerly, according to Canaan (1936: 79), they were found all over the Muslim world. However, Bates is more specific in geographical attribution when she says that they are most common in Turkey, but are also occasionally found in western Iran and India (1991: 58). Magic bowls were used to cure poisoning, and reduce fear or fright, as well as for divination. For the purposes of healing, water is drunk from the bowl, the interior of which is usually inscribed with Qur'anic verses, or various of the other devices already described above, such as numerical combinations, magical squares, figural motifs (Canaan 1936: 89, 94; Bates 1991: 56). The importance of magic bowls is not that they are in anyway universally used, but because they provide a specific example of the translation of Muslim magic into durable material culture, and thus illustrate that a concern with magic could be archaeologically visible.

Higab

The most common example of an item with magico-religious associations, which might be archaeologically detectable, are amulets, or *higab*, which are worn on the person. These were, and to a lesser extent are, popular in certain areas, but absent altogether in others, and can take many different forms, usually consisting of a written text in two parts, the *da'wa* or spell and the *jadwal*, a magic square or other geometric device (Silverman 1991: 22). These are often within a leather, metal or cloth covering, and worn around the neck, waist or arm, or sewn on clothing. They are usually written by a holyman for a specific purpose: safety in travel or protection from disease or attack. Among the Berti of the Sudan, for example, el-Tom (1987) records that the *higab* are believed to contain immense power which can be gained in various ways. These include physically keeping this power on the person through wearing amulets, or less visibly through internalizing the Qur'anic verses or other powerful formulas in the

Plate 4.5 *Higab* (amulet) contents from Qasr Ibrim, Egypt (Egypt Exploration Society)

head by memory or inside the body through drinking the text by washing off the ink and swallowing the water (1987: 243). Amulets have been found archaeologically, for example at Qasr Ibrim, where many *higab* were excavated in various contexts dating from the sixteenth to nineteenth centuries. They have leather outer covers, and inside contained a further package made of cotton, which in turn contained the sacred text (even a blank piece of paper) (see plate 4.5). Other manifestations of amuletic protection occur, for example in Shi'ah chain mail dating from the early nineteenth century which adds spiritual protection through the incorporation of Arabic invocations 'requesting aid and assistance' (Welch 1979: 106) in brass links set within the steel jacket – similar to, though more efficient than, the inscribed cloth jackets of the *Mahdi*'s followers in the Sudan in the nineteenth century. This is a dimension of Muslim magic which is significant to the individual, rather than the group or household, as was apparent in the protection of the domestic environment (see chapter 3).

Bricks, crows' beaks and carpets

The extensive body of ethnographic, anthropological and historical sources dwelling, in whole or in part, upon the subject is of great use to the archaeologist of Islam in recognizing magical items. An informative example is provided by a fragment of text in the Cairo *Genizah*, a medieval synagogue archive, describing contexts for the magical use of Arabic letters. Recorded instances include the use of the letter *Kaf*, engraved on old red potsherds, then steamed until blackened, the result being that vegetable matter will turn 'from one state to another'. Other contexts include fragments of brick inscribed with the letter *Mim* to arouse fear in a person, or engraving the letter *Nun* on a piece of white marble to foil robbers (Ebeid and Young 1974: 405). What at first could appear to be contradictions of normal Muslim practice can also be of relevance within the domain of magic and protection. One might expect, for example, that intimate contact with the crow might be avoided, as it is one of the so-called five nuisances, but it also possesses talismanic properties, and to carry a crow's beak on one's person averts the evil eye (Pellat 1965: 1097). Similarly, the number five, and representations of it, such as the hand, were used to protect inanimate objects such as carpets, guns, bags and pottery from the evil eye in Morocco (Westermarck 1933: 29–31), while the same imagery, the hand, can have a totally different significance in Iran, where it signifies the five most sacred persons of the Shi'ah faith: Muhammad, Ali, Fatima, Hassan and Hussein (Hastings

1911: 459). This again illustrates that meaning is by no means uniform; there are no, or very limited, pan-Islamic interpretative meanings. A belief in magic might be widely found, clothing will certainly be worn, but within each of these broad descriptive categories great diversity exists, a situation broadly comparable to the notions of structuring principles and cultural diversity discussed before. To begin to approach the second level, reconstructing the rich tapestry of Muslim life in all its dimensions, and basing this upon archaeological evidence, requires a variety of factors: an open mind, a rigorous examination of context and analogy, and the consideration of other possible sources of evidence.

War

The final aspect of Muslim life to be touched on here is war. This is a contentious subject but cannot be excluded as it was often intimately connected with the spread of Islam, and must therefore be included within a consideration of the possible archaeology of Islam. Holy war, *jihad* or 'the spread of Islam by arms', often the subject of fear and stereotypes in the West, is, according to Gibb and Kramers, 'a religious duty upon Muslims in general' (1961: 89), and the only type of war authorized and regulated by Islamic law (Peters 1977: 3). Thus, it should be considered as a further area of life which can be imbued with religious significance. According to orthodox Muslim doctrine, two major domains exist in the world: the *dar al-harb*, the land or abode of war, and the *dar al-Islam*, the land of Islam. Within the latter, Muslim rule is established, Islamic law is in place, and non-Muslim peoples have submitted to Muslim control. Creation of this was the object of *jihad*, yet the existence of such a division does not mean that advancing 'the boundaries of the Faith until the whole World acknowledged Allah' (Wheatcroft 1995: 47) is a practical proposition today. Obviously it is not, and a compromise position has been reached. Yet, similarly, the existence of a religious dimension to the pursuit of war within parts of the Muslim world cannot be wholly discounted, even today. Recent conflicts in Afghanistan, Bosnia and Chechnya attest to this, where volunteers, perhaps physically divorced from the immediate conflict, offered their services in aid of fellow Muslims (see plate 4.6). According to Bosworth (1976: 202), 'religious enthusiasm should not be underestimated as a motive all through Islamic warfare.' Certainly, such motivation could be suggested as a possible guiding light behind many of the tragic events which have dominated the media in recent years, including suicide bombings in the Middle East.

Plate 4.6 War scene from *The Khamsa of Nizami* (Browne no. 1424, St John's College, Cambridge)

But what implications does war hold for the archaeology of Islam? First, it is necessary to distinguish somehow between *jihad* and 'general' warfare, which can be started for many reasons all too familiar to us: political power struggles, greed, territorial ambitions. The latter version of warfare was, and sadly is, endemic, but can hardly be classified as religious, though such a label might be sought as a propaganda or motivating device. However, such conflict is essentially secular in nature. Secondly, it is necessary to consider if there is such a thing as a Muslim apparatus of war, thus setting it apart from other conflicts materially. This is the only element possibly approachable by the archaeologist and, indeed, the literature on Islamic weaponry, tactics, fortifications and the like is vast (see, for example, Rahman Zakry 1965; Parry 1970; Parry and Yapp 1975; Nicolle 1976). Distinctive elements might be selected; types of fortifications perhaps (Creswell 1952; Grabar 1978: 66–7) or weaponry or armour of different patterns (al-Hassan and Hill 1992: 96–8) and, of course, inscriptions. But it is impossible to generalize about these within the space available, other than simply to state that the diversity in types and forms was immense. In certain contexts and historical situations, specific machinery of both warfare and defence associated with the Muslim world of course existed, yet at the same time it is necessary to avoid creating stereotypes, such as the Saracen of Hollywood fame with his pointed helmet and curved scimitar. Incidentally, the latter component, at least, is wholly erroneous; according to Bosworth (1976: 208), this type of sword was not common until the fifteenth century (see also Rahman Zakry 1965: 291).

However, one example of specific material culture which might in certain instances prove useful in recognizing the pursuance of *jihad*, or at least in reconstructing military frontier zones over time, should be discussed: the *ribat*. This has been described as 'a base from which to prosecute Holy war' (Hillenbrand 1994: 331), a type of 'fortified monastery', and is found on many of the frontiers of the Muslim world, as in Central Asia and North Africa, dating from the medieval period. Grabar describes the *ribat* form as 'square with halls around a porticoed courtyard' (1973: 180), with essentially the same plan being used as can be found in many caravanserais, and a further example of the interchangeability of Muslim building form often found in medieval Islam. These have been recorded in many areas. For example, an exceptionally large *ribat* dating from the mid-twelfth century, and one of a number of coastal *ribats* built, in the words of Basset and Terrasse, to '*défendre la terre d'Islam contre les débarquements possible des infidèles*' (1927: 119), was recorded close to Mazagan in

Morocco. This was one of the frontier districts, and besides the enclosing wall, defensive towers, gateways and two minarets were all partially preserved. Similar *ribats* on the North African coast are also referred to by King, as at Ajdabiyah in Libya, where they were 'initially associated with the wars of the Aghlabids against Sicily, Italy and the Mediterranean islands' (1989: 197).

Although we have only briefly considered one possible aspect of material culture which might be linked with *jihad*, the *ribat*, the essential point to consider is that the *ghazi*, the warrior of the Faith, did, and perhaps does, exist, pursuing *jihad* for the expansion of Islam. Thus, although we must remember that war is fought more frequently in the name of many causes indistinguishable from those fuelling conflicts perpetuated by non-Muslims, it is possible that another element of Muslim life cannot be wholly separated out and classified as secular. Many, if not all, aspects of life can be imbued with a religious significance, something which we as archaeologists should remember when looking at our evidence, whether fort or faunal assemblage.

Summary and Conclusions

Thus, various areas of life, which are not perhaps always considered by archaeologists, have been shown to be, in many instances, both inseparable from the religious domain and approachable through archaeology. This further enables us to begin to view the archaeology of Islam as a complete entity, ranging from grand mosques and palaces, through individual burials, down to the residue of a meal. All can be, but need not be, affected by a religious element. Life need not be seen as a series of purely economically driven or rationally based decisions, factors which are perhaps increasingly coming to the fore in an age when faith and religious practice are separated out, or absent altogether, from everyday life for many people in the Western world. The multi-disciplinary examples considered in this chapter were drawn from a vast geographical, cultural and temporal range, but serve to illustrate that religious ideals can be translated into practical structuring codes for life. Therefore, the archaeological study of religion should not be conceptualized as confined to a few aspects of life. As was seen with much of the material discussed, multiple interconnections are often evident, with the one running into or influencing the other, as we saw with food and festivals, pilgrimage, trade and travel. All can come together, until their boundaries become blurred.

To return to the concept of the 'umbrella', or superstructure, with many component parts below it, Islam acts as the umbrella, with beneath this our discrete categories of food, war, pilgrimage and so on, with further diversity evident within each of these categories, though still subject to the structuring codes of the religion. Thus variety is produced within the overall entity, or what have been termed structuring principles and cultural diversity. But limitations in how far we can offer interpretations have also been exposed in the face of the bewildering richness apparent. Clothing, food, personal possessions, all can be invested with a social significance and meaning which we can best perceive through ethnography or historical sources; even taking into account the privileged position of the archaeologist interested in Islam, these may be difficult, if not impossible, to reconstruct archaeologically. However, we must be aware of the available possibilities, if only to make us realize that we will never know all the answers, and that archaeology suffers from restricting factors. Finally, much of our discussion has been concerned with the 'ideal', as with the ideal faunal assemblage, but such notions have to be pursued, if only to suggest possible interesting directions of research for the future. The lesser areas of life can be of equal significance to the popularly perceived 'big issues', within the archaeology of Islam, the archaeology of religion and archaeology in general.

5

Art, Trade and Ideas

Believers, do not consume your wealth among yourselves in vanity, but
rather trade with it by mutual consent

Qur'an. Women 4: 29

We now turn our attention to what are, in many respects, much
broader categories: art, trade and ideas. Art is a loose term, defined
by the *Oxford English Dictionary* as 'skill, esp. human skill as
opposed to nature; skilful execution as an object in itself; skill applied
to imitation and design, as in painting etc.' (Fowler and Fowler 1952:
63). Even if we confine ourselves to the latter part of the definition,
it can be seen that 'art' could cover a wide range of techniques,
could be applied in myriad contexts, and rendered in equally
diverse materials. In short, it is something which can be applied in
one form or another to many of the items already discussed, from
tombstones to swords. All can be influenced by art or even be art
objects in themselves, though not necessarily perhaps in the same
way as originally envisaged by the people who made or commissioned them. Therefore, we also come upon the problem of
differentiating between art objects *per se*, and those which are
regarded as such by contemporary observers. It can even be suggested
that academics often 'create' art objects through their researches,
where perhaps such original intentions were lacking, or such a
definition would not have been applied in the original context.
However, it is not the place here to define what constitutes an
art object. Instead, the following discussion will be concerned
with all items bearing decoration of one form or another, thus keeping to the pattern of broad categorizations followed throughout the
volume.

How then do trade and manufacturing enter into the same discussion as art? The link between the three is somewhat created, but at the same time fairly obvious. The connection is the agency through which ideas, including artistic ideas or conventions, and scientific ideas and manufacturing techniques, are transmitted from one place to another, often via trade. Conquest can and obviously did serve as the agent for the spread of Islam and Islamization, but the peaceful movement of ideas, including religious ones, through trade, is often of even greater importance when the spectrum of Muslim history over the centuries is considered. These issues will be discussed in greater detail below; suffice it to say here that trade provides a convenient framework to link a range of material not covered elsewhere, which could, and indeed does, form part of the 'package' which might allow the recognition of a Muslim or Muslim community in the archaeological record.

In many respects this chapter deals with material which has suffered the greatest contemporary disruption. The following discussion is mainly concerned with material dating from before the late sixteenth century and the rise of European power, and the ensuing fragmentation and collapse of the Muslim 'world system'. The form of a mosque and Muslim burial, for example, though affected by modern influences, are, as we have seen, still recognizable for what they are, regardless of contemporary factors. In contrast, distinctive Muslim coinages and sciences have largely ceased to be identifiable in the manner in which they were recognizable in the medieval period. A Muslim science, for instance, is now largely the same as a Western one, though the relevant research might be carried out in a Muslim country. Certainly, the trade patterns that were manifest in the medieval period have long since disappeared. Thus the study of much of this material is ideally approached through archaeology as one of the primary means of furthering our understanding of both artifacts and processes. Art, however, is perhaps the least affected, and contains recurring elements which should allow its recognition as Muslim art today.

Islamic Art or Art of Muslims: Background and Components

A consideration of what is Islamic or, perhaps preferably, Muslim art is a frequently asked question which has been approached by various scholars (see, for example, Ettinghausen 1944; Grabar 1973). However, these studies are usually concerned with the luxury end of production which, when considering a subject such as the formation of Muslim art, is not overly surprising as it was in the courtly

environment that many developments took place which later percola-
ted down through society. A detailed examination of the processes by
which this occurred is beyond the remit of this volume, but has been
well covered elsewhere, both in general and region by region (see
Talbot Rice 1993; Brend 1994).

Nevertheless, briefly summarized, Oleg Grabar (1973) makes the
point that there is no absolute date for the creation of Muslim art. It
can be linked, not surprisingly, to the conquering of each region. As
each area was taken by the Muslims, pre-existing elements of Classical, Byzantine, Sasanian and even Central Asian art were then appro-
priated and adapted in a long drawn-out process (Talbot Rice 1971:
5). An ensuing characteristic was the widespread diffusion of previously restricted decorative motifs from one end of the newly
formed Muslim world to the other (Grabar 1973: 7, 208). General
defining characteristics of Muslim art, according to Philon (1980: 12),
are an 'inherent ambiguity of purpose, function and meaning' with a
universality of decorative forms, and the easy adaptability of buildings for various purposes with only minor changes, leading to 'an
intimate relationship between the monumental and the minor arts'.
What is apparent from this is that Muslim art is a mixture of local and
general components, and that there is no one overall entity; it did not
appear in the saddlebags of the conquering Muslim armies, but was
subject to an evolutionary process.

But what, if any, are the defining characteristics of Muslim art? It is
easy to suggest the frequently cited, though erroneous, statement that
Muslim art is solely a reflection of religious requirements, and that
the primary recognition criterion, for this reason, is an absence of
figural representation. This is wrong, for Muslim art can and has
served both secular and religious purposes, and is by no means devoid
of figural images. At the same time, there are various components to
Muslim art, though they are no more than broad categories and can
be made to 'function' in many different ways. These are: a general
absence of figural representation, especially in overtly religious contexts; a prevalence of calligraphy in the Arabic script; and geometric
and other motifs (arabesques), the latter usually derived from vegetal
prototypes, and both used in repeat forms (Grabar 1973; Ettinghausen 1976; Philon 1980). The existence of these categories could allow
the recognition of Muslim art in archaeological or other contexts, but
the manner in which the three major elements are manifest are
numerous (as is the case with all our categories in the archaeology
of Islam) in both styles and media, and it is worthwhile considering
each of these component parts in a little more detail, beginning with
the issue of figural representation.

Figural representation

To examine the issues surrounding figural representation is instructive both to see how doctrine can be created and to dispute the popular misconception that it does not exist in Muslim art. Within the first two centuries of Islam figural images are found, for example, on coinage, and therefore accessible to much of the population, until the reforms of Abd al-Malik in the late seventh century (discussed below). More frequently, as Arnold notes (1965: 19), it was used within the private domain in the upper echelons of society. Notable examples are provided by the frescos at the eighth-century palace of Qusayr Amra (Jordan) where, among other things, the rulers conquered by Islam are represented, including the Negus of Abyssinia (Ethiopia), the Sasanian ruler and the king of the Visigoths (Talbot Rice 1993: 26–7), and at the palace of Khirbat al-Mafjah (Palestine) where hunting, love, horsemanship and athletics are all represented (Hamilton 1959: 233). That figurative representation was not immediately repressed, or that people were not bothered by it in the early years of Islam, is further reflected in an incident related by Juynboll: when the Muslims assembled for prayers in the great hall of the royal palace at newly conquered al-Mada'in (Ctesiphon), various statues were still standing in it 'which nobody thought of moving', indicating that 'the prohibition against making images of living things had not yet been formulated' (1986: 108).

But it should be noted that an absence of figural art in mosques and other religious buildings has almost universally been in effect, though even in these contexts rare exceptions do exist, as in the carved stone *mihrab* from Mosul (Iraq) described by Talbot Rice, decorated with human figures and dating from the eleventh or twelfth centuries (1993: 98–9). However, a reaction against figural representation did appear, and has been explained as a Muslim reaction to their lack of an effective symbolic vocabulary to counter Christian propaganda, or as a parallel development to Christian iconoclasm. Hence Abd-al Malik's reforms formalized the attitude that 'the prevailing specific use of representations tended to idolatry and no understandable visual system other than writing and of inanimate objects could avoid being confused with the alien world of Christians and by later extension of Buddhists or of pagans' (Grabar 1973: 98). Support for this proposition was sought in the Qur'an and *hadith* (see Isa 1955; Gibb and Kramers 1961: 554; Salman 1969, Ettinghausen 1976: 62) and, although the former 'does not expressly forbid the making of images, the *hadith* are more specific on this issue, and judgements were pronounced against 'all types of artistic creativity in which representational forms are possible' (Bravmann 1974: 15, 16). This was translated into laws, and a condemnation of the representation of living things, among both Sunni and Shi'ah, can be seen to be fully effective by the ninth century. Iconoclasm is also something which could be archaeologically recognizable by, for example, the beheading of statues or the defacing of other figures, as is noticeable in Chinese Central Asia and in parts of India.

Nevertheless, a separation between ideals and practice exists, and figural representation is found in many spheres of Muslim art, though almost totally confined to the secular domain and usually to the upper strata of society. Painting and manuscript illustrations, especially those produced in India and in Iran, are some of the best-known examples of the genre (see, for example, Pinder-Wilson 1969). Subjects include portraits and illustrated epics such as Nizami's *Khamsa* (Five poems) or Firdausi's *Shahnama* (Binyon 1930: 60–73). Much more rare are depictions of Muslim religious history, including pictures of Muhammad which, according to Arnold 'are so rare that some writers have even doubted the existence of any' (1965: 91), but they do exist, and Iranian examples dating from the thirteenth and fourteenth centuries are discussed by Soucek (1988). Otherwise, figural representations could probably be found which have been produced in almost all media at one time or another somewhere in the Muslim world, and various further examples will indeed be referred to later. However, although there are figural representations in Muslim art, they are, on the whole, infrequent, and one of the key components of that loosely defined entity which is Muslim art is their general absence, and this should form one of the criteria allowing its recognition.

Geometry, arabesques and abstract patterns

Further common features of Muslim art are the presence of geometric patterns and designs incorporating miscellaneous abstract and vegetally derived motifs, including the so-called arabesque, defined by Philon as 'based on the infinite leaf scroll' (1980: 14). A certain unity is lent to them as a group through their use in repeat designs, often literally covering a surface in infinite patterns which 'are visual demonstrations of the Oneness of God and His Omnipresence' (Philon 1980: 14). Yet it should be noted that besides the more widely found motifs, such as the star or arabesque, distinct regional styles developed. Space again precludes a detailed discussion, but one representative example will be mentioned, the development of stylistic categories within the Ottoman design repertoire. Its five basic styles described by Petsopoulos (1982: 8–9) are the plain tradition, literally devoid of decoration; the formal and vegetally derived, Abraham of Kütahya; another variant of this called Golden Horn; Saz, a further naturalistic vegetal design; and finally, the mis-named Quatre Fleurs. They are found on metalwork, ceramics, textiles and paper. In fact, this emphasis on surface over shape (Grabar 1973: 194), and the associated techniques developed for surface decoration within Muslim art, is widespread throughout the Muslim world and forms another recognition criterion.

Calligraphy and epigraphy

The third component which should allow the recognition of Muslim art is the use of calligraphy, and its close relation, epigraphy. They will be examined in some detail with reference to case studies, as this is the component of Muslim art which can be encountered on all categories of material. Whereas, for example, the arabesque might be (and largely is) absent in West Africa, calligraphy in the Arabic script is used extensively on metals, paper, stone, ceramics and cloth. It is the medium of Muslim art *par excellence*, encountered from the River Senegal to the Syr Darya and, in fact, wherever Muslim communities are found.

By far the most comprehensive survey of the basic history and background to Muslim calligraphy is provided by Schimmel (1970, 1990). She notes that the importance of writing is stressed in the Qur'an, where it is 'considered to be of divine origin', and, although the Arabic script existed at the time of Muhammad, he was illiterate (this latter point is disputed by other scholars; see, for example, Guillaume 1954: 57). His pronouncements were written down on any available material, and the first Qur'an was assembled during the reign of Uthman, the third caliph, in the mid-seventh century. The sacred character of writing encouraged its spread, and since the language in which God's message was transmitted was Arabic, the Arabic script had precedence over all others, becoming 'the distinctive feature of all Muslim peoples, from West Africa to Indonesia' (Schimmel 1970: 1, 3). The two dominant styles of Arabic script are *kufic* and cursive. (Note the difference between *script* and language; other languages can and are rendered in the Arabic script, including Malay, Swahili, Hausa, Persian, and Turkish.)

Kufic, which originated in Kufah (Roman 1990: ix), is angular in appearance and was used for copying Qur'ans and extensively in inscriptions on buildings and tombstones (see plate 5.1). *Kufic*

Plate 5.1   Tombstone, Dahlak Kebir, Eritrea (*photo*. C. Spence)

inscriptions are almost without exception in Arabic, and various regional styles developed (see figure 5.1). The style declined in usage after the eleventh century, when it either begins to be found in co-existence with cursive scripts, as on the Qutb Minar in Delhi, or is replaced altogether by cursive (Schimmel 1990: 25). Cursive scripts, which are more rounded and easier to use, were developed in Mecca and Medina, and were of use for everyday purposes. They co-existed with *kufic* from the very beginning of Islam, but it was not until the thirteenth to fourteenth centuries that the multitude of cursive scripts which had developed were systematized into six styles: *thuluth, riqa, naskh, tauqi, muhaqqaq* and *rihani* (Schimmel 1990: 22) (see figure 5.2). Calligraphy in the Arabic script, therefore, provides a further category, which is almost universally used, and which can allow the recognition of Muslim art. But besides providing pleasing decoration, art can function in many other, often subtle, ways. The provision of information at various levels is one obvious example, and much interesting research has been undertaken which directly considers this issue with reference to the use of calligraphy and inscriptions.

Sacred and powerful scripts

Beyond the extensive use of inscriptions in explicitly religious contexts, they often transfer a sacred dimension into the secular sphere. Through a deliberate religious invocation or the use of Arabic, the

Figure 5.1 Forms of *basmala* in *kufic* script (after Schimmel 1970: 17)

language of the Qur'an, an inscription might take on a sacred significance even where the meaning might not be understood. For example, Ettinghausen describes a monumental *kufic* inscription on the exterior of a mosque in Washington DC which was 'incomprehensible as verbal communication' to most people, but was not really a fact of any significance as the inscription still served an important function in an area with many new converts, where 'the lettering is the message, rather than its content' (1974: 306, 307).

The power of writing is a factor which appears to recur through Muslim history, even where literacy was restricted, and knowledge of Arabic confined to memorized prayers and a few verses from the

Figure 5.2   Three types of figural representation achieved through calligraphy. Top, Muslim talisman from southern Thailand (after Forbes 1988: 1); middle, face from Yugoslavia (after De Jong 1989: 25); bottom, glass painting from Java (after Fischer 1994: 52)

Qur'an. What could occur was what Edwards (1991: 67) terms the functioning of inscriptions as 'orally revealed scripture'. This might appear a contradiction as applied to epigraphy, but is not necessarily so. Arabic calligraphy functions as a symbol of the faith, an accepted visual image of Islam across the Muslim world, even though it might not be understood or its use was infrequent. Why else would the power of perceived holymen be so important in many areas? The Scottish explorer Mungo Park, for example, though not a Muslim, earned a living for himself writing charms or 'saphies' during his extended travels along the River Niger at the end of the eighteenth and beginning of the nineteenth centuries (see Park 1807). The very fact that he could write was of importance, and the fragments of script served as protective talismans 'by virtue of presence rather than content' (Edwards 1991: 67).

But the meaning of epigraphy cannot, obviously, be discounted as merely visual imagery. The messages carried by inscriptions could serve many purposes, both sacred and secular. At the Dome of the Rock in Jerusalem (see chapter 2), the power and triumph of Islam over other faiths was spectacularly proclaimed, and epigraphy could also be used to settle religious disputes. The series of 14 inscriptions recovered from the site of the harbour town of Daybul (Banbhore) 60 km east of Karachi in Pakistan (Anon 1964: 50–1; Ghafur 1966: 65–9) are of special interest. Two were dated, and all were interpreted as having been fixed to the façade of a central wall in the main mosque 'in a way that met the gaze of the person who entered the mosque' (Ghafur 1966: 89–90). But why was this so? During the second and third centuries AH, one of the intellectual and spiritual debates in the Muslim world was connected with the so-called Mutazalite doctrine which stressed that God could not be seen with the 'physical eye' either in this world or in paradise; the latter belief conflicted with the beliefs of the majority of the faithful and, as Guillaume (1954: 128) records, was 'in spite of the affirmation in the Qur'an'. Mutazilism was the accepted official dogma under Abbasid rule, but during the reign of Mutawakkil this policy was reversed and the Mutazalites were persecuted. The inscriptions, placed as they were in the main place of worship in a major port, and thus open to view by 'Muslims from all corners of the Islamic world' (Ghafur 1966: 90), were used by the orthodox Sunni school to campaign against the Mutazalite doctrines. Hence, one carefully chosen Qur'anic verse espoused the anti-Mutazalite view on 'the vision of God', while a further inscription promoted orthodoxy over the Mutazalite viewpoints concerning the 'creation' of the Qur'an.

This was also the case in the mosque of Abu Ma'ruf at Sharwas (Libya), where the inscriptions were used for specific religious purposes, one of which may be Ibadi in character and records: 'The Qur'an is our Imam,/and the *sunnah* is our Path' (King 1989: 205). Another contains a *surah* (II, 130) which appears to have been selected to appeal, by referring to the prophets of Judaism, Christianity and Islam, to the various religious communities which lived in the area between the mid-tenth and twelfth centuries (Lowick 1974, cited in King 1989). Thus these examples show that inscriptions are not necessarily arbitrary additions of decorative interest placed with little thought as to position.

External symbols

Inscriptions of all types can function in many useful capacities for the archaeologist, as chronological indicators, aids to identifying people or places, but it is worthwhile adding a caution as the presence of Arabic calligraphy and epigraphy need not necessarily signal the presence of Muslims. An apt example of this is shown by the *kufic* or pseudo-*kufic* inscriptions found in churches in southern and central France (Watson 1972, 1989). These are obviously not Muslim contexts, but the textile trade meant that Muslim motifs were copied. Rigid borders do not always exist, and religious or political expansion and contraction must be acknowledged, as noted with regard to the use and adaptation of pre-existing places of worship in chapter 2. The absence of defined boundaries means that various stylistic or cultural elements could circulate and information and stylistic codes be exchanged.

An example of the acceptance of Muslim art in a non-Muslim area is provided by Sicily in the early twelfth century. Here, somewhat surprisingly considering the Christian context, Arabic calligraphy played a central role. Sicily, which had been under Muslim rule until the Kalbids lost control in the 1040s, was invaded by the Normans in the 1060s, but it was not until the early twelfth century that a Norman monarchy was established (Ahmad 1975). In 1130 the new king, Roger II, was crowned, but had 'no trapping of monarchy in which to robe himself' (Johns 1993: 134), and chose those of the Fatimid caliphate, from which he took the external symbols and 'ignored or remained ignorant of their intrinsic significance' (1993: 158). Two Arabic inscriptions which once adorned Roger's palace encouraged the visitor to adore the palace in a manner analogous to the rites employed in circumambulating the Ka'bah, although it is unlikely that these Muslim rites were ever actually followed at

Roger's Christian court. Other facets of Muslim culture adopted included the use of Muslim titles and the Arabic language in bureaucracy; building palaces to architectural plans which mirror structures in Muslim Ifriqiya (approximately equivalent to modern Tunisia); the use of decorative elements such as *muqarnas* or stalactite vaulting; and paintings replicating iconographic themes present in the Fatimid western palace in Cairo. It also appears that Muslim dress was worn not only in the court circle, but perhaps also by the general populace of Palermo (Johns 1993).

Johns' study (1993) shows how easily external symbols can be used to mean different things to different people. Here, Muslim material culture and symbols were being used in a manner which bore no relation to their original context, even though Sicily was a direct heir to over two centuries of Muslim heritage. Society was only transformed to a certain point by the Fatimid imports. However, it would be impossible to mistake this for a true Muslim community even if we only had the archaeological evidence to consider. Key components are absent, which in totality act to construct and perpetuate society, revealing that this was patently not a Muslim society, apparent once a look below the surface is taken.

Visual Imagery

Three general components have thus been isolated which could allow the recognition of Muslim art: an absence of figurative representation, the prevalence of abstract motifs, and calligraphy in the Arabic script. However, the visual imagery of Muslim art is, in a number of regions, drawn from the existing non-Muslim repertoire, which exceeds an abstract or calligraphic vocabulary. Yet which elements might appeal varies considerably, possibly, it can be suggested, according to the specific pre-Islamic heritage. Case studies can be provided to illustrate this from three geographically disparate areas, West Africa, Indonesia and Pakistan.

Al-Buraq is the winged creature who reputedly carried the Prophet on his night journey from Mecca to Jerusalem which is mentioned in the first verse of *surah* 17 of the Qur'an, but the details of the al-Buraq legend were not consolidated until the formulation of the *hadith* literature (Bravmann 1983: 75). The established representation of al-Buraq usually comprises a crowned head, often of a young woman, attached to a winged horse (see figure 5.3). The inspiration for this, according to Arnold (1965: 119), was drawn from many pre-Islamic representative traditions in western Asia, including the

Figure 5.3 Al-Buraq image (after Bravmann 1983: 73)

centaur of Babylon, the 'man-headed bulls' of Assyria and the Sphinx. It was a powerful image among Sufis in Iran, but also of particular popularity in both West Africa and Indonesia. In West Africa, al-Buraq is represented on printed posters imported from Egypt and North Africa, and in stylized amulet form, on masks, and in one instance supporting an initiation drum of the non-Muslim Baga people of coastal Guinea (Bravmann 1983: 82). Al-Buraq images are also found in Indonesia, where the figure has been adapted to the cultural context, 'Indonesianized' almost (Fischer 1994: 50).

Why is this image, which would appear not to be particularly central to Muslim iconography, popular in regions of the Muslim world separated by thousands of kilometres? This is perhaps due to the existence in both regions of long-standing figurative traditions prior to the arrival of Islam, and this had a direct bearing upon the uptake of images and the conception of the strictures concerning certain aspects of Muslim art. In West Africa, masking and sculptural traditions connected with local cult and initiation activities are common, and their inter-relationship with Islam is discussed in detail by

Bravmann (1974). In parts of Indonesia, Java in particular, the pre-Muslim Hindu legacy meant that figurative images had been extensively used and people, as in West Africa, were accustomed to their existence, and continued to produce them once converted to Islam. In Java, figurative art functions in the context of connecting what Geertz (1968: 27) has termed 'Indic Java' with 'Muslim Java'. These images are representative of the syncretism between Islam and traditional practices which occurred in both areas, and it is possible that there was a need for this to occur if Islam were to succeed in appealing to the population. When Islam first reached Java the Muslim missionaries found it useful to use the Wayang, or shadow play, complete with the Hindu deities 'to spread the new religion' (Boediardjo 1978: 112). These were gradually replaced by Muslim heroes (Tjandrasa-mita 1978: 153), thus indigenizing Islam.

Indeed, the vast range of figurative images in Javanese Muslim art is amazing: brass statues, architectural decoration, wooden puppets, ceramics and glass paintings, either wholly non-Muslim in inspiration, such as the depictions of the Panakawan, the attendants of Arjuna and Kresna in the Javanese version of the Mahabharata, or fusing these with Muslim elements such as calligraphy. They reflect what Fischer terms 'the openness, diversity, and ingenuity of a folk art that uses history, indigenous tradition, and a foreign faith, and extols them all' (1994: 50). These are factors paralleled in Muslim West Africa, and are evident historically and ethnographically, as seen in accounts of the masked dance witnessed by Ibn Battuta at the capital of the empire of Mali in the mid-fourteenth century, and in a similar form over 600 years later among the Sanu clan of the Mande Dafing in Bobo-Dioulasso (Burkina Faso) (Bravmann 1974: 49–52). Moreover, this process is traceable archaeologically as syncretic traditions developed to accustom the mass of the population, the sedentary agriculturists (Insoll 1996b: 91–2).

Yet the variations of Muslim art from the orthodox to the syncretic can also be seen to function within relatively circumscribed geographical areas. For example, in West Africa, one Muslim group might have strong figurative traditions, while another might be wholly devoid of them and utilize a more orthodox repertoire of calligraphic, geometric and abstract elements. Likewise, in Indonesia a locally constricted 'spectrum of art' can be seen to function; in contrast to the Javanese figurative tradition, the art and design of Biman, described as 'a staunchly Islamic regency' (Hitchcock 1987: 52), is much more orthodox. Although traces of older belief systems with figurative traditions are found, the use of figurative elements is extremely rare, and there is an emphasis upon geometric and vegetal designs. Even the ancient Indonesian 'ship of the dead' and bird designs are not used, though they are by neighbouring Muslim peoples (Hitchcock 1987: 54). That Islam is an adaptable religion is reflected in material culture, especially art, broadly defined as it is here, and archaeologists are well placed to investigate this, for it in turn sheds light on social issues, such as the varying impact of orthodox as opposed to more diverse Muslim traditions.

The retention of pre-Muslim design elements, and the development of a 'spectrum of art', which can indicate the flexibility of Islam to adapt to particular local or regional circumstances, can be further shown to operate in Swat-Kohistan (Pakistan). Here, the presence of a maze or labyrinth symbol carved in mosques was recorded (Scerrato 1981, 1983), in certain instances placed so as to be at eye level when squatting (as when praying perhaps). This symbol is, according to Scerrato, 'fundamentally alien to Islamic culture' (1983: 26) and, although this point can perhaps be disputed, the presence of the labyrinth motif is of great interest. Islamization of the region occurred in the sixteenth and seventeenth centuries, and a syncretic tradition evolved in this formerly Buddhist area. The hypothesis proposed to account for the presence of these labyrinths by Scerrato is that they are symbols of initiation into knowledge (1983: 28), and possibly linked with Sufi *tariqahs* (brotherhoods) and kept hidden to avoid the censure of the orthodox Mullahs. This scenario is conceivably lent support by the existence of a Muslim mystic visited by Scerrato, who 'lives, apparently not by chance, in a semi-subterranean and labyrinthine dwelling' (1983: 28). By contrast, at the opposite end of the 'spectrum of art', King relates how at the site of al-Faw (Saudi Arabia) a deliberately smashed stone idol of a well-dressed man was found, and though the date of the act of breaking it is unknown, he remarks that 'it is tempting to associate it with the onset of Islam' (1994b: 212). Though uninvestigated, such acts might conceivably have occurred on a large scale as Arabia was transformed 'in a space of some ten years from polytheistic paganism to a strictly monotheistic society' (1994b: 212).

The importance of these examples is to show that Islam can be adapted to suit local contexts, and that it can overlie and intermix with a wide variety of pre-existing traditions; animism in West Africa, Hinduism in parts of Indonesia, ancient traces of Buddhism in northern Pakistan. Although most, if not all, of the components of the archaeology of Islam might be present, 'cultural diversity' can again be seen to operate. Yet equally, no element of syncretism need exist, and orthodox Islam can be wholly apparent. What is again evident is a 'flexible Islam in thought and practice' (Eickelman and Piscatori

1990: xiv). The marriage between the superstructure, Islam, its beliefs and practices and local variety is here evident, and illustrated through art, something which could be archaeologically visible elsewhere.

The Transmission of Muslim Iconography and Other Ideas

The mechanisms behind the spread of Muslim iconography are many and complex, and relate more to the spread of Islam itself than merely the diffusion of artistic repertoire. One of the primary factors was trade. The importance of trade has already been noted as an agent for the spread of ideas including religious ones, and was not confined to Islam; Buddhism, for example, was spread into Central Asia and China partly through the actions of traders. Unfortunately, the agency of trade as a medium for the spread of religion is often neglected by archaeologists, who accentuate the economic aspect and associated issues above all others, thus leading to a one-dimensional emphasis. Yet the investigation of trade mechanisms and processes in all their manifestations is an area to which archaeology can make a significant contribution. Moreover, besides the possible linkage between trade and the initial spread and transmission of religion, religious considerations can also go hand in hand with mercantile and other economic activities on an everyday basis. Eaton provides an example of this when he describes how many early Bengali Muslim saints, represented materially by their shrines, 'are associated with the teaching of wet-rice agriculture, along with, of course, the preaching of Islam' (1984: 26). This is a topic which has already been touched upon in the consideration of local pilgrimage and *hajj* in chapter 4.

Islam and trade were linked from the very beginning. Conversion to Islam could be facilitated through trade. For example, local merchants could benefit from better trade conditions and lower taxes through converting (see Tampoe 1989: 128–9), and greater trust between co-religionists might have been of significance for trade purposes. Certainly, in both Indonesia and West Africa, trade was one of the contributing factors to the initial introduction of Islam, and its continuing spread and acceptance (see Tjandrasamita 1978; Insoll 1996b). Muhammad himself was connected with trade, being born into a trading milieu and trading family. Mecca, according to Ahmed, 'was a busy and wealthy commercial town almost monopolising the entrepôt trade between the Indian Ocean and the Mediterranean trading centres' (1988: 17), and when Muhammad was young he was in charge of a 'trading enterprise of a widow, Khadijah, whom he subsequently married' (Waines 1995: 11). The Qur'an reflects the importance of trade: 'the Qur'an not only shows an interest in it throughout but uses a series of terms of the language of commerce to reproduce religious ideas' (Gibb and Kramers 1961: 56). Besides the religious guidance for trade contained in the Qur'an and *hadith*, laws promulgated dealt with coinage, fiscal administration, crafts, markets, taxation and even economic principles (Lewis 1987: 124). Trade and mercantile activity were thus hardly alien to the nascent Muslim community, and traders followed in the wake of the initial Muslim armies serving to connect up the Muslim world as it took shape in a more peaceable fashion. Traders could even be missionaries, accompanied by missionaries, or preceded or followed by them. Various interconnections could and did exist, both directly and indirectly, via numerous stages over phenomenal distances, periodically during the medieval period. However, it is important to note that the trade routes and commercial centres were not fixed, 'their economic fortunes were not constant unchanging entities in history' (Chaudhuri 1985: 99). Dynasties came and went, merchants died, fashions changed, ports silted up, numerous factors were forever changing; excellent reviews have been provided by Chaudhuri (1985), Tampoe (1989) and Hourani (1995) with regard to the Indian Ocean which illustrate this in some detail. It is only necessary here to show that such systems were in operation, the functions that they could serve, and elaborate upon a few instances of the types of archaeological evidence which might indicate their former presence.

Coinage

Coinage is not only a primary indicator and mechanism of trade, but also provides a direct link back to topics already examined such as figural representation and calligraphy. However, the significance of coinage within the archaeology of Islam is even greater than this because it came to be seen almost as a token of religious identity, as well as a source of evidence which can indicate the very development of Islam. But it should also be noted that, as is evident in many of the other areas of material culture considered in this book, coinage was not part of a fully formed package denoting Muslim identity, which was opened in each newly conquered area. This did not exist, and a transitional period is evident, when all aspects of Muslim material culture were under development.

Coinage had long been in use in all the regions first conquered, and the existing currency of the conquered areas was used. In former Sasanian provinces, the primarily silver coinage underwent a change in the dating system used, and the name of an Arab governor or a pious inscription in *kufic* might be added. Otherwise, the Sasanian issues still bearing the image of the former ruler alongside a fire-altar with attendants were used. Likewise, in former Byzantine areas the existing coinage were utilized; the gold and copper issues might be slightly altered, the name of the emperor suppressed and a mint name in Arabic and Greek added (Grierson 1960: 242). But on the whole these coins were left largely unaltered, and it was not until the reforms of Abd al-Malik that coinage was fully Islamized, with the removal of the figurative images and a change from Greek/Persian to Arabic epigraphy. These reforms took place at the end of the seventh century and have been described by Darley-Doran (1986) as coinciding with theological conflict which was going on between the Umayyads and Byzantines. 'The Islamic coinage reflected this by stressing the unity of God to counter the Trinitarian precepts of Christianity' (Darley-Doran 1986: 10), reminiscent of how the contemporary inscriptions in the Dome of the Rock in Jerusalem were used (see chapter 2). It again illustrates that the development of Islam, and thus of Muslim material culture, was not an instantaneous event.

This issue has been examined by Hoyland, who states that prior to 72 AH (691) 'the archaeological record is strangely silent about Islam, and this despite the fact that we have a fair amount of material from this time' (in press: 4). But, after this date, the sources of evidence multiply, with numerous public proclamations of faith rendered not only on coins, but in inscriptions of many forms (Hoyland 1995). That Abd al-Malik's reform programme served to 'Arabize' government (Welch 1979: 44), and Islamize material culture is evident from the coinage, and also the glass weights (*dinar, dirham, uqiya* and so on) used to test coins (Miles 1948: 2–3, 1951). Coins provided an ideal medium for expressing the new ideology, probably having a wider impact than inscriptions inside mosques which might only be seen by Muslims. Through coins used in trade a much wider audience was reached, and the coin, in addition to serving its primary function as a token of value, could also serve as a symbol for expressing religious identity, alongside an obvious political role. Various messages were carried and functions could thus be fulfilled, though not necessarily all at the same time. Obviously, the uses and messages implied or stated by coinage vary and need not be fixed, but, as Wasserstein argues, the 'family resemblance' of Islamic coinage was there to 'define Islamic coins as Islamic' and 'non-Islamic coins as non-Islamic' (1993: 303).

Muslim coinage is also of interest as a further example to illustrate the diversity which can exist within the spectrum of Muslim art and design. Coins were probably 'art objects' which reached a much larger audience than ever ate from a lustred ceramic bowl or perused the pages of an illustrated manuscript. In this context it then seems surprising that figurative images reappeared at all on coinage, albeit rarely, after the imposition of Abd al-Malik's reforms. One such series of bronze coins bearing portraits and other similar images were produced in Turkish-dominated areas in northern Syria, northern Iraq and eastern Anatolia in the twelfth and thirteenth centuries. Of importance is the fact that the metal from which the coins were struck seems to have influenced whether it bore an image or not. Thus copper coins bore images as 'copper coins in Islam have always been less affected by the conventional taboo against images than have gold and silver' and as 'first and foremost secular objects', used in the market by people of diverse background. In contrast, 'the dinars and scarce silver dirhams are the political manifestos of rulers who took pride in their status as *ghazis* (warriors) on behalf of orthodox Islam' (Lowick 1985: 160, cited in Wasserstein 1983: 316). Images which appear to have been used concurrently included imitations of Byzantine coins bearing explicitly Christian motifs; representations of Muslim rulers, 'first in the likeness of Greek, Roman and Sasanian monarchs, later also in typically Islamic guise wearing up-to-date styles of dress; and thirdly, astrological shapes (Lowick 1985: 172). Thus it is obvious that even here, with an area of material culture readily accessible to much of the population, and outside the private courtly or aristocratic context usually associated with infringements of this prohibition, supposed universals such as the ban on figurative imagery can be shown to be invalid in certain instances.

Trade Routes and Trade Goods

Having briefly considered coins, not only as an agent of commerce, but also as a vehicle for political and religious imagery, it is useful to examine the trade routes and trade goods themselves as possible sources of information. These illustrate how widely the Muslim world was connected with regions beyond its frontiers, which in themselves are often difficult to define. Here, as case studies, trade by sea and land, and three examples of trade items – Chinese ceramics, silver coins and textiles – will be considered.

Although the role of trade as an agent for the spread of ideas, including religious ones, has already been mentioned, it is important to re-emphasize that trade need not only function within the secular economic domain. Many examples can be cited where trade has been accompanied by the spread of ideas associated with 'civilization' or religion, as with the mercantile ventures of the Portuguese in the late fifteenth and sixteenth centuries. However, this is not to say that all trade was underlain by religious intent; it was not. Rather, such impulses can co-exist, and trade need not necessarily be divest of any sacred component, even if this is not explicit to the traders themselves; by the very movement from region to region, colonies and trading settlements might be established, leading to a 'bridgehead' being formed. Places of worship would be established, and over time the religious belief would spread, perhaps even through no overt agency, into the surrounding area. Even fleeting contact with traders or trade goods can have lasting impact, as with the cargo cults of parts of the Pacific region. Religious, technological and philosophical ideas can be transmitted.

Sea trade: the Indian Ocean and beyond

Obviously, trade by sea was not a Muslim invention, but trade via sea routes was of fundamental importance to the Muslim world. Besides the evident trade requirements which were fulfilled, this trade acted as a means of connecting up the various regions of the Muslim world and beyond. One of the most important of these trade systems was centred in the Indian Ocean, the Bay of Bengal and the South China Sea. Many Indian Ocean trade centres, as well as the trade systems themselves, have been examined by historians and archaeologists, and the most convenient study, primarily because it has been recently and extensively updated to include relevant archaeological data, is a study of Arab seafaring (Hourani 1995). Indian Ocean trade was cyclical, and it should not be thought that the same routes operated continuously in the centuries between the beginning of Islam and the disruption caused by the arrival of European merchants in the late fifteenth century. However, when trade connections flourished and trading conditions were good the continuity in the system over centuries, and the sheer geographical distances involved in the trade systems, were phenomenal.

Mechanisms   One such period was between the late seventh and early tenth centuries, with direct sailing via a series of stages from the Persian Gulf to Canton. This sea route was, according to Hourani, 'the longest in regular use by mankind before the European expansion in the sixteenth century' (1995: 61). This route stretched from Siraf and other ports on the Persian Gulf, via Pakistan and India to Sri Lanka, across to Malaysia and Indonesia, and then round to

China; further segments in the western Indian Ocean connected the East African coast, or later under Fatimid impetus the Red Sea to Egypt (Whitcomb 1990–1: 56), and the lands bordering the Mediterranean (see figure 5.4). The concepts of unity and diversity over this vast area are discussed by Chaudhuri (1985: 21–3); social and cultural diversity was rooted in four different civilizations: Hindu, Chinese, Irano-Arabic and Indonesian, with a 'strong sense of unity' lent by the sea trade and the caravan trade in Central Asia. Although Muslim sailors might, and did, sail as far as China, where they founded colonies (the descendants being the Hui, who have been mentioned before, see chapters 2 and 6), this did not mean that they controlled the whole area of the trade route. Various trade centres and their surrounding areas did form parts of the Muslim world but these were not contiguous: 'the political and religious frontiers of Islam ran across trade routes, kingdoms of non-believing princes, and natural boundaries made by deserts, mountains and seas' (Chaudhuri 1985: 21).

The living legacy   Before examining the archaeological evidence, it is as well to note that ample living testimony to Indian Ocean trade is provided by the descendants of traders, adventurers, slaves and pilgrims, dispersed around the various regions and often far from their original homelands. The Hui have been mentioned, and Possehl (1981) refers to the 'living legacy' of the agate miners of the Narmada mines in Gujarat, western India, who are of African descent. These *Siddis* 'are actually more common than one might suspect in western India and Pakistan, especially the coastal areas...This is a result of the lively commerce between India and Africa for at least the past two thousand years' (Possehl 1981: 41). The Arab Muslim communities of southern Thailand show a similar legacy, where Farouk notes that small communities of Arabs of predominantly Hadrami (Yemeni) and Saudi descent are settled and maintain family connections 'with other Arabs across the border in Malaysia' (1988: 7). Arab communities are also found settled in the vicinity of Samarkand in Central Asia (Bennigsen and Enders Wimbush 1986: 125). Though the original 'wave' of Arab immigrants came as conquerors in the eighth century, we can speculate that subsequent influxes were perhaps trade related.

The archaeological legacy   Archaeological evidence attesting to the operation of Indian Ocean trade and the connection which existed between the 'different worlds', which is sometimes represented by, for example, 'made to order goods', is abundant. It illustrates both the

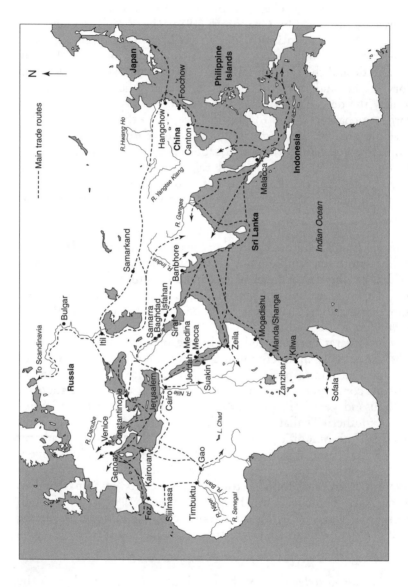

Figure 5.4 Simplified map of trade routes (not necessarily contemporaneous) (after Fage 1978: 25)

earlier 'direct' Indian Ocean trade system and the later 'segmented' one which developed as its successor. The trade centres themselves are archaeological indicators of the trade communities, the trade itself, the goods and the interaction, co-existence and impact of social, religious and political systems which came into contact through the mechanism of trade. Various of these centres which have been archaeologically investigated have already been used as case studies. These have included Siraf on the Persian Gulf (Whitehouse 1968, 1970, 1974), Daybul/Banbhore close to Karachi (Anon 1964; Ghafur 1966), and Shanga on the Kenyan coast (Horton 1996). To these can be added, for example, Mantai on the north-western tip of Sri Lanka (Carswell and Prickett 1984), and other trade centres in Sri Lanka, on the coast of India (Carswell 1979a) and on the Maldive Islands (Carswell 1977). Sohar on the Omani side of the Persian Gulf (Williamson 1974), Kish 200 km south of Siraf (Whitehouse 1976), Kilwa and Manda on the East African Coast (Chittick 1974, 1984), and much further east, Laem Po in Thailand (Dasheng 1995).

Other examples of trade centres which have been archaeologically investigated with varying degrees of competence could be cited. Thus a body of data exists which could, and should, allow an examination not only of economic-related trade process, but also of the accompanying interaction, or lack of it, between the different religious and social traditions as already outlined. Unfortunately, from an archaeological perspective at least, this has hardly yet begun. Preoccupation is still predominantly with the 'harder' economic issues. However, one example can be provided in glazed Chinese pottery of an indicator not only of trade, but also of the interaction and fusion of different cultural elements.

Sherds of Chinese pottery obtained via Indian Ocean trade (ships are admirably suited to the transport of such bulky and fragile commodities) are found scattered on the shores surrounding the South China Sea, Indian Ocean, the Persian Gulf and the Red Sea. They are found at many if not all of the trade centres already mentioned (see also Wijayapala and Prickett 1986; Tampoe 1989, for discussion of Chinese pottery at Mantai and Siraf). Chinese pottery of various types – white wares, celadons, stonewares – has been recorded at numerous other sites dating from the tenth to the sixteenth centuries. Examples connected with the Red Sea coasts, for instance, include Badi on al-Rih Island off the Red Sea coast of the Sudan (Kawatoko 1993), Dahlak Kebir further south on the Dahlak Islands in Eritrea (Insoll 1996d) and, to the north, Quseir al-Qadim in Egypt (Whitcomb 1979; Carswell 1982), and beyond at Fustat in Egypt (Scanlon 1970b; Mikami 1980–1). Chinese pottery has also been recovered from various locations on the opposite, Arabian shore (Mathew 1956; Whitcomb 1988) as at Ayla, the early Islamic town at Aqaba in Jordan (Whitcomb 1990–1). Sherds have been recorded at some distance from the Red Sea (though probably indirectly sourced via this region) at Timbuktu in Mali (Insoll 1996a) and at Douma and other locations in Syria (Carswell 1977, 1979b).

Yet, besides the more obvious economic information which can be derived from this particular source of evidence, Chinese pottery recovered from archaeological contexts has been informative with regard to specific 'Islamization' of products for distinct markets. At Siraf, for example, among the several hundred sherds of imported Chinese stoneware dating from the ninth to eleventh centuries, a fragmentary 'Dusun' stoneware jar was recovered which bore the names Yusuf and either Mansur or Maymun 'incised *before* the vessel was glazed' (Whitehouse 1973: 244). The presence of these Muslim names indicates that 'the jar was made to order for a Muslim trader with contacts, or possibly a factory, in a Chinese port' (1973: 244). This is not a unique instance; Dasheng (1995) mentions Chinese ceramics being made specifically for Muslim markets, and at Laem Po in southern Thailand, a bowl made at the Changsha kilns in Hunan and dating from the ninth century bore an 'Arabic-inspired design' (1995: 55). A water bottle found in Yangzhou in China, of the same date and of Chinese production, also had an underglaze Arabic inscription, interpreted as a 'writing of double Allah in symmetry', but 'clearly painted by ceramic workers who did not know the Arabic script' (1995: 59). Other Chinese wares produced for export markets were also influenced by Muslim forms and decorative motifs. The reverse was also true; Chinese vessel forms and ceramic types like the large white-ware spittoons found at Fustat (Mikami 1980–1: 77) were variously imitated in the Muslim world.

These examples are of importance as they illustrate that there was an element of cultural understanding between the different civilizations and societies involved in Indian Ocean trade. But what does this imply for less visible aspects? Although this remains hypothetical and difficult to test, it can be suggested that producing 'foreign' items for trade might mean that in the process one could get used to these materials oneself, even if only to a slight degree. The 'rub-off' of cultural elements could thus occur, which returns us to the point that we cannot always think in terms of distinctly polarized entities or blocks, the Muslim world as opposed to China, for example. Commerce meant interaction; no matter how strictly one might attempt to control this, trade meant the flow of ideas, and once again complexity is evident and must be allowed for. Thus we can begin to infer and suggest less tangible contacts and influences which a sherd of pottery might indicate.

Land trade: the Scandinavian connection and beyond

The tentacles of Islamic medieval commerce stretched elsewhere by land; for example, north to Europe, in particular to Scandinavia. Such a trade existed, especially in silver coinage from the Muslim world being exchanged for slaves and furs, primarily in the ninth and tenth centuries (Noonan 1981). However, unlike parts of China, India or elsewhere at various Indian Ocean trade centres, there is as yet no evidence that communities of Muslim merchants themselves were established. Thus this trade was not accompanied by conversion to Islam, by all or even part of the population, or it appears by Islamization to any degree.

This Scandinavian trade and the 'Viking contacts' followed routes which either stretched north from Baghdad and the Mesopotamian region or as northern branches of the Central Asian caravan trail, the Silk Road to China. Both of these routes are considered by Herrmann (1991), who describes how the latter branched along the Amu Darya to Urgench, east of the Caspian Sea, and to Bulgar at the confluence of the rivers Kama and Volga, while the former branched north along the western shore of the Caspian via Itil, 'the Khazar Emporium' (Lieber 1981: 25), to Bulgar (see figure 5.4). The furthest the Muslim merchants penetrated was to the Khazar region; beyond this, trade was in the hands of the Vikings, although Arab visitors reached the Upper Volga in the tenth century. The Arabs, according to Noonan (1981: 52–3), developed a pragmatic attitude to the Khazars, and trade flourished when military conflict over control of the Caucausus had subsided. This in itself was important as Noonan notes that 'the Arabs managed to participate in an active trade with a Khazar leadership whose representatives had abjured Islam and then turned to Judaism' (1981: 52).

The most common archaeological evidence of the Viking trade with Muslim lands are the thousands of Islamic silver coins which have been recovered, predominantly in the form of hoards, at various locations in Scandinavia, Russia and on the Baltic coast. Lieber records that nearly 105,000, mostly silver, Islamic coins of various types, all dating from before 970, have been found in Scandinavia (1981: 21–2). The Iraqi origins of this trade are signalled by a hoard unearthed near Zakho in northern Iraq, buried in the early ninth century, and containing 3,306 coins. This hoard contained numerous different issues, including 37 coins from Umayyad Spain and 129

Idrisid Moroccan coins. Rather than representing a hoard buried for future use in Iraq itself, it can be suggested that it was gathered together for onward trade to Scandinavia, where a voracious appetite for silver existed. Glass beads from Muslim areas and dating from the late eighth century are also found in northern and eastern Europe. These, according to Callmer (1995: 51), 'entered the Baltic region from the east, to appear in Finland, the Åland Islands and central Sweden'. Thus here long-distance trade, albeit of little significance compared to the commerce of the Indian Ocean, was in operation, but without any accompanying ideological change.

Land trade: the West African connection

In contrast, several thousand kilometres to the south, the situation was very different. Land-based trade which operated across the Sahara from North Africa to the trade centres of the Western Sahel region of West Africa was accompanied by conversion to Islam and Islamization in general, starting in the late eighth century. Indigenous states, such as the empire of Ghana whose capital was in Mauritania (where only the merchant's quarter, Koumbi Saleh, has so far been found), and indigenously founded towns such as Gao on the eastern Niger bend in Mali, attracted Muslim merchants in pursuit of gold, ivory and slaves to ship north to the wider Islamic world (Thomassey and Mauny 1951, 1956; Insoll 1996b). In return, these merchants brought manufactured luxury goods, glazed pottery, glass and semi-precious stone beads, glass vessels, items of metalwork, textiles, paper and commodities such as cowry shells, one of the currency items in use during the medieval period, and brass (Insoll 1995).

Archaeological limitations   An assessment of this type of trade also allows two general archaeological implications to be noted. Differential survival means that this trade, perhaps inevitably, is skewed in favour of the more durable items. This can lead us to undervalue the importance of certain commodities, especially textiles. In the Western Sahel region no imported textiles have been recovered from the trade centres, yet the corpus of medieval Arabic sources and later European travellers' accounts both tell us how important the textile trade was (see Barth 1965; Levtzion and Hopkins 1981); silk, gauze and linen are all recorded as being imported from North Africa, as well as unspecified cloth from Al-Andalus, and turbans from Ifriqiya during the medieval period (Levtzion and Hopkins 1981: 97). As we saw in chapter 4, clothing, and its obvious links with modesty concerns, are of particular importance within Islam, and textiles were of great general importance within the Muslim world for numerous purposes in all social strata (Ettinghausen 1976: 71–2). To quote Golombek, it became 'a world submerged in textiles, where textiles played a role in every facet of life, for everyone rich and poor' (1988: 33). In certain advantageous conditions, as at Fustat where 3,000 textile fragments were excavated from rubbish heaps dating to the eleventh century (Mackie 1985: 23), or Quseir al-Qadim, also in Egypt, where nearly 4,000 pieces of Mamluk textiles were found (Vogelsang-Eastwood 1993: 87), extensive collections of textiles have been recovered, and the information derived from their analysis has proved of great use in reconstructing trade routes, the significance of the textiles, their uses and the manufacturing techniques employed. But in many areas this profitable avenue of research, like those of paper, perfumes, spices and even slaves, is closed by the lack of evidence.

Secondly, as with certain commodities, so with the means of their transport, which are known mainly from secondary evidence, manuscript illustrations, historical sources, and facilities such as ports and caravanserais; much more rarely are the ships or caravans encountered archaeologically. However, instances do exist, as with the eleventh-century shipwreck excavated at Serçe Liman on the southern Turkish coast. This ship, of apparently Muslim origin, contained a mixed cargo of Byzantine amphora and Islamic glass, as well as glass cullet (refuse glass for re-use) also of probable Byzantine origin. This is of importance as it again attests to the links between Muslims and non-Muslims, 'trade, even in times of war, seldom stopped between Muslim countries, or even between Byzantine and Muslim ports' (Bass and Van Doorninck 1978: 131). Further evidence for the operation of maritime trade between the Muslim world and Christian Europe was recently found off the coast of Devon (England) where a cargo of gold Moroccan coins and jewellery dating from the 1630–40s was discovered by marine archaeologists (Alberge 1997: 3). Similarly, direct evidence for land-based caravan trade has also been found (see plate 5.2). At the 'lost caravan' site in the Ijafen dunes in Mauritania, several thousand cowry shells, once in sacks, along with 2,085 bars of brass were found (Monod 1969). These items, dating from the twelfth century, had been buried for safekeeping by a caravan crossing the desert to the Western Sahel and never recovered.

Trade and social processes Archaeology, in combination with an analysis of existing historical, sociological and anthropological studies, is also beginning to allow a model to be developed to chart the actual processes and rates of conversion to Islam over time in the

Plate 5.2   Salt caravan, Gao, Mali (*photo.* A. Bennett)

Western Sahel (Insoll 1996b: 90–1, 1997b). This owes a debt to Fisher's three-stage model of Islamic conversion (1973, 1985), but equally draws its impetus from trade, and thus we are able to begin to move beyond merely economic concerns, and to consider factors of social relevance, as was argued for earlier.

Islam was brought to the Western Sahel region by Muslim Arab and Berber traders. The primary converts, along with the foreign merchants' local partners in trade, were the local rulers who accepted Islam for a variety of reasons. These included genuine belief (of obvious importance but difficult to assess archaeologically); the advantages conversion might bring in the spheres of magic, ritual and prestige; wealth in trade; and better administration through the adoption of the Arabic script and Muslim officials (Levtzion 1979: 214; Hunwick 1985). Town-dwellers appear to have been early converts, a fact attested archaeologically. Islam may have been attractive, as has been suggested by Trimingham (1959) because, by being universalistic in outlook, it had the power to bring together the different ethnic groups which often made up the population of towns in this region. Often concurrent with townspeople, nomads were early converts, again for a variety of reasons, dominant among which Trimingham (1959) has suggested was the appeal of a lack of a hierarchical priestly system, and the ease of worship Islam enjoys. Lewis (1980: 24) also suggests that the usual pattern of early

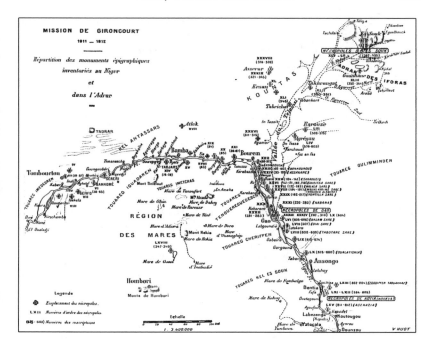

Figure 5.5 Cemeteries in the Niger bend region, Mali (from De Gironcourt 1920: 161)

conversion to Islam by nomadic populations was because they 'found in long-distance trade an attractive and profitable supplement to pastoralism'. This interpretation might help in explaining the cemetery patterning seen in the Niger bend and Adrar des Iforas regions bordering the Sahara (see De Gironcourt 1920), with Muslim cemeteries clustered along trade routes and in areas formerly (and currently) inhabited by nomads (see figure 5.5).

The final group to convert to Islam were usually the sedentary agriculturists, the bulk of the population. Various ideas have been proposed to account for the fact that this group was often last to convert to Islam. It has been suggested that conversion involved more of a fundamental wrench from older systems and ties, with animism and traditional religious cults furnishing the means by which the pressing problems of existence, such as the ensuring of rain, could be comprehended and resolved, turning around the cycle of tending crops, livestock and children (Trimingham 1959: 25; Bravmann 1974: 31). Eventually, through the development of a syncretic Muslim tradition incorporating elements of traditional religious practice and, it should not be forgotten, by the sword as well, conversion among the sedentary agriculturalist population increased (similarly, education and the growth of Sufism were also factors which aided the spread of Islam in West Africa). This, however, was not an instantaneous process, but drawn out over many centuries, and in certain instances is not yet complete, as Islam continues to gain converts among the sedentary populations of West Africa, both in the forest regions, as among the Yoruba, and also in the Sahel, as with the Dogon.

Although the model just presented is local in context and, inevitably, much generalized and simplistic, it is at least providing a start at trying to draw in the archaeological evidence within the frameworks provided by studies utilizing different sources of evidence, as with those already mentioned. It is certainly specific to the West African region, but it would be of interest to see if similar processes are evident elsewhere in the Muslim world, where it is possible that in many instances an implicit link with trade, as in the Western Sahel, existed as the agent of initial Muslim contact.

The Transmission of Islamic 'Civilization'

Trade can also function as the agent of transmission for many other ideas besides religious ones. Visual art has already been discussed and music is another art form which can be transmitted via trade and other cross-cultural connections. Although there is evidently no such thing as a single style of Islamic music, and indeed the legality of listening to music has been much debated by Islamic scholars (Farmer 1929: 22), similarities exist across the Muslim world in both musical styles and certain types of instruments. According to Jenkins and Olsen, 'the musical culture area of the Islamic world stretches for thousands of miles and Moroccans travelling to Turkestan would feel at home with the music despite all local differences (particularly in instruments)' (1976: 85). Yet obviously the types of music are many, 'from learned and sophisticated types of music elaborated in the context of supra-national Islamic civilization, to simple forms of sacred music and nomad or sedentary folk musical traditions' (Shiloah 1995: xv), as are the styles and categories of instrument, and music's varying cultural importance. But this is also a category of evidence which has an archaeological dimension; the discovery of musical instruments in archaeological contexts is well attested in many areas and over various periods. Arav (1993), for example, describes a decorated brass Mamluk conical drum, of probable fourteenth to fifteenth century date which was found near Tel Beth-saida, north of the Sea of Galilee, in Palestine.

Philosophical, technological and all types of scientific ideas can be transmitted through traders. With sciences, for example, the exchange of ideas both across the Muslim world and with other non-Muslim areas, such as China and Europe, was complex and has been much studied (see, for example, Needham 1954– ; Sabra 1976; al-Hassan and Hill 1992). Muslim contributions in many areas of science and technology were great, not only as inheritors and developers of the Graeco-Roman heritage, but also as active innovators (al-Hassan and Hill 1992: 9), and through the unity lent by the existence of Islam across a wide area. Islamic knowledge filtered through to the West via centres of translation such as Cordoba; Greek, Indian, Persian, Arab and Chinese ideas were all transmitted to Europe from the Muslim world (Gabrieli 1970). Add to this the fact that Muslim provinces such as Transoxania bordered scientific 'hot-houses' such as China (and indeed, as we have seen, trade centres were established within it), and a picture of the vitality of Muslim science and technology becomes clear. Elements of this are archaeologically recognizable. Vardjavand (1979), for example, excavated an observatory dating from the thirteenth century at Maraqe in the Azerbaijan region, including what was perhaps the library, a central tower with a diameter of 45 m, and a foundry interpreted as the workshop where astrological instruments were made.

The contribution that archaeological research can make to our understanding of Muslim manufacturing and processing technology is equally significant, but has so far been little pursued, either in investigating relevant sites or bringing modern scientific analytical techniques to bear upon archaeological materials. However, an example of the archaeological investigation of a processing site is provided by recent research near Eilat in southern Palestine. Here, in the Wadi Tawahin (millstone wadi) extensive evidence for the processing of gold-bearing quartz ores was found. This included various structures, a storage pit, outlines of tents and work stations containing tools and millstones dating from between the eighth and tenth centuries. The quartz ore was crushed using anvils and two sizes of hammer before being ground to a powder using the millstones. Subsequently, the gold-bearing dust would have been washed to separate the gold in a complicated process, though no direct evidence was found for this stage of processing (Gilat et al. 1993).

Exciting results were also obtained at Raqqa in northern Syria where a major manufacturing centre has recently been investigated. Conquered by the Muslims in 639–640, it became the Abbasid capital and home of Caliph Harun al-Rashid in the late eighth century. There, between 796 and 808, he built a new palatial and industrial complex (Henderson 1996: 59). Excavations within the industrial complex have provided information on glass technology, with a complete glass workshop dated to c.804. It was here that a major change in Islamic glass technology took place with the development of common Islamic soda lime glass, a glass composition 'which was to last relatively unchanged for about 600 years and which was used throughout the Islamic world' (Henderson 1996: 69). Other industrial evidence found included the site of a pottery industry, and evidence for sugar production, including discarded moulds, and a series of basins and channels which might have been the remains of a sugar factory.

The connection between the development of sugar as a traded commodity and the spread of Muslim civilization has already been referred to (see chapter 4), and it makes an interesting case study. Archaeological evidence for sugar production is not restricted to Raqqa. Whitcomb (1992) mentions the remains of a sugar industry in the southern Ghors region of Jordan, where several sites had the remains of pots and moulds used in the manufacturing process, and at Feifa, the mud-brick walls of a sugar mill itself were recorded (1992: 114–15). At Susa in Iran, further conical sugar moulds, pierced at the base, were found along with the remains of a *sucrerie* (Boucharlat and Labrousse 1979); and Von Wartburg (1983: 313) draws attention to a variety of relevant research which has been conducted elsewhere.

Thus the evidence recovered from Raqqa and other sites has made a direct contribution to our understanding of Muslim manufacturing and processing technology in many ways, another dimension which can be approached through archaeology. Technology was not restricted to one site, but was transmitted around the Muslim world, owing in part to the unity provided by a common religion, and through the agency of trade. Much more could be learnt from excavating and recording sites linked with all aspects of Muslim science and technology, and from examining the objects which fill our museums and stores from past seasons. Similar summaries could be offered of archaeological research on ceramics, metals and textiles, and further information could undoubtedly be derived from the analysis or re-analysis of many categories of item, as with the examples discussed by Henderson (1996): information on enamels (Henderson and Allan 1990), glass composition (Brill 1970; Gratuze and Barrandon 1990; Henderson 1995), source analysis of beads (Saitowitz et al. 1996), study of metals and metallurgy (Weisgerber 1980) and pottery (Frierman and Giauque 1973; Mason and Keall 1990).

These are just a selection of relevant studies which have been undertaken, and numerous further possibilities exist for the application of modern scientific techniques to whole categories of material which have been largely neglected in this respect. There is no reason why style should be privileged over fabric.

Summary and Conclusions

The material discussed in this chapter – art, trade, science and manufactures – appears initially to be only loosely connected, if at all, but as the discussion progressed it became apparent that interconnections between these seemingly disparate subject areas are in fact evident across the Muslim world. Essentially, this is due to the movement of similar modes of thought across great distances through the processes of Islamization: conquest, missionary activity and trade, singly or combined. As a result a certain unity was created. This does not mean that a 'standard Muslim' was created, drawing from a limited pool of binding requirements and ideas; on the contrary, great diversity exists. However, something functioned to allow similarities to be manifest, in music, symbolically in art motifs or with the presence of calligraphy in the Arabic script from Timbuktu to Djakarta; this is Islam, and thus again we return to the point that a Muslim does exist in a recognizable form across the Muslim world, and that this can be evident materially, and therefore approachable by the archaeologist. Why else would common features be found? Why else would sales of 'Islamic art' take place? Yet within this vast entity, this overall framework of structuring principles, myriad diversity is evident, adapting and transforming components of Muslim law and thought, but this is still undeniably Muslim diversity.

Certain implications for the general archaeology of religion also exist. Art is frequently acknowledged as being either wholly religious in intent or having a sacred dimension, whereas trade is not, but this need not be the case. As was shown, trade need not be categorized as entirely secular; it can be associated with the spread of ideas, including religious ones. In the next chapter we will turn to a more orthodox preoccupation of archaeologists in general, death and burial, as a possible further indicator of the former presence of a Muslim community.

6

Death and Burial

Every soul shall taste death. We will prove you all with evil and good.
To Us you shall return.

Qur'an. The Prophets 21: 35

No one escapes death, and theoretically all Muslims should be buried
in accordance with specific rites. Thus the burial is another category
of evidence, and one of primary importance, which might allow the
recognition of a Muslim in the archaeological record. Moreover,
the investigation of funerary evidence allows us to examine further
the social dimension which, as has already been stated, is often much
neglected within Islamic archaeology. Tarlow and Boyd (1992: 4)
make the relevant general point that historical archaeology, of
which Islamic archaeology clearly forms a part, has been notoriously
poor in its development of sophisticated social analyses. While it is
not suggested that the following discussion provides the 'sophisticated social analysis' required, it is hoped that it will show that
Muslim burial, and the often accompanying commemorative structure, constitute more than just a typology of monuments. Both the
burial itself and the funerary monument can have a meaning and
significance which, if unlocked, can provide a wealth of information
on the development and diversity of Islam and the Muslim world and,
of course, on the individuals buried.

Furthermore, it should be remembered that the Muslim community, both past and present, was and is made up of people, individuals
and communities, not merely of 'unquestioning machines' blindly
following the tenets of their religion. This point appears to be often
forgotten. Islamic funerary archaeology is the residue of these individuals and communities and, as with other societies, a desire for

commemoration, to assuage grief, replicate social position and hier-archies in death as in life, to attain piety, establish identity, as well as struggles over authority, can all be manifest in Islamic funerary archaeology and architecture. By studying the patterns of death we can learn much about life.

In the light of contemporary funerary archaeological and anthro-pological theory (see, for example, Hodder 1982a: 139–46; Metcalf and Huntingdon 1991; Tarlow and Boyd 1992; Parker Pearson 1993), a more complex view of Islamic funerary archaeology and architec-ture needs to be taken, acknowledging the diversity which exists and utilizing it to the full for the purposes of interpretation. The rich texture of detailed ethnographic and archaeological evidence available to the archaeologist interested in Islam enables not only information on property, social status and prestige (the usual preserves of the archaeologist dealing with funerary evidence) to be obtained, but also information on possible non-orthodox ritual and beliefs, and perhaps even on the individual, the person who has been buried (an interesting examination of this is provided by Simpson 1995, with regard to the late Islamic Near East).

Within the framework of Islam, where the sacred and secular spheres of life are interwoven until they are inseparable, the archae-ologist cannot succumb to the charge levelled at them by Renfrew (1994: 52) whereby 'the disposal of the dead is generally considered, by archaeologists, under a different rubric from that of religion'. Within Islam, as with most if not all religions, religious belief has an influence over death, its conceptualization, understanding and practicalities (the funerary practices and monuments). Likewise death influences religion, with ideas of resurrection and rebirth after death being a recurring theme. As part of introducing the 'social' into Islamic archaeology, we cannot divorce religion and the disposal of the dead, and thus we have to look at Islamic funerary practices, archaeology and architecture anew, as more than bricks and mortar, but as being of greater social significance. This chapter will thus explore the social dimension of Islamic funerary archaeology, and burial as a category of evidence indicative of the Muslim community in the archaeological record.

Muslim Burial: Ideals and Origins

The origins of Islamic concepts of death, funerary practices and of the earliest commemorative structures have often been discussed (see, for example, Grabar 1966; Ragib 1970), and are the subject of debate. The

Qur'an, though discussing death, contains nothing about funerals or funerary monuments, the details of which are dealt with in the *hadith* and legal texts (Gibb and Kramers 1961: 91; Smith and Haddad 1983; Bowker 1991). Attitudes towards funerary architecture in the *shari'ah* have been examined by Leisten, who makes the point that funerary monuments were not widely used before the ninth century, with common burial practices prior to this date consisting of interment under a pile of stones, or the grave was simply left uncommemorated (1990: 12–13).

Early prohibitions on funerary architecture and commemoration of the dead possibly reflected opposition to the pre-Islamic cult of the dead in the Arabian peninsula, and the fact that ornate tombs were considered 'symbols of worldly pomp' (Leisten 1990: 18). No special attention should be paid to the place of the dead, and they should not become the focus of worship, for all should be equal in death. Such ideals were retained by some sects until today but for others were relatively short-lived, even if disapproval for an ornamented or inscribed gravestone might persist in Muslim law (Simpson 1995: 247). A variety of factors contributed to a growth in the use of funerary architecture; these included the expansion of Islam beyond the Arabian peninsula and the ensuing cultural admixture, pre-Islamic survivals and the desire to express power and authority, both secular and sacred (Hillenbrand 1994: 253–4). The widening gulf between ideals and reality which developed in urban Egypt is commented upon by Edward Lane (1895: 508), who observed a number of funerals in Cairo in the early nineteenth century and remarked that 'it is astonishing to see how some of the precepts of the Prophet are every day violated by all classes of modern Muslims, the Wahabys alone excepted'.

Throughout the Muslim world an essentially uniform funerary rite should be employed and should be straightforward, unostentatious and simple: 'the body is treated with a ceremonial which varies little in different parts of the Muslim world, and is nearly the same for men and women' (Hastings 1911: 501). The funerary rites should entail washing the corpse immediately following death, sealing the body orifices and perfuming the body, which is then enveloped in the shroud or grave clothes. Burial is rapid and the ritual prayer or *salat* for the deceased is said either in the open in the cemetery or the mosque (frequently in the cemetery) or sometimes in the house of mourning. The stretcher or bier is carried to the place of burial by men, followed by the funeral procession. The corpse is lifted out of the bier and placed in the grave (a coffin is not usually used), the head in the direction of the *qiblah*, so that it lies on its right side with the face towards Mecca (sometimes supported in this position by bricks or by a narrower grave-shaft). A confession of faith is said to the deceased which is believed to enable it to answer the questions posed by the interrogating angels Munkar and Nakir, and thus gain entry to paradise. The grave itself should be reasonably shallow to allow the deceased to hear the *muezzin's* call, but also deep enough to allow the corpse to sit up for its interrogation by Munkar and Nakir. Only the place where the head of the deceased is laid may be commemorated with a marker stone or piece of wood, the *shahid* (in this context meaning witness). However, in reality great variety with regard to grave markers is found according to the Islamic legal school or sect followed and geographical area (Hastings 1911: 501–2; Gibb and Kramers 1961: 89–90, 515–17; Dickie 1978: 44–6; Simpson 1995: 241–2, 244–5).

While certain exceptions have to be acknowledged (discussed below), the treatment of the corpse prior to burial, the procedures for its actual interment, and its position within the grave, are fairly uniform and vary little throughout the Muslim world. These should, theoretically, allow the archaeological recognition of a Muslim burial. It is above ground that ideals and realities diverge, and it is the means of commemorating the dead – the funerary monument – and the way in which these structures are manipulated by the living, which offer us an insight not only into death but also into life, and are thus of great importance.

The Place of the Dead

Within Islam, understandable prohibitions on disturbing Muslim graves exist and these must be respected. Hence, the discussion of sub-surface Muslim graves remains largely hypothetical. (The general ethical dilemmas of disturbing the dead have been well covered elsewhere; see, for example, Webb 1987; Day 1990.) It could also be argued that there is little to be gained from the study of individual Muslim graves, due to the pan-Islamic methods of burial employed; theoretically at least, princes and paupers should be buried according to the same rites, and within the grave nothing should be found to differentiate them.

Nevertheless, having emphasized the sensitivities associated with this issue, it must also be stated that the importance of individual interment to the Islamic archaeologist is great, and hence should be included in this discussion. The reasons for this are various; first, obvious useful paleo-pathological and anthropological data can be recovered as, for example, Prominska's study of a thirteenth–fourteenth century Muslim cemetery at Kom el-Dikka in central Alexandria (1971). Secondly, the investigation of burials may allow the recognition of a Muslim in the archaeological record. Thirdly, in most cases the placing of the dead is the result of a conscious decision (excepting accidents and casualties in war) and the logic behind these decisions can tell us much about Muslim life. In order to explore this concept, three levels of analysis will be discussed: the position and treatment of the individual corpse, internal cemetery patterning and intra-cemetery patterning.

The position and treatment of the individual corpse

The concept of the corpse as contaminating, impure and dangerous appears to be almost universal, and Islam makes no exception. The passage or transition of the corpse from this stage to the next has been charted by Leach (1976, summarized in Parker Pearson 1993: 204). He proposes a three-stage framework for the treatment of the dead, with the first phase in the transitory process being the corpse in this pre-burial and dangerous state. This useful framework can equally be applied to the Muslim burial.

The probable absence of direct archaeological evidence for this first and important phase means that without the ethnographic and historical sources our understanding of such concepts within Islam would be limited, thus restricting interpretative possibilities from the beginning. Rites such as washing and perfuming the body would not, obviously, be archaeologically detectable, but clues to the existence of rites of purification might be found. One such indication would be the shroud or grave clothes. Opinion varies as to the number of cloths which should be used – one, two, three or five – but in general they should be simple and usually white (Gibb and Kramers 1961: 89–90). However, in practice, great variety is found. Hillenbrand (1994: 253), for instance, mentions that the use of richly worked silk shrouds was one of the first infringements of the original simple Muslim funerary rites. In itself this possibly reflects the need to move beyond the strictures of an essentially uniform rite, a recurring factor in the elaboration of Islamic funerary practices.

The use of grave clothes could conceivably have opened up another avenue for the display of social status. In Palestine, complete sets of grave clothes, different for men and women, were used (see figure 6.1), which were sometimes prepared by the living ready for their death (Granqvist 1965: 58–9). These are far removed from the simple shroud or shrouds, but still do not reflect the opulence of the ornate

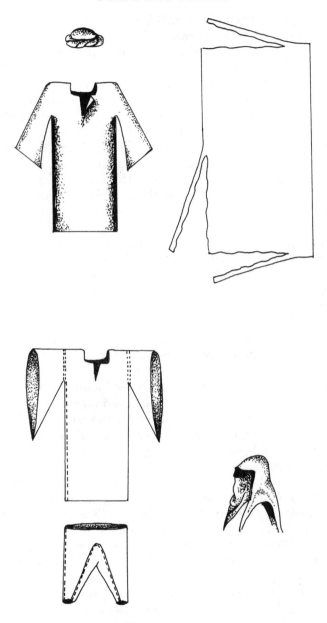

Figure 6.1 Grave clothes formerly used in Palestine. Top, men; bottom, women (after Granqvist 1965: 60–1)

grave clothes of the rich of Egypt, where muslin, cotton and silk were all used (Lane 1895: 506). However, in general, this first stage of the transition of the dead will always be difficult to reconstruct in its entirety based upon archaeological evidence.

The second stage might be of greater importance to the archaeologist; namely, the progress of the corpse into the 'liminal zone' which, according to Parker Pearson (1993: 204), is physically manifest as a cemetery, shrine or temple, where the funeral takes place and where the corpse is separated from the living through burial or other forms of disposal. It is the ritual activities associated with this stage that could allow the recognition of a Muslim burial. The characteristics of Muslim burial have already been outlined, and recognition criteria for the archaeologist could be:

1 The position of the corpse within the grave (right-hand side, face to *qiblah*), and the orientation of the grave pit.
2 The lack of grave goods.
3 The use of single interments, with gender segregation in separate vaults.

This has greater than merely theoretical importance and such criteria have been found to operate in many places. For example, one of the earliest explorations of the archaeology of the Jaulan in south-western Syria found that it was grave orientation that set Muslim Bedouin tombs clearly apart from earlier, and very similar, stone-built 'dolmens'. Both were built of stone slabs and surrounded by stone circles, but the Muslim tombs were oriented differently, 'incumbent upon them from religious motives, whilst the general character of the dolmen has been retained' (Schumacher 1888: 130).

Exceptions to the recognition criteria can be found in all parts of the world. Examples include: the placing of grave goods with Muslim burials dated to between the mid-fourteenth and early eighteenth centuries at Vohemar on the north-east coast of Madagascar (Verin 1986: 221–2; Dewar and Wright 1993: 444), and more occasionally with burials in Palestine (Granqvist 1965: 56, 84, 249; see also Simpson 1995: 245–7, for other examples of grave goods placed in Muslim burials in the Near East). Communal graves were in use in Palestine and the Punyal region of northern Pakistan (Jettmar 1967: 69–72). Burckhardt (1830: 281) records that it was a custom of some of the Bedouin of the eastern provinces of Egypt to 'bury with the dead man his sword, turban and girdle'. At Kossaima (Egypt) the dead man's shirt, head cloth, pipe, camel stick and cap were all left as offerings on, rather than in, the grave (Woolley and Lawrence 1936: 44).

Broomhall mentions further infringements in Muslim burials in China where the corpse was sometimes placed in a sitting position (1910: 230). Islamic prohibition on interfering with the corpse were also broken in Malawi, where the Muslim Yao prepared the body for burial by cutting a hole in the neck and squeezing the intestine empty (Bone 1982: 132). Although flouting Muslim law, such exceptions can be due to the survival of pre-Islamic practices or a lack of religious knowledge, and, though far from exhaustive, these examples indicate that exceptions do exist. But, equally, certain generalities in how the Muslim dead were and are treated can allow the archaeological recognition of a Muslim burial.

The third and final stage in Leach's framework, the passage of the dead into the other world once the ritual activities are over, is of course archaeologically unrecognizable. Nevertheless, material indications as to how the concept of the afterlife might be envisaged could be found, and within the context of Islam these are discussed in the final section of this chapter.

Internal cemetery patterning

Beyond the treatment of the individual corpse, the patterning of the burials within the cemetery can also provide us with information on Muslim communities. While the general archaeological theory and methodology concerning spatial patterning within cemeteries is, of course, applicable to Islamic funerary archaeology (see, for example, Chapman et al. 1981; O'Shea 1984), it should be remembered that there is not always a simple equation between patterns of life and those of death; they are not 'mirror images of life' (Hodder 1982a: 140). What, then, could be specifically gained within the 'archaeology of Islam' from a study of internal cemetery patterning, aside from possible information on population size and descent groups?

Dickie (1978: 46) makes the important point that Muslim cemeteries 'expand as a process of organic growth around a focus of grace, *baraka*', which in many cases is a saint's tomb. This is because it is thought that 'proximity to a holy person will help protect the grave from disturbance and increase the amount of blessing in the afterlife' (Simpson 1995: 244). Similar locational stimuli for burial round a mosque can be provided by the *qiblah*, proximity to which can also be desired. This notion of 'sacred geography' is of importance, and could in certain instances over-ride the presumed logic of inter-cemetery patterning, whereby familial groups congregate together in a manner which perhaps suits the archaeologist more than reality. Religious desires can provide the impetus to cemetery use to such an extent that burial within the vicinity of a more important saint's tomb can lead to severe over-crowding and frequent changing of the occupants of graves in closest proximity to the source of *baraka* (see Gibb and Kramers 1961: 357 for a discussion of this among the Shi'ah). The archaeological recognition of suicides' graves could also be possible. The Prophet disapproved of suicide, and it is forbidden in Islam (Rosenthal 1971: 1246). Therefore, it could be asked whether the graves of suicides are accorded special treatment, perhaps placed in a discrete section of the cemetery, or in another area altogether? This is certainly of relevance as regards children; Simpson records that separate areas or distinct cemeteries for children are frequently found in the Near East (1995: 244).

A further question of increasing relevance within the contemporary world is the archaeological recognition of Muslim space within non-Muslim environments. An instructive example can be provided in the Cambridge city cemetery. The growth in the Muslim community (discussed in chapter 2) dictated the need for a burial ground. This has had obvious material culture implications, clearly visible in figure 6.2, where the Muslim section of this cemetery is both spatially separated and oriented in a different direction from the blocks of non-Muslim and, in the majority, Christian graves. This would be recognizable archaeologically, even if all surface indications had gone, and the presence of a Muslim community would be recognizable.

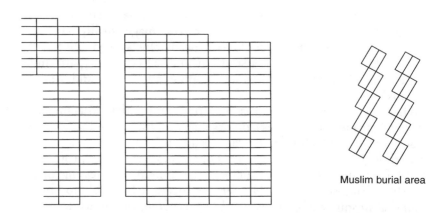

Muslim burial area

Figure 6.2 Alignment of Muslim burial section in comparison to the predominantly Christian burials in the Newmarket Road Cemetery, Cambridge (after the cemetery burial plots plan)

Intra-cemetery patterning

A third level of analysis is the patterning of cemeteries themselves. An interesting example of this can be provided from an ethnographic study in Timbuktu (Mali), where it was found that 'the ecological pattern of the dead strongly reflects that of the living' (Miner 1953: 221). The city was enclosed on three sides by burial grounds (all Muslim), with each cemetery having definite ethnic and quarter identities. The Bela, formerly the vassals of the Tuareg, lived and buried completely separately from the rest of the population. The Arabs also tended to bury their dead in separate cemeteries, with different Arab groups being further buried apart near their paternal kin. However, some burial in the same cemeteries of Arab and Songhai (another major ethnic group in the region) also occurred (Miner 1953). This illustrates that correlations between territorial patterns of life can exist in death, and that in certain contexts ethnic identity and residential patterns might be reconstructed from funerary data. But within Muslim societies, as in all societies, such patterns cannot be taken for granted.

Variation in cemetery patterning can also be found according to region within the Muslim world. For example, in the Arabian peninsula and the Near East, cemeteries were frequently located at the foot or on the slopes of mountains at sites 'imbued with an atmosphere of sanctity' (Ory 1991: 123), and Jewish and Christian cemeteries should not be placed too near 'those of the faithful' (1991: 121). Burton-Page also relates how, in certain areas of India, Muslim cemeteries are situated south of the settlements, 'possibly an extension of the south as the quarter of Yama, the God of death' (1991: 126). Simpson, in considering cemetery location in western Asia, states that where cemeteries are placed outside city walls, as at Mosul, they can become 'the focus of certain other activities considered hazardous or "anti-social", such as pottery production or car-repair garages' (1995: 243).

Indirectly, cemetery patterning might also tell us something about migration, pilgrimage and trade routes, and the borders of the Muslim world as they changed over time. Cemeteries can grow up at nodal points along these routes, perhaps where a saint's tomb, meeting place or caravanserai might have been located (Petersen 1994: 53–4). At the frontiers of the Muslim world, Hillenbrand (1994: 264) mentions that there appears to be a correlation between martyrs' tombs. At Aswan in Egypt, which bordered Christian Nubia, 50 or so Fatimid (969–1171) mausoleums were found clustered in a vast cemetery, and were apparently erected for *ghazis*, warriors who had died fighting for Islam. Similar patterns were also apparent in Central Asia. A more detailed analysis of such cemetery patterning might be of use in charting the fluidity of the frontiers of Islam over the centuries.

The three levels of analysis discussed show that examining the place of the dead in Islam provides a possible starting point for new research. They also begin to hint at the variability which exists, and the variety of information on Muslim society which might be recovered by the archaeologist through examining funerary data. Perhaps most significantly, it was shown that, theoretically at least, a universal and archaeologically recognizable Muslim burial exists, another category of evidence which might allow the archaeological recognition of a Muslim and a Muslim community.

Tombs for the Living and the Dead

As well as 'below ground' aspects of Muslim burial, it is also necessary to consider the Islamic commemorative structure as a medium for conveying a variety information about the deceased, but also about those left behind. Fleming (1973) has described European megalithic tombs as 'tombs for the living', and this notion is transferable to many Islamic funerary monuments which, as well as commemorating the dead, were often designed to impress or convey information to the living. They could become, according to Mujeeb (1967: 183), 'a symbol unifying life, death and eternity'. Moreover, through the use of marble, fired-brick or other materials, a statement could be made concerning power, grief, sanctity or love, and hence, by constructing a funerary monument, the dead could be 'brought to life' and, as Metcalf and Huntingdon (1991) discuss, used to reinforce or legitimize the claims of the living.

There exists no uniform 'meaning' or 'role' for Muslim funerary architecture; it varies regionally, according to doctrinal or sectarian affiliation and to factors such as personal choice and wealth (many people are not at all affected by building mausoleums and a simple tombstone could suffice as a marker, if one is used at all). Among the Shi'ah, for example, there is an emphasis on martyrdom, and pilgrimages to tombs and veneration of martyrs are of importance. In North Africa, the 'cult of the saints' is of significance, and funerary architecture, or rather the saint within, can form a focus for communal identity and belief. Among the Wahhabis of Saudi Arabia, the reverse is true, and the doctrines of early Islam are restored, with simplicity being the essence of funerary practices, and with no veneration of saints. Thus the following examples serve to illustrate some of the diversity which exists within Islamic funerary architecture, and the interpretative possibilities which exist as regards its social function.

Display

Often primary among the factors underlying the construction of a funerary monument are notions of display. Building a tomb is of greater visibility to the living than merely ornate graveclothes, which after burial would soon be forgotten, and offers another way of moving beyond the strictures of the formal Muslim burial rites. Above ground imagination could be freed, and architectural expression and the architect's creativity exploited. Furthermore, the tomb provides a means of creating a lasting legacy, through monumentalising the deceased, and even, it can be argued, placing them within history. Various dimensions are possible and three will be discussed here.

Status The first factor which might be of importance is the demonstration of status, religious or otherwise, and in India such concepts were taken to their extreme. Here, the ultimate secular monuments were created (Taphoo 1974, 1975), a process which culminated in the Mughal period (1626–1858). During this time, single-chambered tombs were replaced by tombs consisting of one large central chamber set within a garden divided into four by axial waterways, the *chahar-bagh*, with a subsidiary pavilion at each corner of the garden (1975: 24). These Mughal garden tombs served as ostentatious symbols of wealth and prestige, indicated by the fact that they were often built by their ultimate occupants well before death, and were used as places for feasting and celebrations prior to fulfilling their primary function (Jellicoe 1976: 112), as a capsule for the dead.

After death, the garden tomb could continue to serve as a symbol of the deceased's wealth and status, but a change in symbolic function sometimes occurred. If the care of the tomb complex was entrusted into the guardianship of a Muslim holyman (as often happened), the occupant of the tomb might thus also take on a more pious identity, more so than in life, and a form of 'legitimization', as discussed by Metcalf and Huntingdon (1991), took place. A social statement might also be made, literally saying 'I am pious', and achieved through utilizing an existing tradition of architectural form and an endowment process, both of which were connected with such ideas of piety. Gibb and Kramers (1961: 334) note that it became a custom for the powerful to prepare a tomb and an adjoining funerary mosque for themselves while alive because 'just as the *qubba* under which the saint lay and the mosque adjoining it was sanctified by him so vice-versa a *qubba* and a mosque could cause a deceased person to become considered a saint'. The benefits of investing in a monumental tomb might therefore be gained twice: first, in life, as a worldly symbol of wealth, and a place to party; and, secondly, after death, by continuing as a symbol of wealth, but perhaps also of piety. Therefore different identities could be created through the use of funerary architecture and accompanying endowments.

Love A second possible dimension associated with building a funerary monument is to display love, and again India offers a fine example, the Taj Mahal on the outskirts of Agra, built by Shah Jahan between 1632 and 1654 for his wife, Arjumand Banu Begam, better known as Mumtaz Mahal. Vast resources were poured into the building of this monumental tomb complex, not for pious reasons, or solely for the purposes of displaying wealth, but, more importantly, as an act of remembrance of, and as a testimony to his love for, his wife. No expense was spared in building the Taj Mahal. Brick, not wood–scaffolding was used, and a ramp over 3 km long was built to lift material to the dome. Both craftsmen and materials were imported not only from different regions of India, but also from other areas of the Muslim world, including Baghdad, Shiraz and Samarkand. White marble set with inlays of precious and semi-precious stones, forming inscriptions and decorative motifs, was used on the exterior, while the interior was equally sumptuously finished with marble filigree screens surrounding the replica tombs (the actual burials were below ground), and furnishings including gold lamps and Persian carpets (Davies 1989: 193–5; see also Nath 1970; Volwahsen 1970; Qaisar 1988). The finished monument is truly magnificent (see plate 6.1). Indeed, it has been described as having 'sexual appeal...a seductive building' (Tillotson 1990: 101), owing to its flesh-like surface of marble. This perhaps could be further interpreted as testimony to Shah Jahan's physical, as well as spiritual, love for the woman who bore him 14 children.

However, it is when dealing with emotion in all its many forms that the process of interpretation becomes most difficult, and thus a consideration of all the intense emotions which inevitably accompany something as traumatic as death is often neglected by archaeologists. Perhaps within the context of such a substantive monument as the Taj Mahal it is easy to begin to say something about the emotions accompanying death, grief for a lost lover perhaps (see Begley 1979 for an alternative and less-convincing interpretation of the Taj Mahal), but equally, with lesser monuments, such emotions could

Plate 6.1 The Taj Mahal, Agra (*photo*. T. Insoll)

also be relevant. The person buried was once in all certainty someone's relative, perhaps their lover, but it is often easier (and safer) to concentrate on the socio-political domain, thus de-personalizing what is after all a very personal event. The fact that emotion of all sorts must be inextricably linked with Islamic death and burial, as with any other, need not be reiterated. Emotion can be displayed on many levels, from the mass emotion which was visibly apparent on our television screens when Ayatollah Khomeini was buried in 1989 to that of numberless family burials which have occurred over the centuries. When considering such a sensitive and personal subject, the archaeologist should bear in mind that funerary evidence is undoubtedly imbued with an 'emotional legacy', unapproachable as that might be.

Muslim identity A third type of information which might be displayed through building a funerary monument is Muslim identity. As we saw with the Taj Mahal, the very materials used in funerary architecture can also serve as a means of conveying information. These materials can range from the more obviously costly, such as the semi-precious stone inlays and white marble of the Taj Mahal, to the less obvious, such as the use of fired-brick in the central and western Sudanic regions of Africa, where its symbolic status depended upon the context in which it was employed. Although it was not imported, it still served as a highly obvious indicator of social status through the amount of resources, primarily water and fuel, which had to be invested in its manufacture in this often resource-poor environment. Thus, fired-brick appears to have served as a 'material of power' in both funerary and other contexts. This is indicated by a comment by Ibn Sa'id (died c.1286–7) who reported that in Barisa (Senegal) 'none builds with plaster and baked bricks except a ruler or a person of wealth and distinction to whom he has given permission to do so' (Levtzion and Hopkins 1981: 185).

This has been recorded archaeologically in the cemetery at Gao-Saney (Mali) where various fired-brick tombs were found (twelfth–thirteenth centuries) (Mauny 1951; Insoll 1996b). The use of fired-brick in this region in the 'palace buildings' at Ouara (Chad) and at Garoumele (Niger) (Binet 1956; Bivar and Shinnie 1962: 4; Lebeuf and Kirsch 1989: 25–6) suggest that fired-brick was a visible material symbol of social status, but possibly also of Islamization. There certainly appears to be a correlation between the use of fired-brick, often only for a short-lived period in selective contexts (tombs, mosques and palaces), and the initial acceptance of Islam by the indigenous rulers. Thus it can be seen that Islamic funerary architecture, both materials and structures, can serve not only to commemorate the deceased but can also display and convey a variety of information to the living.

Inversions of reality

What is displayed, however, can equally be misleading. For example, the presence or absence of a monumental tomb need not be a true reflection of the worldly status of the deceased. Treatment in death is not necessarily consistent with position in life, and doubts are thus cast on any claims for the existence of certainties as regards funerary architecture as a metaphor for social status. This is illustrated by considering a hypothetical case study contrasting the treatment of Sufi saints and Saudi princes after death. The former may have led hermit-like or ascetic existences, perhaps shunning worldly goods, and devoting themselves to a life of contemplation, of reading the Qur'an and religious devotion. Through their saintly reputation, followers might erect a funerary monument totally disproportionate to their worldly status. The archaeologist, lacking any additional information, such as inscriptions, could interpret such a monument as that of someone of great material worth, perhaps an important secular figure, which would obviously be completely inaccurate.

In direct contrast to this are the Wahhabi sect (described in chapter 1), whose essential doctrine Niezen describes as 'true Islam [is] that of the first generation of Muslims, the Prophet and his immediate successors' (1987: 2). They are opposed to 'the cult of saints', and Wahhabi burial is in keeping with the original Muslim custom of commemorating the grave, if at all, by a pile of rocks, a practice originally intended to protect the corpse from wild animals (Laqueur 1992: 284). Kings and paupers should thus be buried in the same way, theoretically at least, which gives rise to the interesting mental picture of the Saudi prince, living in a luxurious house, with a garage full of expensive cars, being indistinguishable in death from the person who burns or collects his rubbish. Thus, it can be seen that the absence of a substantial funerary monument need not always imply that the person buried necessarily lacked social status or material wealth. Diversity and complexity are again the keywords.

Multiple meanings

But just as the meaning of funerary architecture can be misleading, it can equally be very complex. We return again to the fact that many aspects of Islamic material culture can have various meanings depending upon the observer or interpreter. An interesting case study, demonstrating the existence of 'multiple meanings' in funerary architecture, is provided by the local tradition of building 'pillar tombs' on the East African coast. These are so called because the deceased is commemorated by a large pillar (up to 6 m), usually made of coral, which is often inset with imported porcelain dishes. They are associated with the Swahili (see chapter 3) and are found from southern Somalia down the coast into Tanzania, and date from between the fourteenth and seventeenth centuries (Kirkman 1966; Prins 1967; Sanseverino 1983). A group of these monuments on the northern coast of Kenya was analysed by Wilson who found that they seem to have served a variety of functions beyond merely providing 'a suitable resting place for the earthly remains of worthy or wealthy persons' (1979: 33).

They functioned, first, as symbols of ancestry and lineage, or *Waungwana* status, representing people with deep roots in the community who were usually wealthy and in positions of authority, but not necessarily of religious authority. For example, the founder of the *madrasah* in Lamu (Kenya), though revered as a saint, was denied a funerary monument built of permanent materials earlier in this century because he never attained the required *Waungwana* status (Wilson 1979: 34). The possession of this status appears to have overridden religious considerations. Thus, both funerary architecture and 'the ancestors' appear to be used to legitimize social and political claims in this specific context. However, it would also appear that it is the claims of the living that are being pursued, rather than those of the deceased by reinforcing the possession of the all-important *Waungwana* status.

As well as their secular importance to the living, the tombs were also imbued with religious significance, and could be used within rituals of ancestor and spirit worship, which co-existed with orthodox Muslim practice (and in certain instances continue to do so). Archaeological evidence attesting to these non-Muslim rituals has been found, including incense burners, and a pillar tomb, which had what appeared to be a chimney at its centre, was possibly used in sacrificial rites. This evident lack of Islamic orthodoxy has been further indicated by the orientations of certain tombs, which are often many degrees off the almost due north required on the East African coast. This led Wilson (1979: 41) to suggest that the tombs were built by people 'who were outside the firm grip of Islam or who were innocently ignorant of the finer points of orthodoxy or geography'.

Thus, in this example, a variety of functions and meanings appear to underlie the Swahili pillar tombs. These in turn appear to be logical within the context of Swahili society which is a blend of Indian Ocean and African elements, of Islam and traditional beliefs. Physically, the pillar tombs stretch the idea of the Muslim marker stone or *shahid* to its absolute limits, and this is incorporated within, and adapted to, the needs of Swahili society. Undoubtedly, the meaning of these monuments within Swahili society was even more complicated than has been suggested, but part of their former meaning might now be lost forever. How would the interpretative possibilities have been restricted without an understanding of the concept of *Waungwana* status? This was largely gained from historical and ethnographic sources, and would have been difficult, if not impossible, to reconstruct from archaeological data alone. The Swahili tombs were imbued with multiple meanings which could vary according to status and the participant or observer involved. They served to commemorate the dead and, perhaps more importantly, function for the living. Furthermore, the Swahili tombs also provide a salutary lesson as to the interpretative possibilities of funerary architecture, but which equally may elude us.

Tombs as a focus

Muslim funerary architecture may also have social significance in acting as a focus for religious devotion or for the community. Primary among these are the range of structures associated with the mystical and saintly aspects of Islam. Though often strictly opposed by the orthodox and condemned by *fatwa* (formal legal pronouncements such as that made by Ibn Taymiya in the fourteenth century), saints' tombs and the 'cult of saints', Sufi orders and mystical Islam are of great importance in many areas of the Muslim world to both Sunni and Shi'ah, and Islam had to yield to a need for practices such as the veneration of saints. Saints' tombs and 're-incorporated pre-Islamic sanctuaries' (Gibb and Kramers 1961: 324, 629) became of prime importance in many areas of the Muslim world. To the archaeologist interested in Islam this category of structure is of significance, not least in their abundance. They act within 'sacred geography', becoming almost 'sacred markers' within the landscape. Innumerable examples of funerary architecture forming the focus of pilgrimage or the physical or spiritual centres of communities could be cited, and a wide variety of local types of commemorative structure is found, too many to be discussed in detail here. Hence only a couple of examples will be cited to illustrate their importance and the role they can play in the lives of many Muslims by acting not only as tombs for the dead, but also as focal points of great importance to the living.

Saints and Sufis Without parallel as examples of this phenomenon are the tombs of saints and Sufis, but (as noted in chapter 1) to define the saint and Sufi as completely separate entities in every instance is perhaps to categorize them too rigidly. A Sufi is a Muslim mystic who is usually a member of a religious order or *tariqah* (but need not be). A saint is a holy person who need not be a Sufi and can be anyone of sufficient spiritual status. Similarly, a Sufi leader or founder of an order could often acquire saintly status, thus a certain interchangeability of role is possible, though how the funerary monuments are materially manifest might differ. Generally (though, of course, exceptions exist), a Sufi tomb will form part of a larger complex of buildings, a monastery, convent or lodge, while a saint's tomb can be (but need not be) isolated within the landscape.

The appeal of a saint's tomb, Sufi or otherwise, is due to the notion that the soul of the saint lingers around the tomb, *baraka* is present and will aid people who seek the intervention of the saint through petitions, prayers and offerings of various kinds. Typically, around a

Sufi/saint's tomb a complex of buildings will grow up or, if already extant, the tomb of the founder will be centrally placed. These complexes have many forms and names, *zawiyah* (North Africa), *khanaqah* (Central Asia), *dargah* (India), *tekke* (Turkey), depending on where in the Muslim world they are found (the concern here is only with the types of structure which incorporate a tomb). The complex can be composed of a variety of buildings: the tomb of the founder and perhaps of his descendants, a mosque, *madrasah*, public baths, library, accommodation for the resident members of the order, their families and servants, and for pilgrims and travellers, the whole often enclosed by a surrounding wall (Trimingham 1971: 176; Brett 1990: 35; Baha Tanman 1992: 147). Numerous examples of Sufi complexes which incorporate at their centre a saint's tomb could be provided. Golombek (1974), for example, records one at Natanz which was in existence in Iran in the fourteenth century. The shrine was centred around the tomb of a Sufi *shaykh*, with a mosque, cistern, lodgings, minaret, and the corridors and vestibules 'connecting the various parts of the complex' (1974: 420). Of importance is the fact, noted by Golombek, that the focus upon the *shaykh* occurred after his death. 'It is as if the *shaykh* were deemed a more "valuable" asset in his tomb than alive and teaching' (1974: 422).

In contrast to the complete complex is the single tomb or commemorative structure. The *qubba*, or domed tomb, found throughout the Muslim world, is a good example of this type of monument (see plate 6.2), and can range in both design and materials from the humble to the magnificent. The dome is a sign of veneration, but does not itself have a specific funerary attribute (Grabar 1966: 44). *Qubbas* can mark either the actual burial place of the saint or holy person or something associated with them or simply act as a memorial shrine (Trimingham 1949: 142). No binding rules exist, but it should be noted that the domed tomb, and indeed all other types of saints' tombs, can function as a focus of community attention and become the object of pilgrimage.

Martyrs   Another class of Islamic funerary monument which can become objects of pilgrimage are martyrs' tombs and shrines. These range from humble piles of stones to vast soaring edifices. As was discussed in the context of *jihad* (see chapter 4), the significance of martyrdom within Islam should not be understated and is of particular importance for the Shi'ah, with Hussein, the grandson of the Prophet, who was slaughtered at Karbala in 680, 'the *shahid par excellence*' (Gibb and Kramers 1961: 516). Burial at martyrs' shrines is considered an honour, and corpses are brought from afar for

Plate 6.2 *Qubbas* from the air, Old Dongola, Sudan (Institute of Archaeology, London)

interment at the shrines of the most important martyrs. Lassy (1916: 146–9), for example, relates how in Azerbaijan successive burial was sometimes practised: first, in a shallow, temporary grave to allow the flesh to decay; then, once this was complete, the clean bones would be transported to Karbala for reburial in the company of the 'beloved Hussein'. Besides the obvious significance of a vast build-up of funerary remains at certain popular locations, this example also presents the interesting scenario of certain areas devoid of whole strata of people in the funerary archaeological record; namely, those wealthy enough to arrange transport of their remains to sites such as Karbala.

The political role of tombs A further factor of possible importance is the political role that these structures, or rather their contents, can sometimes play in Muslim communities; the saint can function as a focus of religious devotion or communal identity hostile to and beyond the control of the 'accepted' religious or secular authorities, represented by the government and the *ulama*, the Muslim learned class of the cities. Similarly, Sufis could also be regarded with suspicion. Being 'mystics', and often thought to espouse 'semi-socialist' doctrines or to possess loyalties transcending national or ethnic boundaries, they were often seen as 'rebel figures' (Ahmed 1988: 91). Indeed, one of the first acts of the new secular Turkish republic on assuming power in the early years of this century was to close the dervish lodges and to forbid public manifestations of dervish life (Lifchez 1992: 6). Similarly, within the former Soviet Union, Sufi *tariqah* were condemned as 'fanatical anti-Soviet, anti-social, reactionary force[s]', and shrines and tombs were turned into anti-religious museums, as, for instance, the Shah-i-Zenda in Samarkand (Bennigsen and Enders Wimbush 1986: 22, 62).

The role of funerary architecture in politico-religious strife would be difficult to reconstruct archaeologically, but the anthropological and historical literature abounds with examples illustrating this often contentious aspect of the cult of saints and Sufism. In North Africa, the 'cult of the saints', centred on tombs or shrines, is often an important part of religious life, especially significant in rural areas (Montet 1909; Dermengheim 1954; Gellner 1969). In Tunisia, an example is provided by the centrality of the cult of saints in the village of Sidi Ameur, where tombs form not only the physical focus of the community, with the clustering of the habitations of the descendants of the saints around the *zawiyah* or tomb, but also the spiritual focus of pilgrimage and sacrifice (Abu Zaria 1982). Saints' tombs played a major role in life to the extent that the national political party attempted to replace the *zawiyah* and the cult of saints with local party branches, and through education tried to develop a national ideology standing against 'archaic customs' (1982: 194, 201).

Another example in late eighteenth-century Algeria was a conflict between the urban based authorities and a rural Sufi order over the '*baraka*-producing remains' of a Sufi-saint. The saint's corpse was actually stolen from the Kabyles of the Jurjura and taken to Algiers as the burial ceremonies for the saint in the Kabyle *zawiyah* would, according to Clancy-Smith, 'attract large crowds of pilgrims to the tomb seeking divine favours through the saint's intercession, something that could lead to unrest among a fractious population located on the boundaries of Turkish authority' (1993: 167) (Algeria then being under Ottoman control). Eventually a miracle was proclaimed, and the saint, his body duplicated, became the 'man with two tombs', each exuding the all-important *baraka* – one in Algiers and the other in the Jurjura.

But how is this of importance to the archaeologist? For several reasons: first, because we are witnessing the active utilization and manipulation of funerary architecture and funerary remains in the struggle for religious and political loyalties and power. Thus, this provides another example of the potency of funerary architecture as actively, and not passively, constituted, not solely a dead tomb for a dead individual but a tomb acting both for the living and the dead. Furthermore, such conflicts remind us of the 'different Islams' which can exist, urban and rural, orthodox and mystical. But how it might be recognized archaeologically is not at all certain. What, then, are the general implications which can be drawn from this consideration of Islamic funerary architecture for archaeologists? Our examination of the way tombs can function for both the living and the dead has shown that these structures function within Islam at a much deeper level than that of merely providing an attractive resting place for the deceased. In many contexts it might be feasible for the archaeologist to interpret something of the social role and significance of a Muslim tomb, since a rich body of ethnographic, sociological and historical data exists which can help in formulating ways of considering the archaeological data and in suggesting options which might otherwise be neglected. Yet, besides the burial itself and the possible accompanying commemorative structure, a third source of evidence exists: funerary epigraphy and iconography, the 'language of death'.

Funerary Epigraphy: the Language of Death

Although decorated or inscribed gravestones are disapproved of in Muslim law, the fact remains that the use of funerary epigraphy and iconography as a means of signalling a variety of information is a widespread phenomenon, and within Islam much can be learnt from this source of evidence. De Moraes Farias (1990: 69), for example, describes how a common genre of Muslim funerary epigraphy exists: opening with the *basmala* formula, followed by the name of the deceased, the date of death, and 'one or more quotations from, or paraphrases of, or allusions to, the Qur'an'. In many regions, however, the use of Qur'anic inscriptions is rare, the reason being that they might be trodden on or disturbed (Simpson 1995: 247). What is present will vary, and the existence of funerary epigraphic traditions throughout the Muslim world provides a rich source of evidence which is much more varied than merely stating that so-and-so was buried in such-and-such. Funerary inscriptions are used for many purposes: to signal gender, social status, occupation, religious piety, and for claiming origins and ethnicity, ownership or use of something or somewhere through descent, to express religious beliefs, and even to 'indigenize' Islam, bridging the gap between Muslim and non-Muslim practice.

The very existence of an inscribed tombstone can tell us something about the deceased, besides the information gained from reading it. Not everyone could afford an engraved or inscribed tombstone, so often what we are seeing are the wealthier or revered members of society. The 'top-heavy' archaeology of Islam is again apparent, working in favour of the upper echelons, both secular and sacred. Even the crude scratched inscription on an unworked marker stone implies a degree of literacy, which might have been beyond the abilities of a percentage of the population, possibly a sizeable percentage, in an age when literacy could have been restricted.

Symbols

Symbols are one means of overcoming this problem. Among the Lurs of western Iran, for example, complex iconography was employed on funerary stelae dating from the late eighteenth to mid-twentieth centuries. These included figural representations symbolizing both the religious beliefs of this Shi'ah ethnic group, and also providing more practical information on gender and, indirectly, on migration routes. Mortensen (1991: 81–6, 1993: 136–44) isolated a variety of motifs, including a geometric garden design, invoking a mental image of paradise, strings of prayer beads, combs and prayer stones, used by, and so representing, men. Most interesting was an image of a riderless horse, which appears to be a representation of the martyrdom of the Imam Hussein, who is of central importance to the Shi'ah faith. This image served two purposes: to focus attention on the day of judgement and the afterlife and, on a more worldly level, to indicate the pious intentions of the deceased (Mortensen 1991: 86). The combination of pictorial and written information perhaps also served to inform both the literate and the illiterate.

A variety of information is conveyed by these tombstones with their 'value-laden symbols' (Hodder 1982a: 213). However, in this case the code to these highly informative material symbols is being lost through disruptive policies such as the forced sedentarization of the Lurs, which is upsetting the equilibrium of their way of life, and which has led to discontinuation in the erection of pictorial tombstones (Mortensen 1991: 86). This begs the question of how much we are now unable to translate in the repertoire of Islamic iconography and symbolism? There is certainly still much to decode, with a partial solution offered through closer working contacts between 'Islamic' archaeologists, art historians, architects, historians and anthropol-

ogists, as well as the need to utilize general archaeological tools such
as relational analogy and the other contextual interpretative methodologies developed over the past 15 years or so (see, for example,
Hodder 1982a,b, 1986).

Piety, doctrines and human nature

Less overtly symbolic, but equally informative, are the funerary stelae
of the Gao region of Mali. In certain instances, both the gravestones
and the scripts were imported into this region. Five of the tombstones
found at the site of Gao-Saney were imported, ready carved with
name and date, across the Sahara from Muslim Spain (probably from
Almeria) in the early twelfth century (Sauvaget 1950; Vire 1958; de
Moraes Farias 1990; Insoll 1996b). The very presence of these stelae
in the Gao Region meant that the Almoravid dynasty then controlling Al-Andalus had overcome its scruples about using commemorative funerary stelae in providing these items for export. De Moraes
Farias (1990: 76) has suggested that the religious austerity of the
southern Almoravids evident in their home territories of the western
Sahara, was transferred north, hence the dearth of funerary inscriptions dating from their period of control of Spain (1056–1147). But a
desire for such commemorative devices obviously existed at Gao, and
this was fulfilled as the Almoravid appetite for the commodities
which could be sourced from this region (discussed in chapter 5)
was stronger than their religious scruples. Thus, human nature, in
the form of greed, might be expressed in the presence of these stelae.

It would also appear that the funerary stelae at Gao were used for
purposes other than merely commemorating the dead. One of the
factors behind the initial conversion to Islam by local rulers in the
Western Sahel and Sudan, including those at Gao, was prestige, and
even after death the new-found faith could be proclaimed. Three of
the kings commemorated on stelae, including two of the imported
Spanish examples dating from the early twelfth century, in the cemetery at Gao-Saney were recent converts to Islam. Their new identity,
and indeed their piety, were clearly shown by successively adopting
the name of the Prophet, and of the first two caliphs, Abu Bakr and
Umar (Flight n.d.: 1). A century later, other funerary inscriptions in
the Gao region show that Islam had been 'indigenized', with the use
of local names present. For example, one tombstone dated to 1210
and recovered from the cemetery at Gorongobo, bears local Songhai
female names, the dominant sedentary ethnic group in the region.
Thus, we can learn much more from 'the language of death' than
merely who was buried where and when.

Ethnic identity: 'us' and 'you'

The Hui, on the coast of southern China, continue to use Islamic funerary inscriptions in subtle ways. The Chendai Hui, who form part of the Hui ethnic minority, use gravestones bearing inscriptions in Arabic as proof of their 'otherness', their identity, 'etched in stone' (Gladney 1991: 265), in their struggle to create a cultural and ethnic identity and to differentiate themselves from their Han Chinese neighbours with whom they are virtually culturally indistinct (see Dasheng and Kalus 1991, for a list of the inscriptions). This raises the interesting question why, if they are so far removed from Islam and Muslim practices, would Muslim tombs, funerary inscriptions and other Islamic monuments be so important to the Chendai Hui? Gladney (1991) eloquently approaches this issue with reference to the Ding lineage of the Chendai Hui. She suggests that a variety of reasons contributed to the importance placed on the Arabic funerary inscriptions (and other material culture). For example, under the communist government historical cultural traits were essential for proving ethnic identity, and achieving this brought benefits such as economic assistance for an 'underprivileged minority' (1991: 274). Thus, it would make sense to utilize funerary and other monuments pro-actively in such a situation. But it would also appear that the importance of the monuments has altered over time. In periods of stress or need, they could be employed, literally, as historical texts, attesting to the rights, obligations and foreign ancestral traditions of the Hui; equally, they could be quietly forgotten.

The complexities involved in the relationship between the Chendai Hui and their legacy of funerary inscriptions is evident when funerary epigraphy can be seen to function 'the other way', so to speak. While gravestones could be used to affirm different ethnic identity, in this case, Islamic, they could also reflect the problem of being a 'foreign' minority within the midst of a sometimes hostile majority. Hence Arabic and Chinese texts were often combined, possibly as a means of justifying that the Hui also belong, they are not so different as to warrant persecution. In Quanzhou (Canton), an interesting example of an early stage in this process has been recorded, where an inscription dating from the tenth–eleventh centuries has, at the top of the stele, a standard Arabic inscription and, below, a Chinese inscription reading 'grave of the barbarian guest' (Gladney 1991: 191): a juxtaposition of foreign Muslim tradition with what must be a Chinese reflection on the deceased (see figure 6.3). Also in Quanzhou, a trilingual inscription in Arabic, Persian and Chinese dating

Figure 6.3 Bilingual tombstone in Chinese and Arabic from Quanzhou, China, probably dating from the tenth or eleventh century (after Gladney 1991: 191)

from 1750 was recorded set into a tomb. The terminology applied to the deceased differs between the languages; in Arabic he is referred to as 'this feeble man, the deceased', while in Chinese he is the 'pioneer sage' (Broomhall 1910: 113–14).

Yet perhaps the most informative example of the pragmatic and complex interplay between foreign, Islamic and Chinese tradition and terminology is provided by another inscription from Quanzhou. Here, members of the Pu Hui lineage changed their name from the foreign sounding 'Pu' to the Chinese 'Wu' to escape persecution and this was reflected on their tombstones: on the front of their tombs would be inscribed 'Wu's tomb' and on the back, secretly, 'Pu's tomb' (Gladney 1991: 273). This secretive, almost subversive, juggling of Muslim and Chinese tradition, of 'otherness' and 'belonging', is far from fossilized and has been shown to alter over time. The relationship between the two traditions of Islamization and Sinicization, and the resultant implications for Chinese Hui Muslim culture, are encapsulated by Israeli when he remarks: 'the Proposition that Muslims in China have simply become Chinese Muslims is thus, and indeed turns out in historical perspective to be, a superficial observation at worst, a reckless generalisation at best' (1979: 169). More than the outward Sinicization of Islam is apparent, but its intricacies can be approached through material culture, and preserved for the archaeologist, in this instance through funerary inscriptions.

Indigenizing Islam

A group of funerary inscriptions from eastern Java provides an apparently more straightforward instance of the indigenization of Islam in Asia, but without the accompanying subterfuge. Indonesia is today home to the largest Muslim population in the world, with the majority living on the island of Java (Ricklefs 1979: 100). Muslim contacts began when foreign, as opposed to local, Muslim trading communities were established in northern and eastern Java by the eleventh century (Woodward 1989: 58; see also Tjandrasamita 1978). The spread of Islam from these trading communities and its acceptance by the local community has been charted by Ambary (1986) through an analysis of funerary epigraphy. The earliest stele dating from the eleventh century at Leran was imported for a foreign Muslim, but by the fourteenth century local groups were inscribing tombstones in Arabic in a simple form, sometimes incorrectly, as at Tralaya. Dates given in Javanese script indicate the local connection, for instance at Trawulan, where a stone of 1368 was dated *saka* 1290 (Damais 1968), which is of significance, according to Ricklefs, as 'the use of the *saka* era strongly suggests that this is the oldest surviving gravestone of a Javanese, rather than a foreign, Muslim' (1979: 103).

Towards the end of the fourteenth century, the local Javanese script had become more conspicuous, and the use of Arabic declined, a process which continued: 'once Islam had firmly taken root in Javanese society about the beginning of the sixteenth century, local elements once more are prominent in the calligraphy' (Ambary 1986: 25). This is also reflected in the reappearance of pictograms or chronograms to commemorate dates. For example, 1622 is represented on a tomb in Drajat by a carved panel depicting a sea with waves, above which an arrow is extended, symbolism which Ambary interprets as '*segara umob panah tunggal*' or 1544 *saka* (1986: 34). Hence, in eastern Java, where circumstances are wholly different from those experienced by the Hui, Islamic identity could be much more openly proclaimed and, importantly, indigenized without accompanying fears and pressures.

Status and religious affiliation

A final example of the Islamic 'language of death' are the anthropomorphic gravestones of Ottoman Turkey. In the Ottoman empire, with its complex bureaucracy (Inalcik 1973; Wheatcroft 1995), rank and social position were signalled in death as in life. Elaborate iconography and calligraphy carved on to the stones were used to denote secular status and religious affiliation from the sixteenth century onwards. Secular tombstones were carved and painted, with those on men's graves topped with a turban denoting their rank (see plate 6.3), probably derived from pre-Islamic Turkic tradition, while women's were decorated with flowers and children's were made in miniature versions (Goodwin 1988: 62; Laqueur 1992: 284).

Plate 6.3 Ottoman tombstones, Hadarpasha cemetery, Istanbul (*photo.* T. Insoll)

One of the best studied aspects of Ottoman funerary iconography is that connected with the Sufi or dervish orders. The stelae used on dervish graves were used to denote membership of a specific dervish order and even lodge (*tekke*) (De Jong 1989; Lifchez 1992). Laqueur (1992: 286–91) has shown how this art form developed from the sixteenth century, and expanded in the eighteenth century in Istanbul. Representations of the dervish's headgear were carved in the round or incised, in certain cases, the *gul* or rosette design crowning the headgear allowed the specific *tariqat* (Sufi order) to be recognized, with even the internal hierarchy of the *tekke* being sometimes indicated. De Jong notes that tombstones of the Bektashi order (referred to in chapter 5) were easily recognizable owing to the representation of their distinctive twelve-sided felt headgear (*hüseyni tac*) (1989: 11). Though primarily confined to male graves, examples of female dervish graves are also found.

With the Ottoman dervish tombstones, although an orthodox monument was employed, orthodoxy was stretched to its limits (or beyond) through the use of complex epigraphy and figural iconography. These symbolic devices can be used to replicate after death two

Plate 6.4   Muslim cemetery, Borneo (Haddon Collection, Cambridge)

major, and often conflicting, themes of Ottoman life: the secular order of status concerns and bureaucracy, and religious affiliation. Once again, funerary epigraphy and iconography can be seen to act at a deeper level than purely commemorating a deceased Muslim. But, at the same time, the over-riding link is still there; these tombstones, from those of the Lur in Iran to West Africa, China, Indonesia and Turkey, are all indisputably and recognizably Muslim (see plate 6.4). Great diversity is apparent, but they are of one family; both structuring principles and cultural diversity are evident.

The Apple and the Olive

So far we have seen that the significance and symbolism of the burial, the tomb, the gravestone and the 'language of death' in Islam can go far beyond the merely functional. A similar symbolic significance, again very revealing, can be seen in much of what can be associated with death and funerary rituals in various areas of the Muslim world.

In much of the Muslim world that is dry and inhospitable there is a preoccupation with water, symbolically and practically, as a source of life (Lings 1968). As will be discussed below, water is intricately linked with Qur'anic imagery of paradise, and the Islamic garden, an earthly paradise, was created as a reflection of this. At a more mundane level (obviously not everyone was buried in a tomb set in a formal garden or even had access to such a garden), the ideas of water, fertility and verdure are frequently linked with both life and death. In opposition to the concept of life-giving water, there is another, of heat and dryness oppressing the dead. The person who neglected their prayers in life would have to atone for this after death, by making their ablutions with fire: 'all that is done here with water, must be done there (eternity) with fire' (Granqvist 1965: 69). Although such concepts are not, however, confined to Islam (Humphreys 1981: 10), the association between water, particularly moving water, and life, and dryness and death, serve as a lesson in contextual associations which could be of use to the archaeologist concerned with a fuller understanding of all facets of Muslim societies.

Within Islam, the heat–death association had a direct influence upon the materials used in tomb construction. Leisten (1990: 15–16) describes how, in the early Islamic period, it was believed that a tomb should not be made of brick and sealed with lime mortar as these materials had been in contact with fire and would dry out the grave, a continuation of certain pre-Islamic beliefs that the soul of the dead would suffer thirst. An archaeological example of the need to cool the corpse is provided by the grave shafts which were linked to above-ground brick tomb towers found in Rayy in Iran and dated to between the tenth and twelfth centuries (Adle 1979, cited in Leisten 1990: 21). These perhaps served to provide ventilation for the dead, as wind towers do for the living. Similarly, in Turkey, Goodwin (1988: 66) relates how by the end of the seventeenth century there was a fashion for having open ironwork domes on the Ottoman *türbe* (tomb or mausoleum). This, according to one legend, served to 'admit the fire-quenching rain', a 'vehicle of purification [and] a source of nourishment' (Dickie 1978: 45).

The reverse of the heat–death association, that of water/verdure–life, is of equal significance, and both are tied together. An example of this is provided by considering the apple and the olive, two trees of importance to the Shi'ah Turkic peoples of Azerbaijan. These trees provide fruit and hence sustain life, and on another level they, along with the willow, symbolize life. Lassy (1916: 143, 147) describes how the olive, with its green leaves throughout the year, actually represents life, and how the willow through its blossoming in spring, exhibits a new vitality, as people also do at that time of year. Green, the colour of the leaves and of Islam, as well as signifying life, can also signal purity: 'my father's house is green', meaning the family was blameless, was a phrase used in Palestine (Granqvist 1965: 63). But green can also be the colour of death, of grave clothes for example, as well as reminding people of paradise, and thereby acting as the 'last and highest colour in the gamut of mystical experience' (Schimmel 1976: 29). The apple also assumed significance in a funerary context among the Azerbaijan Turks. This was due to its 'extraordinary fruitfulness', a vital power which the dead needed, and its association with Hussein, whose 'wonderful apple' never decreased in size no matter how much he ate it (Lassy 1916: 150).

At a practical level this information is of use to the archaeologist interested in Islam. The significance of a colour such as green can be seen, and the physical survival of green-coloured clothing, shrouds and the like in funerary contexts is obviously possible. Secondly, the fact that corpses can be interred, as in Azerbaijan, with material symbols or parts of life-giving or vitalizing substances is of import-ance. Stones representative of apples, 'apple-smelling' sand from the tomb of Hussein, and willow sticks could all be placed with the corpse. Furthermore, such ideas and practices are not confined to the Shi'ites of the Caucasus. In North Africa, the exceptional ver-dure of trees planted on saints' tombs is attributed to their *baraka*, and sacred trees often indicate the burial place of a saint, with offer-ings left at these trees and pieces of cloth tied into their branches as a form of supplication (Lassy 1916: 143–9), something frowned upon by the orthodox as incompatible with monotheism, but as Guillaume notes, neither Judaism nor Christianity has been able to get rid of such practices 'so it need not surprise us if Islam has not been more successful' (1954: 9). Simpson also records that aloes, myrtle and palm fronds were frequently placed above graves in various areas of the Near East, and that flowers were grown over graves in Turkey and Iran (1995: 247).

Besides the practical importance of such information, perhaps of greatest significance to the archaeologist is that it can be seen how all aspects of death and funerary rites in Islam can be imbued with a deep significance, beyond the act of merely disposing of the dead. They can be tied with, and inextricable from, life. But how could the significance of the apple or the colour green in a funerary context be guessed at without the ethnographic and historical accounts? When does a pebble become an apple, for example? The truth is that it would be extremely difficult, if not impossible, to reconstruct this solely from archaeological evidence.

The Archaeology of Paradise

The final aspect of material culture associated with death and burial which will be touched upon here is the Islamic garden. Although the archaeology of paradise might seem a strange concept, within Islam man-made versions exist in the Islamic garden. This is more than a random collection of plants, buildings and watercourses; it is structured by 'sacred geography' and concepts of the afterlife, and can, as we have seen with the Taj Mahal, form the setting for a tomb. The significance of the garden as a metaphor for paradise is shown in the Qur'an, where gardens are frequently alluded to, or explicitly described, as in *surah* 55 (The Merciful), where the four gardens of paradise are described thus: 'But for those that fear the majesty of their Lord there are two gardens...planted with shady trees...Each is watered by a flowing spring...And besides these there shall be two other gardens...of darkest green...A gushing fountain shall flow in each.' The origins of the paradise garden predate Islam and, as Moynihan notes, 'the English word "paradise" is simply a transliteration of the old Persian word *"pairidaeza"* referring to a walled garden' (1980: 1). The ancient Persian belief in the world divided into four by two axes with a pool at the intersection, the 'spring of life', gave rise to the *chahar-bagh* or 'fourfold' garden (Dickie 1976). This is a motif found represented on ceramics dating from as early as 4,000 BCE

(Wilber 1979: 3), with the earliest Persian garden or park yet known dating from around the sixth century BCE at the palace of Pasargadae near Isfahan (Brookes 1987: 31).

The incorporation of Persia into the Muslim world 'allowed the concept of the Persian garden to be carried to Syria, Egypt and the Maghrib' (Pinder Wilson 1976: 73). Thus similar gardens developed in many regions of the Muslim world (see studies in MacDougall and Ettinghausen 1976), with a physical form usually consisting of a square or rectangular unit divided into four by two crossing axes, often watercourses. At the centre, if a funerary garden, would be the tomb, so that the deceased could continue to enjoy the pleasures of the garden and also 'foretaste heavenly bliss' (Dickie 1976: 90–1, 1978: 47; Schimmel 1976: 18). Otherwise a pavilion might be placed in the same position. Perhaps the greatest examples of Islamic gardens dating from the medieval period are those of Persia, India and Spain; some survive to this day, others have been excavated and reconstructed. An example of the latter is provided by the excavations in the Alcazar in Seville where, Dickie notes, pollen analysis showed that orange trees had been planted in each corner of the four flower-beds (1976: 98), which were themselves sunk to a level of 2 m below the height of the walkways (Ruggles 1993: 167). This use of elevated walkways between the quadrants of the garden created the impression of walking on a floral carpet 'with flowers instead of threads' (Dickie 1976: 100).

The creation, maintenance and even access to gardens was obviously beyond much of the population. Rulers such as Babur, the founder of the Mughal dynasty, might create gardens almost wherever they went (Moynihan 1980), but this was not an option open to everyone. Therefore gardens were created on carpets which could contain representations of all the features of real gardens: plants, pools, watercourses, birds and fish (Ellis 1982: 15–17). According to Goody, 'gardens became a standard theme of the Oriental carpet used by nomads, peasants and city-dwellers alike. Few could have gardens; most could have carpets, which do not need watering and flower all year round' (1993: 112). The Islamic garden as a metaphor for paradise functioned so successfully for all strata of society partly as a reaction to the arid environment found across much of the geographical range of the Muslim world. As Dickie notes (1976), the Arabs amplified the Persian idea through their fear of death, dryness and desert. Moreover, the garden can be seen to signify much more than just a physical setting for displaying plants and elegant architecture. In this instance it is something to enjoy, but can also be a physical reflection of the commonly held Muslim understanding of paradise, which can be entertained by all classes of society throughout the Muslim world.

Summary and Conclusions

The preceding examples, drawn from the archaeological, ethnographic and historical literature, have shown the diversity which exists, both in meaning and form, in Muslim funerary practices which certainly involve more than just disposal of the dead. The living, the deceased and their myriad varieties of funerary monuments can be inextricably interlinked in ways more complex than an archaeologist, for reasons of interpretative simplicity, would perhaps like to acknowledge. The deceased can be used by the living, and the living can be used by the deceased, not for any single reason, but for many – economic, religious, political and social. Numerous agendas, needs, hopes and emotions are expressed and, one trusts, fulfilled through the medium of funerary ceremonies and monuments.

What, then, does this contribute to our understanding of funerary archaeology in general? In short, it is apparently impossible to assign any one 'universal' interpretation to a burial, even within a supposedly 'clear-cut category', such as Islam. The burial cannot be neatly categorized or separated as something clinical, as merely a way of disposing of the dead or as only an arena for the display of social status, removed from the individual, either the dead or living. As we have seen, death forms a part of life: the corpse can form a communal focus; imagery of the afterlife can serve as an instructive device; tombs are built to serve a variety of purposes; and funerary epigraphy is utilized in many different ways. The diversity found in one example of funerary archaeology, within the spectrum of Muslim death and burial, is quite phenomenal, and this perhaps should be more frequently remembered by archaeologists concerned with the application of cross-cultural 'catch-all' models.

Within the context of the archaeology of religion, what has been learnt? The point made by Renfrew (1994) that the study of the disposal of the dead is too often divorced from religion by archaeologists, was referred to in the first section. Death and funerary practices are in most cases 'serviced' by some form of religious rite, or are incorporated within the religious whole, for, as part of the human condition, we usually require something more than just disposing of what fast becomes a putrefying and distasteful hazard to health. This object was once personalized, as relative or friend, and religion can provide a means of coming to terms with grief and loss.

To adopt a polarized approach, whereby the disposal of the dead and religion are separated out, is wrong. It severely restricts interpretative possibilities and does not reflect reality.

Finally, what conclusions are there to be drawn from a study of funerary practices within the archaeology of Islam? It can be seen that 'diversity' and 'complexity' are again the keywords, and the recognition of this diversity supports the notion that within our conceptual frameworks we need to incorporate the 'multiple centres of Islam', rather than a defined 'core and periphery' (see chapter 1). But within the range of Muslim death and burial practices there are common identifying characteristics and a unifying structure; Muslim tradition and dogma tend to act over the whole, and orthodoxy is apparent. To the archaeologist, the overall recognition criteria would be the essentially uniform treatment of the corpse within the grave. A Muslim burial should be recognizable in the archaeological record. It is above ground that we begin to see the egalitarian nature of Muslim burial become corrupted in certain instances; yet below ground one is still a good Muslim.

What of this diversity today? What are the lessons for the Islamic archaeologist looking at funerary practices in the future? The increased 'franchise' of Islam means that its material culture correlates can now be found in a wider geographical area than ever before: Muslim burials will be encountered in Berlin, London and Washington. Yet, it is possible that the regional identity which has characterized much of this discussion will not be encountered by the archaeologist of the future. In certain respects it might be easier to identify a Muslim buried in the 1990s, eight hundred years hence, than one buried eight hundred years ago. Increasing standardization of material culture has occurred, reflecting a general world-wide trend facilitated by easier communications and a homogeneous global media, allied with a desire to present a unified face to a more hostile non-Muslim world and increased Islamic revivalism and fundamentalism (Ali 1996). Thus, though dogma might be fixed, the all-important material culture remains resulting from Muslim death and burial cannot be regarded as static and unchanging.

7

The Community Environment

'I swear by this city (and you are a resident of this city), by the begetter
and all whom he begot: We created man to try him with afflictions.
                                                          Qur'an. The City 90: 1–4

A consideration of the kinds of environment in which Muslim life
finds expression, and its possible archaeological implications, will
bring together many of the elements discussed in preceding chapters,
for a settlement is a conglomeration of domestic and other structures.
All of these have been considered in some detail, and are here placed
in context, settlements varying from villages to cities and the wider
landscape as well.

Rapoport makes the important point that 'houses, settlements, and
landscapes are products of the same cultural system and world view,
and are therefore parts of the single system' (1969: 73). Just as we
viewed the domestic environment as a social construct, so should we
see the settlement. This does not necessarily mean that a 'culturally
deterministic' approach is being proposed; on the contrary, the factors
which can underlie settlement form are many – environmental, economic and so on – but a social component must also be included.
Somewhat surprisingly, archaeological studies of settlements, landscapes and environments have until recently infrequently considered
such social, sacred or symbolic factors as of great importance (see
Bender 1993). This is in obvious contrast with the archaeological
studies of the domestic environment which have already been discussed (see, for example, Locock 1994; Parker Pearson and Richards
1994, and chapter 3); to quote Rapoport, 'man lives in the whole
settlement of which the house is only a part' (1969: 69). To neglect
this area emphasizes what Rykwert has termed 'the poverty of much

urbanistic discourse', whereby occupied space is studied only 'in physical terms of occupation and amenity' and the 'psychological space, the cultural, the juridical, the religious' are neglected (1976: 24).

Relevant archaeological studies might consider spatial patterning with reference to economic geography (Fletcher 1977; Hodges 1987) or to geography in general (Wagstaff 1987), but until recently it was again anthropologists, historians, geographers and art historians who frequently emphasized the possible social, symbolic and sacred aspects of settlements; iconography of landscape (Cosgrove and Daniels 1988); cosmological reasoning underpinning settlement form (Lebeuf 1967); the place of the settlement within sacred geography (Ortiz 1969); the possible significance of the centrality of either settlements or components thereof (Wheatley 1971) (see also Rapoport 1969: 50; Parker Pearson and Richards 1994: 12–19, for other examples). Recently, however, archaeologists have come to consider settlements and the whole environment as more than products of economic decisions, but as social constructs (Hodder 1990).

Muslim Cities and Settlements

Study of the Muslim city

As the Muslim urban settlement is one of the best-studied aspects of Muslim material culture, it is given prominence in the following discussion. However, at the same time it is recognized that to reflect only on the city, at the expense of the town, village or camp, is wrong, but it is hoped that this will in part be excused by the large-scale absence of archaeological studies concerned with these other settlement types.

The Muslim city has in the past provided a convenient unit of study and, based upon a limited number of examples, mainly drawn from North Africa and the Near East, wide-ranging generalizations were made as to the overall character of the Muslim city everywhere. These studies were one of the first manifestations of the orientalist approach, whereby the structure of the city was defined in terms of religious requirements, and a similar form was said to exist from Morocco to Indonesia. This process of the creation of a stereotypical Muslim city has been examined by a number of scholars, most notably by Bonine (1977) and Abu-Lughod (1987) and, more recently, region by region across the Muslim world (excluding sub-Saharan Africa and south and South-east Asia) by Haneda and Miura (1994). The stereotype created, based on North African or sometimes

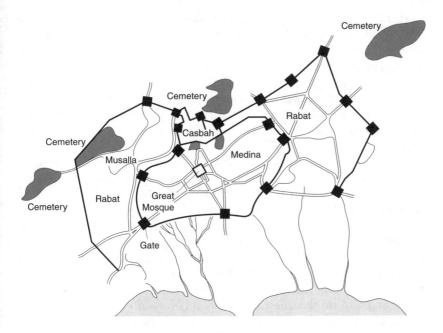

Figure 7.1 Stereotypical city layout based on Tunis (after Hakim 1986: 59)

Syrian examples, comprised a standard kit of elements: the *medina*, or central urban entity, within which was the *casbah* or walled citadel, a city within the city containing the ruler's residence, mosque, barracks, stores and so on. The *medina* would be walled with several gates, and perhaps surrounded by *rabad* or *rabat*, outer suburbs. The inhabitants lived in distinct quarters according to ethnic or economic background in groups of courtyard houses connected by winding alleyways and narrow streets, supposedly characteristic of the 'oriental' or Islamic city (see figure 7.1). The *medina* would also contain a number of core elements: the Friday mosque, other local mosques, *suq* or *suqs* (markets) arranged spatially according to the goods sold, baths, hostels for travellers, schools, shops, cemeteries perhaps (usually outside the city) and all the other prerequisites of urban life.

The process by which this was achieved has been aptly described by Abu-Lughod (1987: 155) as an *isnad*, a chain of transmitters, in this instance a succession of Western scholars. W. Marcais (1928), according to Abu-Lughod, initiated this approach, followed by G. Marcais (1945) and, most influentially, G. Von Grunebaum (1955), who used the North African examples in a generalized way and applied these to the creation of an idealized 'Islamic city'. This process has perpetuated to this day in many respects, as in Hakim's (1986) volume on Arabic Islamic cities (admittedly North African in focus). Various reasons to account for this 'created' Muslim city have been proposed: 'to attempt to explain everything in terms of a dichotomy between an advanced Europe and a stagnant Islamic World' (Haneda 1994: 4) or, alternatively, as Bonine reports (but does not agree with), as a model which evolved with a central premiss that 'Islam is an urban religion because only in a town can faithful Muslims adhere to all requirements of the Qur'an and *shari'ah*' (1977: 148).

The view that Islam is only truly at home in an urban setting is often held; for instance, Sopher remarks on 'the strong predilection for the city which runs through Islam' (1967: 28). This is often based upon notions of legalistic interpretation; for example, the requirement of certain legal schools that valid Friday prayers must take place with a congregation of over 40 people, which, as Lapidus notes, is non-sensical, as neither 40 nor two 'make a place a city as opposed to a village or other settlement' (1973a: 60). Lapidus adopts a sensible approach to urbanism, both in its place within the wider environment, and also on the question of Islam being only an urban religion; nomads or village dwellers are no less good Muslims for their settlement types. It is due more to 'historical circumstance' (Lapidus 1973a) that Islam and cities became the environment in which the legal schools were established, and the surroundings in which the early Muslim conquerors initially settled, either in newly founded cities or pre-existing conquered ones.

But is it necessary to deny completely the existence of any common features within Islamic cities or Muslim settlements, and to deny religion as a structuring principle to a greater or lesser degree? As with much 'revisionist' scholarship, there is the danger that the opposite to the equally inaccurate generalizing approach is achieved and diversity is pushed to the fore to the exclusion of any common patterns. Perhaps a 'mix and match' approach is best here, whereby certain common features could be expected, but these will by no means be the same in every situation (if anything, questions of scale will rule this out: a village will obviously not have all the facilities of a city). A complex of factors underlie the structuring of a Muslim settlement, and these will be discussed in greater detail below.

To press wholly for specific local circumstances as the primary agent behind the establishment and structure of the larger Muslim city would appear to be flawed. Topography, climate, economy and pre-Islamic traditions were all of obvious importance, and the city was not structured solely according to religious requirements, but nor need they play an insignificant part. If we accept that a domestic environment can be structured according to religious or resultant social requirements, why not the larger city as well? If the domestic environment can be regarded as both the outcome and perpetuator of social codes and requirements (see chapter 3), so the city or settlement can be so regarded, in many instances, on a larger scale. To use a general point made in another context by Gilsenan, 'space is crucial in thinking about culture and ideology because it is where ideology and culture take on physical existence and representations' (1982: 187). The Muslim settlement is an ordered and created space, and not neutral from society or individuals, but it is not an isolated entity either. Obviously, the settlement is defined or bounded, and how this is achieved varies, but at the same time it is also an integral part of its surroundings. Too often this has been ignored from an archaeological perspective, and settlement examined as somehow divorced from its surroundings. What we need is a 'total approach' whereby the settlement is considered as part of the whole, connected physically to the landscape and the environment.

There is also the issue of 'regionalism' which is a factor in much research into Muslim urbanism. Archaeological research has contributed greatly to the debate on Muslim urbanism in Central Asia thanks to several decades of research by Soviet scholars (Komatsu 1994), whereas in Turkey, until very recently, the opposite was true. What is fashionable in terms of research in one area need not be in another, leading to a frequent lack of a comprehensive overview, or what has been termed the absence of common paradigms in favour of particularist studies (Haneda and Miura 1994).

Definition and origins of the Muslim city

Definitions of what constitutes a city, a town or a village vary immensely. Is it size, number of inhabitants, administrative nature, facilities? General definitions do not always seem to apply (see, for example, Weber 1958) in the Muslim world. Kisaichi (1994: 66), for instance, argues that certain Muslim Uighur 'towns' in China lack clear boundaries between themselves and the surrounding farm lands so that 'it might be more accurate to call it [sic] an enormous rural village'. However, Hakim (1986: 56) uses more orthodox definitions based upon administrative criteria and drawn from Arabic historical sources such as al-Maqadisi (died 990) who differentiates the misr (plural amsar), metropolis, qasabah, (plural qasabat), provincial capital, medina (plural mudun), provincial or market town, and qaryah (plural qura), village. Hakim also considers that urban settlements should include a Friday mosque, a suq, and a governor and/or qadi.

General common sense would appear to be a fairly straightforward guide to the type of settlement being considered; size is obviously important, but beyond this it would seem that any type of restrictive definition as to settlement form could be challenged with examples that do not conform. However, many larger Muslim towns and cities prior to the modern age can be recognized on the basis of certain criteria, and these have been divided into various types in the Near and Middle East. These include the created cities (often garrisons) of the early Muslim conquests; the *amsar*, Fustat and Kufah for example, and the adapted pre-existing cities of antiquity, such as Jerusalem and Damascus (Stern 1970: 30; Elisséeff 1980: 91). This created/adapted model is simple but in many ways effective, as it can equally be applied outside the heartlands, and thus provides a generalizing element within a mass of diversity.

Yet a Muslim city in West Africa has different local antecedents from those of Arabia, as does one in Central Asia or Indonesia (for the latter see Behrend 1984). In Arabia, Whitcomb has suggested that the city 'may be an urban type based on tribal organization and its structure, like the tribal society which produced it, was an important element in the spread of Islam' (1996: 46). The form of the Muslim city does not owe its origins solely to Islam even in Arabia; it has a pre-Islamic heritage. The walled citadel, a recurring feature already mentioned, is not a Muslim creation but found in earlier cities in the Byzantine and Sasanian worlds. Similarly, the frequently encountered central cluster of religious and administrative buildings is a focus of power which predates Islam. Habitation in quarters according to ethnic affiliation or social category was not an Islamic invention, nor could a seemingly random town plan of myriad winding alleys be accepted as the result of Qur'anic injunction or the implementation of *shar'iah*. Islamic cities were not new phenomena as regards their form, but the result of a variety of factors, new and old, and were not solely dictated by religious requirements.

Archaeological recognition of Muslim cities and settlements

Could there then be said to be a Muslim city? And is this archaeologically recognizable? There is, or can be, but this does not mean that the sort of criteria outlined by Hakim (1986: 60–90) will be found in every instance, though they can allow the archaeological recognition of Muslim cities. Typological approaches are weak: not every city will have a walled citadel, surrounded by a *medina* and outer suburbs, defined by quarters of courtyard houses with an emphasis upon inward orientation, alongside ward mosques, with a central mosque/palace and administration complex either inside or outside of the citadel. *Suqs* need not be centrally placed and graded according to the trades or goods being sold and the degree to which they might be considered polluting; *madrasahs* (religious schools), cemeteries, water-storage facilities, caravanserais, *hammams* (baths) and *maristans* (hospitals) need not all be present. Only in a few selective contexts, as in North Africa and Islamic Spain where a great degree of uniformity in city type appears to have existed, may near-complete examples of the model be found.

Yet it is true to say that many of these elements can be present, and that these constitute a Muslim city, as opposed to a non-Muslim one. It cannot be disputed that core characteristic elements exist, even if only reduced to the simplest form of a mosque and Muslim burials in a settlement (the burials more usually surrounding it). It is these more basic criteria, which are more likely to be applicable to smaller towns and villages, which have been neglected thus far in the discussion, and which could allow their archaeological recognition. Certain criteria do exist which set apart a Muslim settlement from a non-Muslim one from Senegal to Saudi Arabia, from Kazakhstan to Indonesia. They are far from mirror images of each other, and are subject to many structuring factors other than religious requirements, but at the same time exhibit certain aspects in common which relate to a mutual religion.

A much looser structure is needed in assessing the Muslim settlement, and its archaeological recognition; some core features will be present, but a pre-ordained blue-print does not exist. Possible keys to identification might include all or any of the above, but even these changed over time. For example, it might be possible to say that narrow streets and alleyways with courtyard houses having largely blank façades and multiple dead ends were due to Muslim concerns with privacy and the protection of the family, but in some instances this might be due to the climate (providing shade) or, as Bulliett (1975: 224) has suggested, to the existence of a society without wheels, rendering wider streets unnecessary. The invocation of a single factor to explain structuring features behind Muslim settlements is often impossible, but neither should economic or practical necessity be given precedence over social or religious needs.

Social Dimension of the Muslim Settlement

The settlement can act both as a mirror and sustainer of social codes. It is an active area of material culture and may provide information on the societies it maintains and replicates, something which may be approachable by the archaeologist. Once again utilizing archaeological and other sources of evidence, we will see that the settlement, our final area of the archaeology of Islam, need in no way conform to a mundane stereotype, but can be informative, vibrant and, unfortunately, elusive.

Authority at a central core

The relationship between sacred and secular authority in Islam, frequently referred to, and its importance stressed, especially in the Early Islamic period, is manifest in the Muslim city and, much less frequently, in other forms of settlement as well (perhaps understandably, as rulers tended towards inhabiting, or having grow up around them, larger settlements). Yet more than just a simple juxtaposition of mosque and palace as a focal point of sacred and secular authority is sometimes apparent. A significant, but not typical, example of a central core is provided by Caliph al-Mansur's round city at Baghdad. This circular city, which though only occupied between 762 and 766, and reconstructed from historical data (excavation has yet to be carried out), provides an 'image of rule', of how al-Mansur perceived his authority and how this changed over time. The city was a circular double walled 'citadel', surrounded by a moat, with at its centre the caliph's palace and the congregational mosque, expressing 'the intimate relationship between religion and state' (El-Ali 1970: 93) (see figure 7.2). Surrounding this was an inner ring of buildings with the offices of state, and the residences of the Caliph's children, slaves and bodyguards, and a further outer ring, the details of which are hazy, but which would have been occupied by other functionaries and soldiers (Lassner 1970a,b).

Although this complex was recognizably Muslim, expressed if anything by the congregational mosque, it was also the continuation of pre-Islamic traditions. Lassner (1970b) records that the general features of the round city are found at pre-Islamic sites in both Iraq and Iran, while Beckwith (1984) suggests that it was the culmination of the fusion of a mix of traditions, most notably Iranian royal ones, with the design being the work of a converted Central Asian priest (see also Creswell 1952: 94–9). Leaving aside its ancestry, the central notion of the mosque/palace core was not new in Baghdad. It is found in certain Umayyad government palaces, as at Kufah (Lassner 1970b: 133), but the concept of centralizing authority is almost a universal; in the ancient Chinese city, the seat of secular authority was likewise placed centrally (Wheatley 1971: 462). The theme of

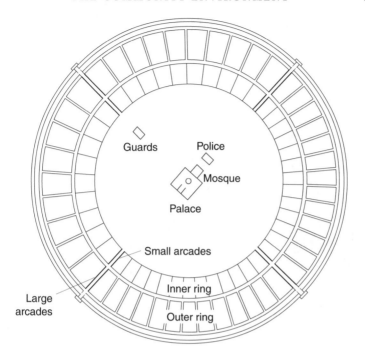

Guards
Police
Mosque
Palace

Small arcades

Inner ring

Large arcades

Outer ring

Figure 7.2   Reconstruction of the round city, Baghdad (from Lassner 1970b: 207)

amalgamating power in a central core occurs through history, and to give it an Islamic identity is wrong, though an Islamic version of it was certainly developed.

What is also of importance is that the round city in Baghdad was used as a means of unifying the disparate ethnic groups which formed the population. Large suburbs spread in all directions, containing Arabs (sedentaries and nomads), Africans and Persians, with the round city as the core, separate, but 'vocal' at the same time. To achieve this, the pre-Islamic heritage was skilfully utilized by al-Mansur. The circular plan and other aspects of 'visual language' which the local population understood were used to aid his search for legitimacy and as a 'tangible' expression of authority (Lassner 1970b: 131). The focus of authority both spiritual and secular was centred in the round city, and the caliph welded both secular and temporal power in himself through the fusion of palace and mosque, a further factor which helped in creating unity in the population. Grabar explained the round city as 'a conscious attempt to make an

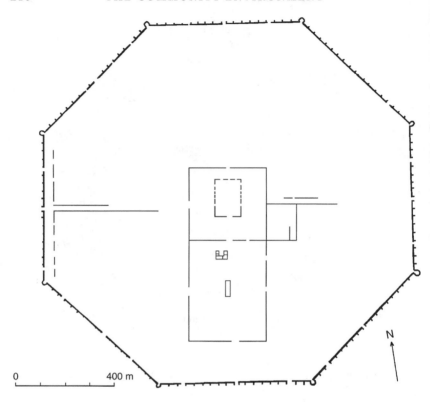

Figure 7.3   The Octagon of Husn al-Qadisiyya (after Northedge and Falkner 1987: 152)

entity that would symbolize the total rule of the Muslim prince' (1973: 71). This was perhaps of some success as a round plan was also used at the town of Qsar es-Seghir in Morocco, and the so-called 'octagon of Husn al-Qadisiyya' at Samarra, built by Harun al-Rashid at the end of the eighth century, also drew upon al-Mansur's round city for inspiration – a walled octagonal enclosure of over 1,500 metres in diameter, with a gate set in each side (see figure 7.3). But it was the interior where parallels with Baghdad were to be seen: 'with its large area, avenues, central square, mosque and palace, the Octagon can be seen to be a copy of the arrangements of Mansur's Round City of Baghdad' (Northedge and Falkner 1987: 155; see also Northedge et al. 1990).

The concept of power represented as an architectural component has been studied as a mirror of historical changes in Muslim society by Bacharach (1991), who has charted three phases in how the 'loci' of power changed over time. In the first administrative and mosque complexes of the early Islamic period, physical proximity of the *dar al-imara* and the mosque illustrated 'the inter-related importance of the roles of governor and religious leader' (1991: 126). These centres were located within and on the same 'geographic plane' as the areas of population, a factor which altered in the second phase when the religious, social and educational requirements of the population began to be met by the main urban mosques. Authority began to change, with the *ulama* becoming responsible for guiding the 'Islamic way of life' especially in the cities; palace complexes were now placed at some distance from the population (as at Samarra in the ninth century) and, according to Bacharach (1991: 121), this 'second era coincides with the transformation of urban centres into Muslim cities'.

The third phase in the late eleventh and twelfth centuries sees the appearance of the citadel as 'a major locus of Muslim rule'. This was perhaps related to the fact that the users of the citadels were often 'ethnically alien' to those they ruled, the Seljuks in Anatolia for example. The factor of height as well as distance also appears to become important; rulers were now often above the ruled, as at the Alhambra in Granada. Thus Bacharach's analysis has shown that changes in authority and even the nature of society can be manifest in settlement form, with distance and topography utilized as a signifier of power in a manner which could be archaeologically distinct, and which also exposes the flaws in models which state the existence of a citadel as a given everywhere from the first appearance of the idealized 'Islamic city'.

Class, society and ethnicity

To take this analysis one stage further, beyond examining the role and manifestations of authority, it is necessary also to consider the settlement as a metaphor for society. As with many of the areas considered in this volume, there is usually a departure point between ideals and reality, and in this instance the ideal is represented by *ummah*, the whole Muslim community devoid of class or racial distinctions. The existence of this seems to conflict with practical realities. From the outset, Muslim cities were composed of disparate ethnic groups, as at Baghdad, but also manifest at Fustat, one of the *amsar* or garrison cities founded in 640 and the predecessor of Cairo. A hierarchy existed in the first conquest situation: at the top were members of the Prophet Muhammad's tribe, the Quraysh, and the Ansar, the Prophet's supporters, then the other Arab Muslim tribes, and below them non-Arab Muslims (Persians, blacks and so on), and finally non-Muslims. These patterns were visible in the great semi-circular camp city of tents and reed and clay huts grouped into 30–40 tribal and multi-tribal units, which quickly grew more permanent (Abu-Lughod 1971; Kubiak 1982). To help create *ummah*, the Umayyad rulers practised a 'conscious policy to level tribal differences' (Kubiak 1982: 216), as apparent in residential patterns, through, for example, the promotion of a multi-tribal central quarter, Ahl ar-Raya, the place of government and the congregational mosque.

However, it can be argued that this did not usually proceed much beyond an ideal. People usually live with those they know best or feel at ease with, ethnically, socially or as co-religionists, and it is likely that residence according to ethnic or other affiliation is probably to be expected in many cases, but whether this will always be manifest in distinct quarters cannot be certain without evaluating each particular case. Nevertheless, this type of residence pattern is to be found frequently in the archaeological record and attested in historical sources. At Otrar in Kazakhstan, for example, where Tamerlane died in 1405, excavations in levels dated to between the sixteenth and eighteenth centuries uncovered distinct quarters composed of units of between six and 15 houses inhabited by people of different social groups and, according to the excavator, perhaps grouped by family (Baipakov 1992: 108). In certain instances, tribal marks on the pottery even allowed a reconstruction of the ethnicity of the inhabitants.

Numerous other examples could be provided, and anthropology offers more to show notions of class, ethnicity or family impinging upon the ideal of *ummah* in settlement patterns. Gerholm's research in the town of Manakha in the Yemen has already been mentioned in the discussion of the domestic environment, and is equally pertinent to the settlement, with the townscape described as 'a mirror of the social order' (1977: 161). Topography and elevation were used to express both authority and social distinctions (reminiscent of the way the tower house in Yemen functioned in the vertical axis), with the noble families in Upper Manakha, the rank and file or 'middle strata' in Lower Manakha, and the low-ranking townspeople, not considered as part of tribal society, even further below, a material construct of society across the settlement. Similar patterning was evident in the form of the traditional Palestinian village up until the 1930s. Amiry and Tamari (1989) relate how each village was made up of a number of separate quarters named after patrilineal descent groups, with again the more influential groups inhabiting the elevated areas, and the others in the lower quarters.

What is apparent from these examples is that, once again, to isolate one over-riding reason why people should live with their peers does not work. In one instance, it could be due to religion (Christians living apart from Muslims, for example); in another, by ethnicity or class in an all-Muslim settlement. It could also be because of stigma attached to occupation, as with blacksmiths or tanners frequently living in their own distinct area on the edge of a settlement because they are subject to fears and prejudices or because of the polluting aspects of their work. Various factors underlie residential patterning within the Muslim settlement, which often shows that a religiously egalitarian Muslim community is more of an ideal than a practical reality. This is something which archaeology is ideally suited to investigating.

Spatial domains

The notion of spatial domains – public, semi-private and private spheres – can be of great importance as we saw with the domestic environment. In the idealized 'Islamic city' rigidly defined boundaries between different spatial domains exist: the public mosque and market, the semi-private quarters with their lockable gates, and the private domestic environment of the houses themselves, separated into public and private areas. This idealized model has, as with most generalizations, exceptions. Differences in settlement form, as have been described for Yugoslavia and India, will preclude the uniform existence of semi-private quarters in every instance, and even the *suq* does not always qualify as a wholly public space, but is sometimes gender restricted as at Riyadh (Saudi Arabia), where in 1917 Philby recorded a female *suq* alongside the ruler's palace (1920: 162) (see figure 7.4). Which space can be considered as falling within the category of private or public can, as was discussed in chapter 3, depend upon gender.

It is perhaps not surprising that if a public/private spatial divide is evident in the domestic environment, it should also be visible on a larger scale in the community environment composed of agglomerations of these units. These larger units, while they signal an evident spatial concern, could not then be expected to sit neutrally in their relationship with the other components of a settlement. A great degree of spatial coding does or did exist in many Muslim settlements, and is manifest archaeologically, as well as recorded by anthropologists and historians.

Gerholm (1977) gives an anthropological perspective on these issues. He describes how in his study area in the Yemen the public

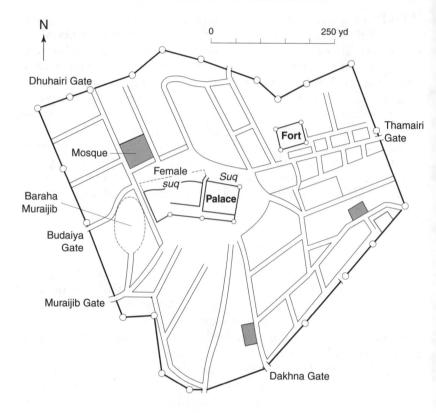

N

0   250 yd

Dhuhairi Gate

Mosque

Baraha
Muraijib

Budaiya
Gate

Muraijib Gate

Female
suq

Suq

Palace

Fort

Thamairi
Gate

Dakhna Gate

Figure 7.4   Plan of Riyadh, Saudi Arabia (after Philby 1920: 162)

sphere (male) is associated with the congregational mosque, the *suq*, the administrative buildings, the *mafraj* (described in chapter 3), and even the football field. Within this public sphere, status considerations are important, and gradations emerge between, for example, the market, where social status is linked with how little you are seen to do, and the mosque, which is less hierarchical (1977: 176); this information could not be deduced from the archaeological record alone. A similar case exists for semi-private and private space. Gated town quarters could be used to demarcate spatial domains, and Akbar (1993) relates how gates could be used to maintain privacy and identity. Even subquarters within the larger entity could themselves be shut off to create a kind of communal living room for residents (Akbar 1993: 145). The sequence of gates from the public one in the city wall, to the quarter gate which is less public, to the subquarter gate which is in turn semi-private, and, finally, to the house entrance which is regarded as private, all demarcate different spatial zones, patterning which should be kept in mind when considering a Muslim settlement.

Archaeologically, the existence of spatial demarcation in Muslim settlements has been well recorded, a particularly useful example being the walled town of Qsar es-Seghir in Morocco. Here the Muslim occupation levels of the twelfth to mid-fifteenth centuries are overlain by a period of Portuguese occupation dated to between the mid-fifteenth and mid-sixteenth centuries, therefore providing two distinct settlement patterns for comparison. According to Redman, 'the Qsar es-Seghir sequence provides a fascinating glimpse of a stepwise series of modifications ultimately leading to the total transformation of an Islamic town into a European-Portuguese town' (1986: 165). These included a greater concern by the Portuguese with public space, represented by a 25 per cent increase in area covered by streets and plazas. Focus was placed upon decorating house entrance ways in comparison to the plain Muslim ones. The centralized core of the Muslim town, consisting of the congregational mosque, public bath and market, while the buildings obviously changed, was also de-emphasized in the Portuguese town. This was interpreted as reflecting a more individualized and segmented system, 'probably resulting from a diminished sense of shared values and less centralised tradesmen' (Redman 1986: 246).

The example from Qsar es-Seghir illustrates that a Muslim settlement plan when juxtaposed with a Christian one can be archaeologically recognizable. As with the mosque, so with settlement form, archaeology can enable differentiation between different 'religious layers'. Interestingly, such a change in the nature of public and private space was also recorded in Spain after the Christian re-conquest, where Violich mentions that more direct access to the church, plaza and market was often opened up (1962: 174). But it should also be noted that a correlation between the presence of a Muslim community and an emphasis upon private space at the expense of public space does not always hold true. Changes in the use of space before the Muslim conquest were evident at Baysan (Bet Shean) in Palestine, with a decline in the use of public space evident with the abandonment of the amphitheatre. Pre-Muslim 'Christianization' had an impact upon urban life and was also 'reflected by the city plan and architecture' (Tsafrir and Foerster 1994: 101).

Having seen that a Muslim settlement overlain by a Christian one was archaeologically recognizable, it is interesting to look at the reverse process to ensure that we are not observing any peculiar anomalies. The second case study is Bierman's (1991) architectural analysis of how Ottoman occupation transformed Venetian Crete. The capital, Heraklion (Candia, Qandiye), was founded by the Arabs in 827, captured by the Byzantines, and sold by the Franks to the Venetians in 1204, who occupied it until the Ottomans took the city in 1669, following on from their successful capture of the towns of Khania and Retimo. The Venetians had literally 'Venetianized' Retimo and Candia by building 'provincial versions' of the Basilica, Piazza San Marco and the Palazzo Ducale; thus, in Bierman's words, 'the central monumental core of these Cretan cities was developed to replicate that of Venice itself, thereby reinforcing and perpetuating Venetian political and religious values and attitudes by their presence and their spatial relationships' (1991: 57).

Prior to the Ottoman occupation a distinct spatial system was in place. This was not in itself indigenous, and was certainly at odds with Ottoman concepts of spatial construction. Hence the Venetian spatial overlay was in turn 'Ottomanized' in what Bierman terms an 'external' and 'internal' manner. The former was effected most prominently through the siting of the Sultan's *cami*, the main mosque complex, visible from afar, which in both Candia and Retimo correlated with the position of former Christian buildings, a Franciscan monastery church and a San Marco replica respectively. Conspicuous spatial positioning was not an Ottoman prerogative, but the focus of the cities was altered to centre on the Sultan's marker. Cemeteries, fountains, church to mosque conversions and *madrasahs* were all used in the process of spatial transformation, especially through the alteration of the Venetian piazza system, thereby allowing access and sight of the Grand Vezir's mosque, the former Greek Orthodox cathedral (Bierman 1991: 66). Thus it can be seen that spatial alteration to reflect prevailing religious belief and social/cultural requirements can obviously be a two-way process. Yet it should also be noted that, although a Muslim spatial system was being created, this was also very much a specifically Ottoman construct, with their distinctive *cami* and cemeteries proclaiming both Ottoman and the individual identity of the founders.

Nomad settlements

So far the discussion has created an imbalance in favour of sedentary city-dwellers. These, along with the inhabitants of towns and villages, do not have a monopoly on settlement and Muslim society. Nomads, as has been discussed already, are widespread in the Muslim world and their settlements should be studied just as much as cities, towns and villages, even if they are often more ephemerally fixed. The archaeological recognition of nomadic settlements has already been touched upon with reference to the domestic environment (see chapter 3), and besides tent outlines and the other evidence already mentioned, wells, corrals, storage facilities, all could indicate their former presence (see Cribb 1991). The frequently cyclical nature of nomadic pastoralist activities of larger base camps and smaller way stations might be recognizable; differences between camel, cattle and horse keepers might equally be evident (see Cribb 1991). It is not my aim here to exhaust the possibilities which a Muslim nomadic community might suggest for archaeology. Rather, two examples of settlement types with nomadic associations will be considered, as interesting case studies with a social emphasis: a 'Bedouin station', and the enigmatic *qusur* (singular *qasr*) or so-called 'desert castles', which are a feature of the Early Islamic period in parts of Syria and Jordan. Both have been suggested as having functioned in a variety of ways in nomadic society, symbolically and practically, and the two archaeologically investigated examples suggest possible frontier relationships between states and nomads.

The first site is ar-Risha in Jordan, separated by a distance of 3 km into ancient and modern, but surprisingly similar in character. Ancient ar-Risha, founded perhaps as early as 650 and lasting until the eleventh–twelfth centuries, is made up of a variety of structures: a mosque, houses of varying sizes, one with a reception area, and stables, about which tents must have been erected. It has been described as a 'steppic reflection' of the ideal Islamic city, containing all the necessary urban components and of approximately the same date as the first *amsar*, and it is claimed to offer an insight through architecture and settlement structure into Bedouin politics and polities (Helms 1990: 5, 131). It functioned, like its modern counterpart, where garages replace stables, as a service centre and stopping point but, more importantly, as physical testimony to 'direct diplomacy between the state and the tribes' (1990: 170). It drew upon pre-Islamic models, such as that provided by neighbouring Qasr Burqu, but used these in new ways through the transfer of diplomacy from the boundaries of the previous Byzantine state to the tribal territory. Thus, it can perhaps be suggested, it wholly rather than partially included a group of nomadic Bedouin within the new Umayyad state and its successors.

The second site is that of Qasr al-Hayr East in Syria, which, though differing in several respects from ar-Risha, has also been claimed to illustrate a concern with including the nomadic population within the larger Muslim community and state. Excavated over a number of years (Grabar et al. 1978), Qasr al-Hayr East was found to contain a variety of distinct components. These included a walled outer enclosure, 15 km in perimeter, and containing evidence of an attempt to ensure a permanent water supply through the use of underground channels leading to a water supply 25 km away. Within this was a 'large enclosure', interpreted as a *medina* containing several residences and a mosque, and a 'small enclosure' interpreted as a caravanserai. Created originally in the eighth century, and thus another Umayyad foundation, it was partially abandoned in the tenth century, reoccupied in areas in the twelfth century, abandoned again in the fourteenth century, with thereafter intermittent small-scale use continuing.

If the interpretations of the excavators are believed, it was created as 'a means for controlling and settling turbulent tribes' (1978: 157). This, it was suggested, was achieved through providing, besides facilities for travellers, a *medina*, which was a role model of central authority, a mosque, the symbol of a unified Muslim community, and a source of income from the water supply and the outer enclosure which could be used for pastoral activities. It could have become a focal point for periodic gatherings of nomads. The second phase of occupation was apparently divest of the symbolic function, if that is the correct term, as it became a 'motel town', with the service components coming to the fore. Therefore it is with the former phase that the greater interest would appear to rest, if Qasr al-Hayr did indeed function as an imprint of government within a tribal territory. Indeed, it is this visual imagery which would then appear to be of great significance, the 'transference' of stone architectural components from the urban centre, whose function is encapsulated, in a point made by Whitcomb, 'as definitional elements for an urban entity, rather like towered walls used as the symbol for cities on early maps' (1995: 491). It provided an image of the state, if anything, and, although it is only a hypothesis, it provides an interesting scenario regarding possible relations between nomads and the state.

A Total Approach: the Landscape

A settlement should not be divorced from its overall context, its surrounding physical environment. Nomadic populations, for example, are not autonomous. Relations with either rural or urban sedentary communities are common and mutual obligations and trading networks between these groups exist. Protection was often provided to caravans and town-dwellers by nomads, as in areas of Saudi Arabia until recently (Cole 1975). Town or city-dwellers can be linked to their rural sedentary counterparts through marketing networks, and the larger settlements can act as market and service centres (see chapter 5). Numerous permutations are possible, but the point is that these links exist and, although not specifically Muslim, their importance lies in the fact that the archaeology of Islam must be viewed as the sum, the totality of all these elements. To separate one element out, urban studies for instance, and to examine it on its own is frequently restricting, as is privileging the urban environment at the expense of looking at its place within the landscape.

Lapidus recognized that emphasizing dichotomies between city and country are not a useful paradigm (1973b: 21), and it is in evaluating these links that archaeologists can make a contribution (see Sjöström 1993; King and Cameron 1994). Physical links between settlement and surrounding area will exist in many instances, providing a body of material for the archaeologist. These can range from irrigation and water supply systems to field systems, nomad, trade and pilgrimage routes, and fortifications. All mechanisms by which the landscape can be tied together, settlement to settlement, nomads to sedentaries, feature to feature deserve study. Connecting landscape features are many, and we can look at water supply as an example. It is important as a necessity of life, subject to much technical ingenuity in its provision, as a 'landscape element' and also because it has a significance beyond the purely practical in Islam as was shown in the Muslim concept of paradise (see chapter 6).

Water supply

Many areas of the Muslim world are arid or semi-arid, and access to an adequate water supply is of particular importance; a variety of mechanisms have been developed to supply and store water. Although much of this technology predates Islam and cannot be said to be Muslim in character, it is intimately linked with a large part of the Muslim world from North Africa to Central Asia. Notable among the available traditional technologies are the 'horizontal wells', the *qanat, foggara, karez* and *falaj*, where water from a 'mother well', a vertical shaft, is channelled, often over a considerable distance, by a horizontal channel or conduit (slightly sloping and usually covered) to source. Secondary shafts are usually dug at measured intervals along the covered shafts for removal of debris and for ventilation, as with the *qanat*, for example, common in Iran (Cressey 1958; Goblot 1979; al-Hassan and Hill 1992). These are often highly visible in aerial photographs and provide a prime example of links between settlement and environment, with tentacles of *qanats* and roads stretching out from the larger settlements.

The very visibility of these systems lends them particularly to archaeological investigation. A good example is the study of the *falaj* and associated structures in various parts of Oman by Costa (1983), and the work by Wilkinson (1975, 1976, 1977) in the vicinity of the ninth–tenth century trade centre of Sohar, a site already mentioned in the context of Indian Ocean trade (see chapter 5). The stated aims of the latter project, in particular 'to describe the methods of water supply used and in general to understand how the land was used by the inhabitants of medieval Sohar' (1975: 159–60), are precisely what are often needed to tie Muslim settlements to their surroundings in a 'a total approach'. Also of interest would be relating the type of information provided by Brookes (1987) to the archaeological evidence derived from settlement studies. He describes the 'strict system of priorities' (Brookes 1987: 193) enforced as to water access from the *falaj* in Oman. Drinking had universal first priority both inside and outside a settlement; after drinking, inside a settlement, male bathing took priority, followed further downstream by female bathing, in turn succeeded by the place for washing the dead (mosques may have had their own access to water from the *falaj*), and finally for agricultural use.

Add to the hydraulic systems already described, waterwheels and equipment such as the Egyptian *shaduf*, a lever-type mechanism used to draw water, along with the range of options available for storing water – tanks, cisterns, wells and pools – and the material remains of this one aspect of settlement 'periphery' are many. Indeed, in one case the analysis of water technology has helped in totally rethinking the role of a settlement; the study of the settlement devoid of this component would have been wholly misleading. The site in question is Dahlak Kebir situated on the island of the same name off the Eritrean coast of the Red Sea. Dahlak Kebir is located in an extremely arid environment, yet functioned as a trade centre for several hundred years, and thus would have had not inconsiderable demands for water (Insoll 1996c, d). These were met by over a hundred cisterns cut out of the coral, of varying dimensions, and often linked to rock-hewn channels functioning as catchment systems to collect the sparse rains. Surprisingly, although the existence of this site has been known for many years, only one aspect has been adequately studied, the Arabic funerary inscriptions (Bassat 1893; Schneider 1983), thus providing a far from unique example of skewed analysis in favour of a single privileged component, divorced from context, and leaving the observer perhaps thinking that Dahlak Kebir functioned only as a city of the dead. Obviously it was wholly dependent on its surroundings for its very existence but this fact seems to have been ignored.

The significance of water beyond the practical in Islam is something a number of scholars allude to. At Qsar es-Seghir (Morocco), for example, alongside the evident spatial differences between the Muslim and Portuguese occupations, it was noticeable how the Portuguese did not display in the surviving evidence the same concerns for latrines, drains, sewers and washing facilities evident in the Islamic period (Redman 1986: 243). This does not necessarily mean that the Portuguese were particularly dirty, but could be connected with the emphasis upon cleanliness and purity which is a recurring feature in Islam, exemplified by ritual cleansing prior to prayer, which should take place five times a day (see chapter 2). A general preoccupation with hygiene is also something remarked upon by the excavators of Daulatabad, ancient Devgiri, in India (see plate 7.1). Well-constructed drains, latrines and pipes were all recorded, both to supply and dispose of water, leading Mate to remark that 'if cleanliness was next to godliness, here was a society that strove after it' (1983: 337).

The *hammam*, or bath-house, is a well-known feature of urban Muslim society indicative of the concern with cleanliness and copied or continued from Byzantine or Indian traditions. Examples have been found archaeologically, and are well attested architecturally in many areas of the Muslim world, though many are falling into disuse

Plate 7.1   The citadel and later town, Daulatabad, India (*photo*. T. Insoll)

today. Various types exist, though a similar plan might be followed (for details on all aspects of the *hammam*, see Sourdel-Thomine 1971). Public baths were frequently built, as attested in areas which were formerly part of the Muslim world, in Ottoman Bulgaria, for example (Kiel 1974: 652) or in many areas of Spain (de Epalza et al. 1989). Besides their obvious hygiene purposes, baths could serve 'as a meeting place for relaxation and communication' (Grabar 1973: 155) (see plate 7.2). Al-Janabi (1978: 190) also describes a further type of bath, which he interprets as one used for the ablution of corpses, at Kufah in Iraq and which dates from the Ilkhanid period (1258–1337). Private baths could also exist. Recently, the so-called 'Moorish baths' in Gibraltar have been given just such an attribution, having possibly formed part of the governor's residence (Finlayson 1997). Excavations revealed the presence of the plunge bath in the hot room, as well as part of the hypocaust found to be filled with a thick deposit of black sludge, residue from the furnace (Benady 1988: 8–10; see also Torres Balbás 1942: 206–10). Numerous other examples illustrating the importance of cleanliness and an adequate water supply could be provided. The main point to emphasize is that the discussion of water-related structures is only one example of possible settlement–landscape links, but it illustrates how important it is to apply a 'total approach' in considering all aspects of settlement and their possible interconnections.

Sacred geography

A final question to consider within the context of landscape studies or settlement positioning is what actually constitutes sacred geography. The networks of pilgrimage trails, local and international, have already been discussed (see chapter 4), and these could be said to form a part of 'sacred geography'; similarly, the role of tombs within this has also been described (see chapter 6). But what of other elements? Do these exist? Even city orientation, as Bonine (1990) has shown, is not necessarily reflective of *qiblah* direction but more the result of topography, and, as Sopher (1967) remarks, Islam does not impress cosmological representations upon the landscape: explicit sacred connotations, aside from the obvious centrality of the holy places of Mecca and Medina, are restricted to saints' and martyrs' tombs. Exceptions nevertheless exist, as at In-Teduq in Niger, a pre-sixteenth century site, which has been interpreted as indicative of Sufism and monumentalization of the *qiblah*, through the clustering of the stone-built tombs, houses and shops around the mosque (Cressier 1992: 75–7).

Plate 7.2 Bathing scene from *The Khamsa of Nizami* (Browne no. 1424, St John's College, Cambridge)

Yet this is an under-researched field, and the environment itself is certainly not a sterile concept in Islam, but considered as something entrusted to mankind by God, which should be maintained in a sustainable way (Pedersen 1995: 263). Similarly, Schimmel (1991) has illustrated how the landscape and environment can be represented in spiritual terms in mystical poetry, and a study by Lahiri (1996) has gone one stage further and managed to tie together various elements of Muslim sacred geography in the landscape of late medieval Ballabgarh, north of Delhi. Here, 'shared social norms and tolerances' (1996: 263) led to a homogeneity of Hindu and Muslim religious geography. In summary, sacred geography, as with physical or human geography, should surely be considered more fully in future, even if only to be discounted as of little relevance within the archaeology of Islam, once we are more certain of its importance. This is a further component of the 'total approach' towards settlement studies.

The Contemporary and Future Situation

The relevance of much of the above for archaeologists of the future dealing with the material residue of the present can be questioned. As with many other areas of life and aspects of material culture, Muslim settlements have recently undergone radical change. A situation exists whereby, on the one hand, increasing diversity might be manifest in certain matters and an increasing uniformity in others. Fundamental agents of change are many and include prosperity, secularism and Westernization, the impact of the motor car, the availability of new materials and new technologies. No one cause is wholly responsible, but it is undeniable that change has been felt across the Muslim world. Riyadh, as described by Philby (1920) within living memory, has gone forever.

Yet the pace of change is so quick and the impact so far reaching that rapid changes in society will offer challenges to the archaeologists of the future. A single example will be mentioned here. Akbar (1988) has offered an interpretation to account for certain recent changes in Muslim cities concerning issues of control and ownership of property. Basically, he suggests that the traditional settlement is an 'ordered' one, with more people having a stake in society through ownership or control of property, whereas a modern society is more 'organized' and, consequently, 'people who neither own nor control are irresponsible and dissipate the resources of the society' (Akbar 1988: 200). Whether this is true is debatable (and is in many ways reminiscent of a certain spectrum of current British political thought), but this is not the essential point. Rather, it raises the question of how such issues could be examined by archaeologists interested in Islam in the future. Are issues such as changes in ownership of property and their possible fundamental societal consequences approachable by the archaeologist through material culture? In this instance they are related to material culture; Akbar (1988) goes on to define five 'forms of submission of property'. Again the validity of the categories is open to debate but the importance of such models is to illustrate what might be considered through moving beyond a limited corpus of standard archaeological paradigms. The Muslim settlement is not (and never was) a fossilized entity, and if it is considered as a mirror or result of society, as it is here, recent behaviours and their possible material outcomes must also be considered.

Summary and Conclusions

Settlements have been considered here as a facet of the material culture which in totality constitutes the archaeology of Islam, and, although certain commonalties appear, a generalizing model along the lines of the once-popular 'orientalizing' approach is not acceptable; too much emphasis has to be given to factors such as environment and topography. The Muslim city has developed as an environment for those following the requirements of their faith. Yet the direct religious component within the Muslim city is negligible beyond a notion of public/private spatial considerations which as a social concern are a by product of religious convention. (We can disregard the central mosque/palace core as being wholly religious; as we have seen, this appears to owe its origins in part to a pre-Islamic heritage of power symbolism.) Nevertheless, there was something definable as a Muslim city, and recognizable as such, regardless of the opinions of the proponents of diversity to the extent that no uniformity is supposed to exist, even if it is only reduced to the core elements of mosques and cemeteries. But frequently, as has been discussed, much more than this will be found, which will entail the archaeological recognition of a Muslim city. Manifest patterns are apparent which can differentiate it from other settlement types, best exemplified in juxtaposition as was illustrated using the Moroccan and Cretan examples. Villages and pastoral encampments have fewer possible recognition criteria, and were perhaps less affected, but again mosques and burials might allow their recognition as Muslim settlements. If Islam is to be regarded as a complete system for life, it could be expected that this would be apparent in the settlement. Muslim identity could not be expected to be wholly exempt from this important aspect of material culture. It is how this is achieved which is subject, as with all the categories of material culture discussed, to great diversity.

8

An Archaeology of Islam?

God creates you weak: after weakness He gives you strength, and after
strength infirmity and grey hairs.

Qur'an. The Greeks 30: 54

The conclusions which can be drawn from this study are varied, and
are certainly both positive and negative in terms of their implications.
On the positive side, and in answer to the fundamental question raised
at the very beginning of this volume, it can be seen that many
categories of material culture which can be recognized as specifically
Islamic are present cross-culturally. These can also be manifest archaeologically, and can range from a city structured according to specific
spatial requirements down to items such as a seal ring. However, it
must also not be forgotten that much of what has been presented is an
ideal scenario, an ideal Islamic material culture, and it is very unlikely
that such a 'suite' of evidence would ever be found in totality. Exceptions to every proposed structuring principle can and will occur, in all
probability outweighing the residue of orthodox behaviour. People
will be buried with grave goods, not all Muslims lived in courtyard
houses, mosques can be mis-aligned and built without a *mihrab*,
turbans might be rare, alcohol was drunk, the list continues. Equally,
traditional criteria are of little validity in many areas of the modern
Muslim world, but people are still Muslims, and it is possible to be a
Muslim with few outward manifestations. Archaeology can and does
attest to this, and comparative studies illustrate how flawed it is to
create an ideal Muslim, who just does not exist, except perhaps in the
Arabian Nights or in a Hollywood stereotype where the landscape is
studded with minarets and peopled with characters wearing turbans,
baggy trousers and shoes with pointed curling toes.

Many Muslims do not live life according to Qur'anic prescript or the injunction of the *shar'iah*. The notions of ideals and realities are both plainly apparent. The concept of *ummah*, or community, for example, is in effect an ideal: glance around Muslim societies today and it can be seen that they are beset with the same problems of inequality and the like which are found in any other society or community. Add to this the huge cultural diversity found, and the problems involved in identifying an archaeology of Islam seem immense. Further limitations are apparent. The geographical emphasis in this volume has had to be selective, and in fact concentrates on certain areas. Many of the examples of material culture given do not apply, or have never applied, outside certain specific contexts. Likewise, the masculine emphasis is noticeable: male rulers, male artisans, soldiers and scholars predominate, and the female dimension, where acknowledged, is often considered in what could be termed clichéd contexts, relating to the domestic environment and food preparation. This imbalance reflects much of the current literature, and it is highly probable that archaeologists will be able to define the female presence within the archaeology of Islam in a more credible manner in the future, once greater attention is paid to this area of study.

Thus, in the face of the problems outlined, the purpose of the exercise could be questioned if, for example, one of the main conclusions is the recognition that the gulf between ideals or 'structuring principles' and reality or 'cultural diversity' is largely insurmountable. This makes us consider the positive points which have also been isolated – not least the practical advantages of illustrating that it is possible to consider religion as exerting a potential influence over all areas of life, and thus the archaeology of religion as constituting the residue of this 'total picture'. All aspects of life, from birth in the domestic environment to death and burial, can be structured according to religious, and the resultant social, codes. The archaeology of Islam must be regarded as a complete system, not an abstracted set of 'princely' artifacts or vague statements based upon a few grand monuments, but the residue of millions of individuals spread over time and space. In this respect it is perhaps easier to approach the study of Islam as a distinct entity compared with many other world religions; for example, Christianity, of which, according to one involved party, a priest, it may be better 'to talk more about family resemblances rather than an essential essence' (Shakespear 1995). Islam is perhaps more easily defined, and this would certainly appear to be correct as regards the categories of relevant material culture which are related to it.

Yet it also needs to be remembered that religion is not merely a monolithic entity superimposed according to divine will. The individual is again of great importance, and individual religious experience varies. According to Geertz, 'for one man, his religious commitments are the axis of his whole existence...for another man, not necessarily less honestly believing, his faith is worn more lightly' (1968: 111–12). This has obvious implications for material culture and, in turn, archaeology. Muslim and other religious interpretation is subject to many different meanings at various scales. At a group level, for instance, as was noted in chapter 1, these can include the different legal schools, the two main Muslim traditions of Sunni and Shi'ah, esoteric Sufi Islam, and many other interpretations and manifestations. Within these each individual can bring his or her own perspective to bear, creating further diversity – but diversity, it is argued, within a Muslim framework.

Similarly, what material culture 'means' can vary. Of all the case studies cited in this volume, the one examining the Norman court in Sicily perhaps provides the best example of the different meanings which can be inherent in material culture with Islamic associations (see chapter 5). But this was an extreme example, contrasting what was in the end a Christian court composed of people who held a specific vision of Muslim material culture as it had connotations of how they perceived a court should appear. Yet similar diversity in the meaning of material culture was apparent within a wholly Muslim context, as was seen with the role of epigraphy. Inscriptions can mean different things to different people: as a symbol if the viewer is illiterate or cannot read it for other reasons, or as an instructive device at a much more fundamental level if the message can be read. Add to this context, remove our inscription from the hypothetical mosque, say, place it in a museum and its meaning can change again depending upon the observer. Notions such as plurality in meaning and interpretation, and contextual examination as an interpretative device are well-trodden theoretical paths in recent years and are not worth travelling further down just for the sake of it. Archaeologists should now be aware of such fundamental issues, and that Islamic archaeology should in any way be exempt from such considerations is insupportable. In fact this aspect of the 'post-processual' approach has direct and fundamental practical implications for many aspects of Islamic archaeology. An awareness that material culture can function in different ways at different levels would appear obvious, but neglected. Why else could Austin and Thomas raise the question: 'how and why has it been possible for medieval historians to systematically ignore the work of medieval archaeologists?' (1990: 47).

Replace 'medieval' with 'Islamic', and the sentiments are the same, and the simple answer is that they could because much of the research was irrelevant.

Besides an improved theoretical awareness, contributions can also be made to Islamic archaeology at a more practical level. It was noted in chapter 1 that the individual is often denied, as are frequently whole strata of society; what was not mentioned is the relationship between Muslims and archaeology. This might seem strange, like considering a particular relationship between Hindus and the past for example, but in the context of Islam this is important because of the concept of *jahiliyyah*, the 'age of ignorance', which existed before Islam. At one end of the scale it might then be thought that Muslim interest in the past, at least before Islam, was and is likely to be negligible, but this is a false conception. As both Trigger (1989: 183) and Lindholm (1996: 33) note, the pre-Islamic past and archaeology can be of importance to Muslim peoples. The Shah's celebration at Persepolis for the supposed anniversary of 2,500 years of the Persian kings in 1971, or Arabs reciting the poetry of the warriors of the *jahiliyyah*, are prime examples. Similarly, in Libya the government was responsible for starting a major archaeological project, *The UNESCO Libyan Valleys Archaeological Survey*, as it was thought that lessons from the past might be learnt to benefit agricultural practices today (Barker 1996: 1).

Yet how conceptions of the past and of archaeology exist will vary depending on cultural context and, of course, from individual to individual. An interesting, and rare, study of such issues is provided by Blau (1995), who examines attitudes towards the past in the United Arab Emirates. Elsewhere such studies are lacking, even though reviews of the relevant archaeology in different regions might be undertaken or varying attitudes to the past considered (see, for instance, the studies on the Near East, Soviet archaeology, Israeli archaeology, and Indian archaeology in Trigger and Glover 1981, 1982; also Layton 1989; Masry 1994; Insoll 1996c). Such a study or studies would be of great interest for comparative purposes in assessing the relationship between archaeology, the general study of the past and of Islam.

This in turn leads to a consideration of the possible practical significance of archaeology for the study of the very origins of Islam. Archaeology can and has contributed to our understanding of the component parts, the structuring principles of material culture: the Muslim burial, the mosque, the domestic environment. In respect of these a largely orthodox position has been followed in the previous pages, but the origins of the mosque, for example, are currently the subject of a re-evaluation (Johns 1995), a process of review based on archaeological and historical evidence. Much more controversial is the examination of direct events associated with the origins of Islam, Qur'anic 'history' almost, through archaeology, although it is extremely unlikely that this will ever take place to any significant degree; for example, archaeological research in Mecca and Medina, obvious key sites, is impossible. Furthermore, from a Muslim perspective it is not necessary; nothing will be found that will add to the religion, no equivalent of the Dead Sea Scrolls or a hidden gospel will appear (al-Sharekh 1995). The truth is already revealed and material culture, and therefore archaeology, cannot confirm or deny the faith of believers. In this respect there are differences from other areas of religious archaeology; biblical archaeology, for example, in which there sometimes appears to be an emphasis upon proving or disproving actual events (see, for example, Keller 1965; Bartlett 1997).

Such a viewpoint returns us to questions of faith touched upon in chapter 1. How far should one probe when examining something as personal as religious experience? This is perhaps for the individual to decide but some sort of threshold of restraint surely needs to be observed. Similar issues are considered by Waines (1995: 267–79) with reference to the historical study of Islamic origins, and he provides a convenient summary of the pertinent research trends. These fall into two main groups: first, that of the faithful, the 'insider' Muslim perspective, and, secondly, that of secular, Western, usually European scholars. He notes that, until recently, a 'dovish' perspective was adopted by scholars in treating the Arabic sources relating to Islamic origins, but within the past two decades a much more 'hawkish' school has appeared, exemplified by, for example, Crone and Cook (1977) and Wansbrough (1977, 1978). The Qur'an was subjected to 'literary analysis' in the latter study, for instance, where it was seen as 'salvation history', presenting not a history of events but 'simply theological rationalizations of those events' (Waines 1995: 277).

Archaeology could have a significant role to play in assessing the development of Islam and the validity of the Qur'an as a historical source for those who think such an approach permissible. But essentially we are as yet in no position to achieve this, not only because of the practical impossibility of attempting it, but also because the theoretical and even moral implications have to be considered further. Yet it is also necessary to accept, as the material culture makes plainly apparent, that Islam and Islamic civilization did not emerge fully fledged, but were subject, as with most things, to a developmental process. This is especially obvious when Muslim material culture in the first conquest situation is considered. In Spain, for example, most of which was conquered in 711, Grabar (1973) notes that no Muslim monument or text has been found until the formation of the Umayyad caliphate in 756, with the Cordoba mosque, construction of which started in 785–6, the first building 'of any sort of signifi-cance in Muslim Spain' (1973: 20–1). Whether this information is now out of date, as is likely in the light of 25 years further archaeological research, is largely irrelevant because the importance of this example lies in the fact that it illustrates that the pack of material culture 'cards' was not instantaneously laid out each time a new territory was taken by the Muslim armies. Rather, as we have seen, this material culture was itself developing; moreover, buildings could be adapted and re-used and ephemeral materials employed leaving little or no visible traces. The ninth century would appear to be the turning point when it could be said that many typically Islamic features had developed in a recognizable form. This prompts the question of whether it was coincidental or connected with fundamental religious issues, such as the standardization, transcription and evaluation of the *hadith* in the ninth century?

It is pertinent to finish this volume by re-stating that, although great complexity and diversity, ethnic, cultural, geographical, is evi-dent, it is obvious that structuring principles are in operation which create categories of material culture identifiable cross-culturally as Muslim. This unity can in part be attributed to the existence of the Qur'an, which should structure the life of all Muslims. Yet to say this does not mean that an 'other' is created, reminiscent of past orientalist approaches; rather, this material culture is now part of the contem-porary 'world picture', from Mecca to Cambridge, and this has been shown. The archaeology of Islam is of relevance for us all, not only in offering a further dimension of material culture of which to be aware, but also because of the conceptual implications in an era where we are constantly reminded of the globalization processes at work around us. The archaeology of Islam is not a Muslim archaeology but every-one's archaeology.

References

Abdulak, S. 1977: Tradition and Continuity in Vernacular Omani Housing. *Art and Archaeology Research Papers* 12, 18–26.

Abu Zaria, N. 1982: *Sidi Ameur: a Tunisian Village*. London: Ithaca.

Abu-Lughod, J. L. 1971: *Cairo: 1001 Years of the City Victorious*. Princeton, NJ: Princeton University Press.

Abu-Lughod, J. L. 1987: The Islamic City – Historic Myth, Islamic Essence, and Contemporary Relevance. *International Journal of Middle Eastern Studies* 19, 155–176.

Abu-Rabia, A. 1994: *The Negev Bedouin and Livestock Rearing: Social, Economic and Political Aspects*. Oxford: Berg.

Adams, N. 1990: Life in Ottoman Times at Qasr Ibrim. In C. H. Bonnet (ed.), *Seventh International Conference for Nubian Studies: Pre-publication of Main Papers*. Geneva: University of Geneva, pp. 1–16.

Adams, W. Y. 1987: Islamic Archaeology in Nubia: an Introductory Survey. In T. Hagg (ed.), *Nubian Culture Past and Present*. Stockholm: Almqvist and Wiksell, pp. 327–61.

Adams, W. Y. 1996: *Qasr Ibrim: the Late Medieval Period*. London: Egypt Exploration Society.

Adle, C. 1979: Constructions Funéraires à Rey: Circa Xe–XIIe Siècle. *Akten des VII Internationalen Kongresses für Iranische Kunst und Archäologie*. Berlin: Dietrich Reimer Verlag, pp. 511–15.

Ahmad, A. 1975: *A History of Islamic Sicily*. Edinburgh: Edinburgh University Press.

Ahmed, A. S. 1984: Religious Presence and Symbolism in Pukhtun Society. In A. S. Ahmed and D. M. Hart (eds), *Islam in Tribal Societies: from the Atlas to the Indus*, London: Routledge, pp. 310–30.

Ahmed, A. S. 1988: *Discovering Islam: Making Sense of Muslim History and Society*. London: Routledge.

Ahuja, S. 1979: Indian Settlement Patterns and House Designs. *Art and Archaeology Research Papers* 15, 32–8.

Akbar, J. 1988: *Crisis in the Built Environment: the Case of the Muslim City.* Singapore: Concept Media.

Akbar, J. 1993: Gates as Signs of Autonomy in Muslim Towns. *Muqarnas* 10, 141–7.

Al-Azzawi, S. H. 1969: Oriental Houses in Iraq. In P. Oliver (ed.), *Shelter and Society*, London: Barrie and Jenkins, pp. 91–102.

Alberge, D. 1997: Curious Diver Struck Gold from 17th Century. *The Times*, 8 November, p. 3.

Alexander, J. 1979: The Archaeological Recognition of Religion: the Examples of Islam in Africa and the Urnfield in Europe. In B. Burnham and J. Kingsbury (eds), *Hierarchy and Settlement* (BAR. S59), Oxford: British Archaeological Reports, pp. 215–28.

Alexander, J. 1988: The Saharan Divide in the Nile Valley: the Evidence from Qasr Ibrim. *African Archaeological Review* 6, 73–90.

Alexander, J. 1994: Islamic Archaeology: the Ottoman Frontier on the Middle Nile. *Sudan Archaeological Research Society Newsletter* 7, 20–6.

Alexander, J. 1997a: Qalat Sai: the Most Southerly Ottoman Fortress in Africa. *Sudan and Nubia* 1, 16–20.

Alexander, J. 1997b: Personal communication, 20 May.

Al-Hassan, A. Y. and Hill, D. R. 1992: *Islamic Technology: an Illustrated History.* Cambridge: Cambridge University Press.

Ali, M. M. (ed.) 1951: *A Manual of Hadith (Sahih Bukhari).* Lahore: The Ahmadiyya Anjuman Ishaat Islam.

Ali, T. 1996: Personal communications, 14 March and 11 September.

Al-Janabi, T. 1978: A Ruined Ilkhanid Bath at Kufa. *Sumer* 34, 189–95.

Al-Janabi, T. 1983: Islamic Archaeology in Iraq: Recent Excavations at Samarra. *World Archaeology* 14, 305–27.

Allan, J. 1978: Khātam, Khātim. In *The Encyclopedia of Islam*, vol. 4, 2nd edn. Leiden: E. J. Brill, pp. 1102–15.

Allan, J. W. 1982: *Nishapur: Metalwork of the Early Islamic Period.* New York: Metropolitan Museum of Art.

Al-Rashid, A. 1980: *Darb Zubaydah: the Pilgrim Road from Kufa to Mecca.* Riyadh: University Libraries.

Al-Rashid, A. 1986: *Al-Rabadhah: a Portrait of Early Islamic Civilisation in Saudi Arabia.* Riyadh: King Saud University.

Al-Sharekh, A. 1995: Personal communication, 26 October.

Ambary, H. A. 1986: Epigraphical Data from 17th–19th Century (AD) Muslim Graves in East Java. In C. D. Grijns and S. O. Robson (eds), *Cultural Contact and Textual Interpretation*, Dordrecht: Foris, pp. 25–37.

Amiry, S. and Tamari, V. 1989: *The Palestinian Village Home.* London: British Museum.

Andrews, P. A. 1971: Tents of the Tekna, South-western Morocco. In P. Oliver (ed.), *Shelter in Africa*, London: Barrie and Jenkins, pp. 124–42.

Andrews, P. A. 1987: The Generous Heart or the Mass of Clouds: the Court Tents of Shah Jahan. *Muqarnas* 4, 149–65.

Andrews, P. A. 1995: The Hassaniya-speaking Nomads, Tekna, Trarza, and Brakna. In L. Prussin (ed.), *African Nomadic Architecture: Space, Place and Gender*. Washington, DC: Smithsonian Institution Press, pp. 66–73.

Anon. 1964: Excavations at Banbhore. *Pakistan Archaeology* 1, 49–55.

Arav, R. 1993: A Mamluk Drum from Bethsaida. *Israel Exploration Journal* 43 (4), pp. 241–5.

Arnold, T. W. 1965: *Painting in Islam*. New York: Dover.

Arrowsmith-Brown, J. H. (ed.) 1991: *Prutky's Travels to Ethiopia and Other Countries*. London: Hakluyt Society.

Asher, C. B. 1984: Inventory of Key Monuments. In G. Michell (ed.), *The Islamic Heritage of Bengal*. Paris: Unesco, pp. 37–140.

Asher, M. 1986: *In Search of the Forty Days Road*. London: Penguin.

Athamina, K. 1989: The Black Banners and the Socio-political Significance of Flags and Slogans in Medieval Islam. *Arabica* 36, pp. 307–26.

Austin, D. 1990: The 'Proper Study' of Medieval Archaeology. In D. Austin and L. Alcock (eds), *From the Baltic to the Black Sea: Studies in Medieval Archaeology*, London: Unwin Hyman, pp. 9–42.

Austin, D. and Alcock, L. (eds) 1990: *From the Baltic to the Black Sea: Studies in Medieval Archaeology*. London: Unwin Hyman.

Austin, D. and Thomas, J. 1990: The 'Proper Study' of Medieval Archae ology: a Case Study. In D. Austin and L. Alcock (eds), *From the Baltic to the Black Sea: Studies in Medieval Archaeology*, London: Unwin Hyman, pp. 43–78.

Bacharach, J. L. 1991: Administrative Complexes, Palaces and Citadels: Changes in the Loci of Medieval Muslim Rule. In I. A. Bierman, R. A. Abou-El Haj and D. Prezoisi (eds), *The Ottoman City and its Parts*. New York: Caratzas, pp. 111–28.

Baha Tanman, M. 1992: Settings for the Veneration of Saints. In R. Lifchez (ed.), *The Dervish Lodge*. Los Angeles: University of California Press, pp. 130–71.

Baipakov, K. 1992: Les Fouilles de la Ville d'Otrar. *Archéologie Islamique* 3, 87–110.

Banning, E. B. and Köhler-Rollefson, I. 1992. Ethnographic Lessons for the Pastoral Past: Camp Remains near Beidha, Southern Jordan. In O. Bar-Yosef and A. Khazanov (eds), *Pastoralism in the Levant: Archaeological Materials in Anthropological Perspectives*. Madison: Prehistory Press, pp. 181–201.

Barker, G. (ed.) 1996: *Farming the Desert: the UNESCO Libyan Valleys Archaeological Survey*, vol. 1. London: Society for Libyan Studies.

Barth, H. 1965: *Travels and Discoveries in North and Central Africa*. London: Frank Cass.

Bartlett, J. R. (ed.) 1997: *Archaeology and Biblical Interpretation*. London: Routledge.

Barton, S. W. 1986: *The Bengali Muslims of Bradford*. Leeds: University of Leeds.

Bartosiewicz, L. 1996: Camels in Antiquity: the Hungarian Connection. *Antiquity* 70, 447–53.

Bashear, S. 1991: Riding Beasts on Divine Missions: an Examination of the Ass and Camel Traditions. *Journal of Semitic Studies* 356, 37–75.

Bass, G. F. and Van Doorninck, F. H. 1978: An Eleventh Century Shipwreck at Serçe Liman, Turkey. *International Journal of Nautical Archaeology and Underwater Exploration* 7, 119–32.

Bassat, R. 1893: Les inscriptions de L'Ile de Dahlak. *Journal Asiatique* 9, 77–111.

Basset, H. and Terrasse, H. 1927: Sanctuaires et fortresses Almohades: le Ribat de Tit. *Hesperis* 7, 117–56.

Bates, U. 1991: The Use of Calligraphy on Three-dimensional Objects: the Case for 'Magic' Bowls. In C. G. Fisher (ed.), *Brocade of the Pen: the Art of Islamic Writing*. Michigan: Michigan State University, pp. 55–61.

Beck, L. 1978: Women among Qashqa'i Nomadic Pastoralists in Iran. In L. Beck and N. Keddie (eds), *Women in the Muslim World*. Cambridge, MA: Harvard University Press, pp. 351–73.

Beckwith, C. I. 1984: The Plan of the City of Peace: Central Asian Iranian Factors in Early Abbasid Design. *Acta Orientalia Academiae Scientiarium Hungaricae* 38, 143–64.

Begley, W. E. 1979: The Myth of the Taj Mahal and a New Theory of its Symbolic Meaning. *The Art Bulletin* 61, 7–37.

Behrend, T. E. 1984: Kraton, Tamon, Mesjid: a Brief Survey and Bibliographic Review of Islamic Antiquities in Java. *Indonesia Circle* 35, 29–55.

Benady, T. (ed.) 1988: *Guide to the Gibraltar Museum*. Grendon: Gibraltar Books.

Bender, B. (ed.) 1993: *Landscape: Politics and Perspectives*. Oxford: Berg.

Bennigsen, A. and Enders Wimbush, S. 1986: *Muslims of the Soviet Empire: a Guide*. London: Hurst.

Betts, A.V.G. 1990: Ancient ar-Risha: Stone Implements. In S. Helms (ed.), *Early Islamic Architecture of the Desert: a Bedouin Station in Eastern Jordan*, Edinburgh: Edinburgh University Press, pp. 159–68.

Bierman, I. A. 1991: The Ottomanization of Crete. In L. A. Bierman, R. A. Abou-El Haj and D. Prezoisi (eds), *The Ottoman City and its Parts*. New York: Caratzas, pp. 53–75.

Binet, Capitaine. 1956: Notes sur les ruines de Garoumele (Niger). *Notes Africaines* 53, 1–2.

Bintliff, J. 1991: The Contribution of an *Annaliste*/Structural History Approach to Archaeology. In J. Bintliff (ed.), *The Annales School and Archaeology*. Leicester: Leicester University Press, pp. 1–33.

Binyon, L. 1930: Painting. In E. Denison Ross (ed.), *Persian Art*. London: Luzac, pp. 60–73.

Birge, J. K. 1937: *The Bektashi Order of Dervishes*. London: Luzac.

Bivar, A.D.H. and Shinnie, P. 1962: Old Kanuri Capitals, *Journal of African History* 3, 1–10.

Blau, S. 1995: Observing the Present – Reflecting the Past: Attitudes towards Archaeology in the United Arab Emirates. *Arabian Archaeology and Epigraphy* 6, 116–28.

Bloom, J. 1989: Minaret: Symbol of Islam. *Oxford Studies in Islamic Art*, vol. 7. Oxford: Oxford University Press.

Boediardjo, S. 1978: Wayang: a Reflection of the Aspirations of the Javanese. In H. Soebadio and C. A. du Marchie Sarvaas (eds.), *Dynamics of Indonesian History*. Oxford: North-Holland, pp. 97–121.

Bone, D. S. 1982: Islam in Malawi. *Journal of Religion in Africa* 13, 126–38.

Bonine, M. E. 1977: From Uruk to Casablanca: Perspectives on the Urban Experience of the Middle East. *Journal of Urban History* 3, 141–80.

Bonine, M. E. 1990: Sacred Direction and City Structure: a Preliminary Analysis of the Islamic Cities of Morocco. *Muqarnas* 7, 50–72.

Bosworth, E. 1976: Armies of the Prophet. In B. Lewis (ed.), *The World of Islam*. London: Thames and Hudson, pp. 201–12.

Boucharlat, R. and Labrousse, A. 1979: Une sucrerie d'epoque Islamique sur la rive droite du Chaour à Suse. *Cahiers de la Délégation Archéologique Française en Iran* 10, 155–76.

Bourdieu, P. 1973: The Berber House. In M. Douglas (ed.), *Rules and Meanings: the Anthropology of Everyday Knowledge*. London: Penguin, pp. 98–110.

Bourdieu, P. 1977: *Outline of a Theory of Practice*. Cambridge: Cambridge University Press.

Bowker, J. 1991: *The Meanings of Death*. Cambridge: Cambridge University Press.

Braudel, F. 1972: *The Mediterranean and the Mediterranean World in the Age of Phillip II*. London: Collins.

Bravmann, R. 1974: *Islam and Tribal Art in West Africa*. Cambridge: Cambridge University Press.

Bravmann, R. 1983: *African Islam*. London: Ethnographica.

Brend, B. 1994: *Islamic Art*. London: British Museum.

Brett, M. 1990: Islam in North Africa. In P. Clarke (ed.), *The World's Religions: Islam*, London: Routledge, pp. 23–47.

Brill, R. H. 1970: Chemical Studies of Islamic Lustre Glass. In R. Berger (ed.), *Scientific Methods in Medieval Archaeology*. Berkeley, CA: University of California Press, pp. 351–77.

British Museum 1998: *Art and Culture of the Islamic World: Newsletter* 1. London: British Museum.

Brookes, J. 1987: *Gardens of Paradise: the History and Design of the Great Islamic Gardens*. London: Weidenfeld and Nicolson.

Broomhall, M. 1910: *Islam in China*. London: Morgan and Scott.

Brown, K. and Palmer, M. 1987: *The Essential Teachings of Islam*. London: Rider.

Bruce, S. 1995: *Religion in Modern Britain*. Oxford: Oxford University Press.

Bulliet, R. W. 1975: *The Camel and the Wheel*. Cambridge, MA: Harvard University Press.

Bulliet, R. W. 1992: Annales and Archaeology. In A. B. Knapp (ed.), *Archaeology, Annales and Ethnohistory*. Cambridge: Cambridge University Press, pp. 131–4.

Burckhardt, J. L. 1830: *Notes on the Bedouins and Wahabys*. London: Colburn and Bentley.

Burton, R. F. 1898: *Personal Narrative of a Pilgrimage to Al-Madinah and Meccah*. London: George Bell.

Burton-Page, J. 1991: Maḳbara (India). In *The Encyclopedia of Islam*, vol. 6. 2nd edn. Leiden: E. J. Brill, pp. 125–8.

Callmer, J. 1995: The Influx of Oriental Beads into Europe during the Eighth Century AD. In M. Rasmussen, U. Lund Hansen and U. Nädman (eds), *Glass Beads: Cultural History, Technology, Experiment and Analogy*. Lejre: Historical–Archaeological Experimental Centre, pp. 49–54.

Campo, J. E. 1991: *The Other Sides of Paradise: Explorations into the Religious Meanings of Domestic Space in Paradise*. Columbia: University of South Carolina Press.

Canaan, T. 1936: Arabic Magic Bowls. *Palestine Oriental Society Journal* 16, 79–127.

Carmichael, D., Hubert, J., Reeves, B. and Schanche, A. (eds) 1994: *Sacred Sites, Sacred Places*. London: Routledge.

Carsten, J. and Hugh-Jones, S. (eds) 1995: *About the House: Lévi-Strauss and Beyond*. Cambridge: Cambridge University Press.

Carswell, J. 1977: China and Islam in the Maldive Islands. *Transactions of the Oriental Ceramic Society* 41, pp. 121–98.

Carswell, J. 1979a: China and Islam: a Survey of the Coasts of India and Ceylon. *Transactions of the Oriental Ceramic Society* 42, pp. 24–58.

Carswell, J. 1979b: Sin in Syria. *Iran* 17, 15–24.

Carswell, J. 1982: Imported Far Eastern Wares. In D. S. Whitcomb and J. H. Johnson (eds), *Quseir al-Qadim 1980: Preliminary Report*. Malibu: Undena, pp. 193–9.

Carswell, J. and Prickett, M. 1984: Mantai 1980: a Preliminary Investigation. *Ancient Ceylon* 5.

CEN 1973: Moslems Plan Mosque in City House. *Cambridge Evening News*, 26 January.

CEN 1976: Terraced House is Mecca for City's Islamic Faith. *Cambridge Evening News*, 6 July.

CEN 1981a: Moslems in City Can Keep Spiritual Home. *Cambridge Evening News*, 12 February.

CEN 1981b: Cash Available for Building Mosque in City. *Cambridge Evening News*, 21 July.

CEN 1982: Muslims Find New Home. *Cambridge Evening News*, 6 September.

CEN 1985: Peaceful Haven where Muslim Faithful Meet. *Cambridge Evening News*, 29 November.

CEN 1988: Small Building is Spiritual Centre for County Muslims. *Cambridge Evening News*, 9 June.

CEN 1990: Untitled. *Cambridge Evening News*, 13 September.

Champion, T. 1990: Medieval Archaeology and the Tyranny of the Historical Record. In D. Austin and L. Alcock (eds), *From the Baltic to the Black Sea: Studies in Medieval Archaeology*, London: Unwin Hyman, pp. 79–95.

Chapman, R., Kinnes, I. and Randsborg, K. (eds) 1981: *The Archaeology of Death*. Cambridge: Cambridge University Press.

Chatty, D. 1978: Changing Sex Roles in Bedouin Society. In L. Beck and N. Keddie (eds), *Women in the Muslim World*. Cambridge, MA: Harvard University Press, pp. 399–415.

Chaudhri, R. A. 1982: *Mosque: its Importance in the Life of a Muslim*. London: London Mosque.

Chaudhuri, K. N. 1985: *Trade and Civilisation in the Indian Ocean*. Cambridge: Cambridge University Press.

Chittick, H. N. 1974: *Kilwa: an Islamic Trading City on the East African Coast*. Nairobi: British Institute in Eastern Africa.

Chittick, H. N. 1984: *Manda: Excavations at an Island Port on the Kenya Coast*. Nairobi: British Institute in Eastern Africa.

Clancy-Smith, J. 1993: The Man with Two Tombs: Muhammad Ibn 'Abd Al-Rahman, Founder of the Algerian Rahmaniyya, c.1715–1798. In G. M. Smith and C. W. Ernst (eds), *Manifestations of Sainthood in Islam*. Istanbul: Isis Press, pp. 148–69.

Cole, D. P. 1975: *Nomads of the Nomads: the Al Murrah Bedouin of the Empty Quarter*. Chicago: Aldine.

Conkey, M. and Gero, J. 1991: *Engendering Archaeology: Women in Prehistory*. Oxford: Blackwell.

Conkey, M. and Spector, J. 1984: Archaeology and the Study of Gender. *Advances in Archaeological Method and Theory* 7, 1–38.

Content, D. J. (ed.) 1987: *Islamic Rings and Gems: the Benjamin Zucker Collection*. London: Phillip Wilson.

Cordwell, J. M. and Schwarz, R. A. (eds) 1979: *The Fabrics of Culture: the Anthropology of Clothing and Adornment*. The Hague: Mouton.

Cosar, F. M. 1978: Women in Turkish Society. In L. Beck and N. Keddie (eds), *Women in the Muslim World*. Cambridge, MA: Harvard University Press, pp. 124–40.

Cosgrove, D. and Daniels, S. (eds) 1988: *The Iconography of Landscape: Essays on the Symbolic Representation, Design and Use of Past Environments*. Cambridge: Cambridge University Press.

Costa, P. M. 1983: Notes on Traditional Hydraulics and Agriculture in Oman. *World Archaeology* 14, 273–95.

Cressey, G. B. 1958: Qanats, Karez, and Foggaras. *The Geographical Review* 48, 27–44.

Cressier, P. 1992: Archéologie de la devotion Soufi. *Journal des Africanistes* 62, 69–90.

Creswell, K.A.C. 1932: *Early Muslim Architecture*, vol. 1. Oxford: Clarendon Press.

Creswell, K.A.C. 1952: Fortification in Islam before AD 1250. *Proceedings of the British Academy* (unnumbered), pp. 89–125.

Creswell, K.A.C. 1958: *A Short Account of Early Muslim Architecture*. London: Penguin.

Cribb, R. 1991: *Nomads in Archaeology*. Cambridge: Cambridge University Press.

Crone, P. and Cook, M. 1977: *Hagarism: the Making of the Islamic World*. Cambridge: Cambridge University Press.

Cunningham, A. 1880: *Report of Tours in the Gangetic Provinces from Badaon to Bihar: Archaeological Survey of India*, vol. 11. Calcutta: Superintendent of Government Printing.

Cunningham, C. E. 1964: Order in the Atoni House. *Bijdragen tot de taal-, land-en Volkenkunde* 120, 34–68.

Damais, L-Ch. 1968: L'Epigraphie Musulmane dans le Sud-Est Asiatique. *Bulletin de l'Ecole Française d'Extrême Orient* 54, 567–604.

Darley-Doran, R. 1986: *Centuries of Gold: the Coinage of Medieval Islam*. London: Zamana Gallery.

Dasheng, C. 1995: Chinese Islamic Influence on Archaeological Finds in South Asia. In R. Scott and J. Guy (eds), *South East Asia and China: Art, Interaction and Commerce*. London: Percival David Foundation, pp. 59–63.

Dasheng, C. and Kalus, L. 1991: *Corpus d'inscriptions Arabe et Persanes en Chine*, vol. 1: *Province de Fujian (Quanzhou, Fuzhou, Xiamen)*. Paris: Geuthner.

Davies, P. 1989: *The Penguin Guide to the Monuments of India*, vol. 2: *Islamic, Rajput, European*. London: Penguin.

Dawood, N. J. (trans.) 1993: *The Koran*. Harmondsworth: Penguin.

Day, M. 1990: Archaeological Ethics and Treatment of the Dead. *Anthropology Today* 6, 15–16.

De Epalza, M., Llobregat, E. A., Azuar Ruiz, R., Lauado, P. J., Bevià, M., Irars Perez, J., Gisbert, J. A., Boigues, C. and González Baldovi, M. 1989: *Banos Arabes en el Pais Valenciano*. Valenciano: Conselleria de Cultura, Educacio I Ciencia.

De Gironcourt, G. R. 1920: *Missions De Gironcourt en Afrique Occidentale, 1908–1909, 1911–1912*. Paris: Société de Géographie.

De Jong, F. 1989: The Iconography of Bektashiism: a Survey of Themes and Symbolism in Clerical Costume, Liturgical Objects and Pictorial Art. *Manuscripts of the Middle East* 4, 7–29.

Denny, W. B. 1990: Saff and Sejjadah: Origins and Meaning of the Prayer Rug. *Oriental Carpet and Textile Studies* 3(2), pp. 93–104.

Dermengheim, E. 1954: *Le culte des saints dans l'Islam Maghrebin*. Paris: Gallimard.

Dewar, R. E. and Wright, H. T. 1993: The Culture History of Madagascar. *Journal of World Prehistory* 7, 417–66.

Dickie, J. 1976: The Islamic Garden in Spain. In E. B. MacDougall and R. Ettinghausen (eds), *The Islamic Garden*. Washington: Dumbarton Oaks, pp. 89–105.

Dickie, J. 1978: Allah and Eternity: Mosques, Madrasas and Tombs. In G. Michell (ed.), *Architecture of the Islamic World*. London: Thames and Hudson, pp. 15–47.

Donaldson, B. A. 1939: *The Wild Rue*. London: Luzac.

Donley, L. 1982: House Power: Swahili Space and Symbolic Markers. In I. Hodder (ed.), *Symbolic and Structural Archaeology*. Cambridge: Cambridge University Press, pp. 63–73.

Donley, L. 1987: Life in the Swahili Town House Reveals the Symbolic Meaning of Spaces and Artefact Assemblages. *African Archaeological Review* 5, 181–92.

Donley-Reid, L. 1990: A Structuring Structure: the Swahili House. In S. Kent (ed.), *Domestic Architecture and the Use of Space*. Cambridge: Cambridge University Press, pp. 114–26.

Douglas, M. 1966: *Purity and Danger: an Analysis of Concepts of Pollution and Taboo*. London: Routledge.

Douglas, M. (ed.) 1984: *Food in the Social Order: Studies of Food and Festivities in Three American Communities*. New York: Russell Sage Foundation.

Dunlop, D. M. 1958: Bīmāristān. In *The Encyclopedia of Islam*, vol. 1, 2nd edn. Leiden: E. J. Brill, pp. 1222–4.

Eaton, R. M. 1984: Islam in Bengal. In G. Michell (ed.), *The Islamic Heritage of Bengal*. Paris: UNESCO, pp. 23–36.

Ebeid, R. Y. and Young, M.J.L. 1974: A Fragment of a Magic Alphabet from the Cairo Genizah. *Sudhoffs Archiv* 58, 404–8.

Edwards, H. 1991: Text, Context, Architext: the Qur'an as Architectural Inscription. In C. G. Fisher (ed.), *Brocade of the Pen: the Art of Islamic Writing*. Michigan: Michigan State University, pp. 63–75.

Ehrenberg, M. 1989: *Women in Prehistory*. London: British Museum.

Eickelman, D. F. and Piscatori, J. (eds) 1990: *Muslim Travellers: Pilgrimage, Migration, and the Religious Imagination*. London: Routledge.

El-Ali, S. A. 1970: The Foundation of Baghdad. In A. H. Hourani and S. M. Stern (eds), *The Islamic City in the Light of Recent Research*. Oxford: Bruno Cassirer, pp. 87–101.

Elisséeff, N. 1980: Physical Layout. In R. B. Serjeant (ed.). *The Islamic City*. Paris: UNESCO, pp. 90–103.

Elisséeff, N. and el Hakim, R. 1981: *Mission Soudano-Française dans la Province de Mer Rouge (Soudan)*. Lyon: Maison de l'Orient Méditerranéen.

Ellis, C. G. 1982: Garden Carpets and their Relation to Safavid Gardens. *Hali* 5, pp. 11–17.

El-Rashedy, F. 1997: Personal communication, 20 October.

El-Tom, A. O. 1987: Berti Qur'anic Amulets. *Journal of Religion in Africa* 17, 224–44.

Emeljanenko, T. 1994. Nomadic Year Cycles and Cultural Life of Central Asian Livestock Herders before the Twentieth Century. In C. Van Leeuwen, T. Emeljanenko and L. Popova (eds), *Nomads in Central Asia*. Amsterdam: Royal Tropical Institute, pp. 37–68.

Engestrom, T. 1959: Origin of Pre-Islamic Architecture in West Africa. *Ethnos* 24, 64–9.

Ettinghausen, R. 1944: The Character of Islamic Art. In N. A. Faris (ed.), *The Arab Heritage*. Princeton, NJ: Princeton University Press.

Ettinghausen, R. 1974: Arabic Epigraphy: Communication or Symbolic Affirmation. In D. K. Kouymjian (ed.), *Near Eastern Iconography, Epigraphy and History: Studies in Honour of George C. Miles*. Beirut: American University of Beirut, pp. 297–317.

Ettinghausen, R. 1976: The Man-made Setting. In B. Lewis (ed.), *The World of Islam*. London: Thames and Hudson, pp. 57–72.

Evans, J. M. 1975–6: The Traditional House in the Oasis of Ghadames. *Libyan Studies* 7, 31–40.

Ewert, C. 1971: El Mihrab de la Mezquita Mayor de Almeria. *Al-Andalus* 68, pp. 391–460.

Faegre, T. 1979: *Tents: Architecture of the Nomads*. London: John Murray.

Fage, J. D. 1978. *An Atlas of African History*. London: Edward Arnold.

Farb, P. and Armelagos, G. 1980: *Consuming Passions: the Anthropology of Eating*. Boston: Houghton Mifflin.

Farmer, H. G. 1929: *A History of Arabian Music to the XIIIth Century*. London: Luzac.

Farouk, O. 1988: The Muslims of Thailand: a Survey. In A.D.W. Forbes (ed.), *The Muslims of Thailand*, vol. 1: *Historical and Cultural Studies*. Bihar: Centre for Southeast Asian Studies, pp. 1–30.

Fedorov-Davydov, G. A. 1983: Archaeological Research in Central Asia of the Muslim Period. *World Archaeology* 14, 393–405.

Feilberg, C. C. 1944: *La Tente Noire*. Copenhagen: National Museum of Ethnography.

Fentress, E. 1987: The House of the Prophet: North African Islamic Housing. *Archeologia Medievale* 14, 47–68.

Fernández-Puertas, A. 1994: Spain and North Africa. In M. Frishman and H-U. Khan (eds), *The Mosque: History, Architectural Development and Regional Diversity*. London: Thames and Hudson, pp. 101–17.

Finlayson, C. 1997: Personal communication, 10 April.

Fischer, J. 1994: *The Folk Art of Java*. Kuala Lumpur: Oxford University Press.

Fischer, K. 1973: Archaeological Field Surveys in Afghan Seistan. In N. Hammond (ed.), *South Asian Archaeology*. Park Ridge: Noyes Press, pp. 131–55.

Fisher, H. J. 1973: Conversion Reconsidered: Some Historical Aspects of Religious Conversion in Black Africa. *Africa* 43, 27–40.

Fisher, H. J. 1985: The Juggernaut's Apologia: Conversion to Islam in Black Africa. *Africa* 55 (2), pp. 153–73.

Fitzgerald, E. (trans.) 1970: *The Rubaiyat of Omar Khayyam*. London: The Folio Society.

Fleming, A. 1973: Tombs for the Living. *Man* 8, 177–93.

Fletcher, R. 1977: Settlement Studies (Micro and Semi-micro). In D. L. Clarke (ed.), *Spatial Archaeology*. London: Academic Press, pp. 47–162.

Flight, C. n.d.: Thoughts on the Cemetery at Sane. Unpublished paper, Centre of West African Studies, University of Birmingham.

Forbes, A.D.W. (ed.) 1988: *The Muslims of Thailand*, vol. 1. *Historical and Cultural Studies*. Bihar: Centre for Southeast Asian Studies.

Fowler, H. W. and Fowler, F. G. 1952: *The Concise Oxford Dictionary of Current English*. Oxford: Oxford University Press.

Frierman, J. D. and Giauque, R. D. 1973: Saljuq Faïence and Timurid Earthernware from Tammisha: Some Preliminary Technological Notes. *Iran* 11, 180–4.

Frishman, M. 1994: Islam and the Form of the Mosque. In M. Frishman and H-U. Khan (eds), *The Mosque: History, Architectural Development and Regional Diversity.* London: Thames and Hudson, pp. 17–41.

Frishman, M. and Khan, H-U. (eds) 1994: *The Mosque: History, Architectural Development and Regional Diversity.* London: Thames and Hudson.

Gabrieli, F. 1970: The Transmission of Learning and Literary Influences to Western Europe. In P. M. Holt, A. Lambton and B. Lewis (eds), *The Cambridge History of Islam,* vol. 2b. Cambridge: Cambridge University Press, pp. 851–90.

Gardet, L. 1970: Religion and Culture. In P. M. Holt, A. Lambton and B. Lewis (eds), *The Cambridge History of Islam,* vol. 23. Cambridge: Cambridge University Press, pp. 569–603.

Garlake, P. 1978: An Encampment of the Seventeenth to Nineteenth Centuries on Ras Abaruk, Site 5. In B. de Cardi (ed.), *Qatar Archaeological Report: Excavations 1973.* Oxford: Oxford University Press, pp. 163–71.

Garwood, P., Jennings, D., Skeates, R. and Toms, J. 1991: Preface. In P. Garwood, D. Jennings, R. Skeates and J. Toms (eds), *Sacred and Profane.* Oxford: Oxbow Books, pp. v–x.

Gassong, S. 1987: Turkoman Prayer Rugs. *Oriental Carpet and Textile Studies* 3 (1), pp. 83–95.

Geertz, C. 1966: Religion as a Cultural System. In M. Banton (ed.), *Anthropological Approaches to the Study of Religion.* London: Tavistock, pp. 1–46.

Geertz, C. 1968: *Islam Observed: Religious Development in Morocco and Indonesia.* New Haven, Conn.: Yale University Press.

Geertz, C. 1976: Art as a Cultural System. *Modern Language Notes* 91, 1473–99.

Gellens, S. I. 1990: The Search for Knowledge in Medieval Muslim Societies: a Comparative Approach. In D. F. Eickelman and J. Piscatori (eds), *Muslim Travellers. Pilgrimage, Migration, and the Religious Imagination.* London: Routledge, pp. 50–65.

Gellner, E. 1969: *Saints of the Atlas.* London: Weidenfeld and Nicolson.

Gellner, E. 1981: *Muslim Society.* Cambridge: Cambridge University Press.

Gerholm, T. 1977: *Market, Mosque and Mafraj: Social Inequality in a Yemeni Town.* Stockholm: University of Stockholm.

Ghafur, M. A. 1966: Fourteen Kufic Inscriptions of Banbhore: the Site of Daybul. *Pakistan Archaeology* 3, 65–90.

Gibb, H. A. R. and Kramers, J. H. (eds) 1961: *The Shorter Encyclopedia of Islam.* Leiden: E. J. Brill.

Gibb, H. A. R., Kramers, J. H., Lévi-Provençal, E. and Schacht, J. 1960: *The Encyclopedia of Islam.* Leiden: E. J. Brill.

Gibb, H.A.R. (trans.) 1993: *The Travels of Ibn Battuta.* Delhi: Munshiram Manoharlal.

Giddens, A. 1979: *Central Problems in Social Theory.* London: Macmillan.

Gilat, A., Shirav, M., Bogoch, R., Halicz, L., Avner, U. and Hahlieli, D. 1993: Significance of Gold Exploitation in the Early Islamic Period, Israel. *Journal of Archaeological Science* 20, 429–37.

Gilsenan, M. 1982: *Recognizing Islam*. London: Tauris.

Gladney, D. C. 1991: *Muslim Chinese: Ethnic Nationalism in the People's Republic*. Cambridge, MA: Harvard University Press.

Goblot, H. 1979: *Les Qanats: une technique d'acquisition de l'eau*. Paris: Mouton.

Golombek, L. 1974: The Cult of Saints and Shrine Architecture in the Fourteenth Century. In D. K. Kouymjian (ed.), *Near Eastern Iconography, Epigraphy and History: Studies in Honour of George C. Miles*. Beirut: American University of Beirut, pp. 419–30.

Golombek, L. 1988: The Draped Universe of Islam. In P. P. Soucek (ed.), *Content and Context of Visual Arts in the Islamic World*. University Park: Pennsylvania University Press, pp. 25–49.

Goodwin, G. 1988: Gardens of the Dead in Ottoman Times. *Muqarnas* 5, 61–9.

Goody, J. 1982: *Cooking, Cuisine and Class*. Cambridge: Cambridge University Press.

Goody, J. 1993: *The Culture of Flowers*. Cambridge: Cambridge University Press.

Grabar, O. 1959: The Umayyad Dome of the Rock in Jerusalem. *Ars Orientalis* 3, 33–62.

Grabar, O. 1966: The Earliest Islamic Commemorative Structures. *Ars Orientalis* 6, 7–46.

Grabar, O. 1971: Islamic Archaeology an Introduction. *Archaeology* 24 (3), 197–9.

Grabar, O. 1973: *The Formation of Islamic Art*. New Haven, Conn.: Yale University Press.

Grabar, O. 1976: Islamic Art and Archaeology. In L. Binder (ed.), *The Study of the Middle East*. New York: John Wiley, pp. 229–63.

Grabar, O. 1978: Palaces, Citadels and Fortifications. In G. Michell (ed.), *Architecture of the Islamic World*. London: Thames and Hudson, pp. 65–79.

Grabar, O., Holod, R., Knustad, J. and Trousdale, W. 1978: *City in the Desert: Qasr al-Hayr East*. Cambridge, MA: Harvard University Press.

Graham-Campbell, J. (ed.) 1994: Archaeology of Pilgrimage. *World Archaeology* 26.

Granqvist, H. 1965: *Muslim Death and Burial: Arab Customs and Traditions Studied in a Village in Jordan*. Helsinki: Helsingfors.

Grant, A. 1991: Economic or Symbolic? Animals and Ritual Behaviour. In P. Garwood, D. Jennings, R. Skeates and J. Toms (eds), *Sacred and Profane*. Oxford: Oxbow Books, pp. 109–14.

Gratuze, B. and Barrandon, J-N. 1990: Islamic Glass Weights and Stamps. *Archaeometry* 32, 155–62.

Greenlaw, J. P. 1995: *The Coral Buildings of Suakin*. London: Kegan Paul.

Grierson, P. 1960: The Monetary Reforms of Abd al-Malik. *Journal of the Economic and Social History of the Orient* 3, 241–64.

Guillaume, A. 1954: *Islam*. London: Penguin.

Hakim, B. S. 1986: *Arabic-Islamic Cities: Building and Planning Principles*. London: Kegan Paul.

Hallet, S. I. and Samizay, R. 1980: *Traditional Architecture of Afghanistan*. London: Garland.

Hamilton, R. W. 1959: *Khirbat al-Mafjah: an Arabian Mansion in the Jordan Valley*. Oxford: Clarendon Press.

Haneda, M. 1994: Introduction: an Interpretation of the Concept of the Islamic City. In M. Haneda and T. Miura (eds), *Islamic Urban Studies: Historical Review and Perspectives*. London: Kegan Paul, pp. 1–10.

Haneda, M. and Miura, T. (eds) 1994: *Islamic Urban Studies: Historical Review and Perspectives*. London: Kegan Paul.

Hastings, J. 1911: *Encyclopedia of Religion and Ethics*. Edinburgh: T. and T. Clark.

Hastorf, C. 1991: Gender, Space and Food in Prehistory. In M. Conkey and J. Gero (eds), *Engendering Archaeology: Women in Prehistory*. Oxford: Blackwell, pp. 132–59.

Hattox, R. S. 1991: *Coffee and Coffeehouses: the Origins of a Social Beverage in the Medieval Near East*. Seattle: University of Washington Press.

Hawting, G. R. 1993: The Hajj in the Second Civil War. In I. R. Netton (ed.), *Golden Roads: Migration, Pilgrimage and Travel in Medieval and Modern Islam*. Richmond: Curzon Press, pp. 31–42.

Helms, S. 1990: *Early Islamic Architecture of the Desert: a Bedouin Station in Eastern Jordan*. Edinburgh: Edinburgh University Press.

Henderson, J. 1995: Investigations into Marvered Glass II. In J. W. Allan (ed.), *Islamic Art in the Ashmolean Museum. Oxford Studies in Islamic Art*, vol. 10. Oxford: Oxford University Press, pp. 31–50.

Henderson, J. 1996: New Light on Early Islamic Industry: Excavations in Raqqa, Syria. In R. J. A. Wilson (ed.), *From River Trent to Raqqa*, Nottingham: University of Nottingham, pp. 59–71.

Henderson, J. and Allan, J. W. 1990: Enamels on Ayyubid and Mamluk Glass Fragments. *Archaeomaterials* 4, 167–83.

Herrmann, J. 1991: Some Remarks on Eastern European Branches of the Silk Road. *Pakistan Archaeology* 26, 241–50.

Hillenbrand, R. 1986: Madrasa: Architecture. In *The Encyclopedia of Islam*, vol. 5, 2nd edn. Leiden: E. J. Brill, pp. 1136–54.

Hinton, D. A. (ed.) 1983: *25 Years of Medieval Archaeology*. Sheffield: University of Sheffield.

Hitchcock, M. 1987: Islamic Influences on Indonesian Design. In A. Al-Shahi (ed.), *The Diversity of the Muslim Community: Anthropological Essays in Memory of Peter Lienhardt*. London: Ithaca Press, pp. 51–7.

Hodder, I. 1982a: *The Present Past*. London: Batsford.

Hodder, I. 1982b: *Symbols in Action*. Cambridge: Cambridge University Press.

Hodder, I. 1986: *Reading the Past*. Cambridge: Cambridge University Press.

Hodder, I. 1990: *The Domestication of Europe*. Oxford: Basil Blackwell.

Hodges, R. 1987: Spatial Models, Anthropology and Archaeology. In J. M. Wagstaff (ed.), *Landscape and Culture: Geographical and Archaeological Perspectives*. Oxford: Blackwell, pp. 118–33.

Horton, M. 1991: Primitive Islam and Architecture in East Africa. *Muqarnas* 8, 103–16.

Horton, M. 1996: *Shanga: the Archaeology of a Muslim Trading Community on the Coast of East Africa.* London: British Institute in Eastern Africa.

Hourani, A. 1991: *Islam in European Thought.* Cambridge: Cambridge University Press.

Hourani, G. F. 1995: *Arab Seafaring* (expanded and rev. edn by J. C. Carswell, with additional notes from H. Frost, M. Horton, D. King, G. King, P. Morgan, G. Scanlon and H. Wright). Princeton, NJ: Princeton University Press.

Hoyland, R. 1995: Personal communication, 1 December.

Hoyland, R. (in press): *Seeing Islam as Others Saw It: a Study of the Non-Muslim Sources Relating to Early Islamic History.* Princeton, NJ: Princeton University Press.

Hubert, J. 1994: Sacred Beliefs and Beliefs of Sacredness. In D. Carmichael, J. Hubert, B. Reeves and A. Schanche (eds), *Sacred Sites, Sacred Places.* London: Routledge, pp. 9–19.

Hugh-Jones, S. 1985: The Maloca: a World in a House. In E. Carmichael, S. Hugh-Jones, B. Moser and D. Taylor (eds), *The Hidden Peoples of the Amazon.* London: Museum of Mankind, pp. 78–93.

Humphrey, C. 1974: Inside a Mongolian Tent. *New Society* 31, 273–5.

Humphreys, S. C. 1981: Introduction: Comparative Perspectives on Death. In S. C. Humphreys and H. King (eds), *Mortality and Immortality: the Anthropology and Archaeology of Death.* London: Academic Press, pp. 1–13.

Hunwick, J. 1985: Songhay, Borno and the Hausa States, 1450–1600. In J. F. A. Ajayi and M. Crowder (eds), *The History of West Africa*, vol. 1. Harlow: Longman, pp. 323–71.

Inalcik, H. 1973: *The Ottoman Empire.* London: Weidenfeld and Nicolson.

Insoll, T. 1995: A Cache of Hippopotamus Ivory at Gao, Mali; and a Hypothesis about its Use. *Antiquity* 69, 327–36.

Insoll, T. 1996a: Archaeological Research in Gao and Timbuktu: October and November 1996, Preliminary Report. Unpublished paper, University of Cambridge.

Insoll, T. 1996b: *Islam, Archaeology and History: Gao Region (Mali) c.AD 900–1250.* Cambridge Monographs in African Archaeology 39. BAR International Series 647. Oxford: Tempus Reparatum.

Insoll, T. 1996c: The Archaeology of Islam in Sub-Saharan Africa: a Review. *Journal of World Prehistory* 10 (4), 439–504.

Insoll, T. 1996d: A Report on an Archaeological Reconnaissance Made to the Dahlak Islands. Unpublished paper, University of Cambridge.

Insoll, T. 1997a: Mosque Architecture in Buganda, Uganda. *Muqarnas* 14, 179–88.

Insoll, T. 1997b: Medieval Gao: an Archaeological Contribution. *Journal of African History* 38 (1): 1–30.

Isa, A. M. 1955: Muslims and Taswir. *The Muslim World* 45, 250–68.

Israeli, R. 1979: Islamization and Sinicization in Chinese Islam. In N. Lev tzion (ed.), *Conversion to Islam.* London: Holmes and Meier, pp. 159–76.

Jellicoe, S. 1976: The Mughal Garden. In E. B. MacDougall and R. Etting-hausen (eds), *The Islamic Garden*. Washington: Dumbarton Oaks, pp. 109–24.

Jenkins, J. and Olsen, P. R. 1976: *Music and Musical Instruments in the World of Islam*. London: Horniman Museum.

Jenkins, M. and Keane, D. 1982: *Islamic Jewellery in the Metropolitan*. New York: Metropolitan Museum.

Jettmar, K. 1967: The Middle Asiatic Heritage of Dardistan (Islamic Collective Tombs in Punyal and their Background). *East and West* 17, 59–83.

Johns, J. 1993: The Norman Kings of Sicily and the Fatimid Caliphate. *Anglo-Norman Studies* 15, 133–59.

Johns, J. 1995: Personal communication, 1 December.

Juynboll, G. H. A. 1986: The Attitude towards Gold and Silver in Early Islam. In M. Vickers (ed.), *Pots and Pans: a Colloquium on Precious Metals and Ceramics in the Muslim, Chinese and Graeco-Roman Worlds, Oxford 1985*. Oxford: Oxford University Press, pp. 107–15.

Kalesi, H. 1978: Oriental Culture in Yugoslav Countries from the 15th Century till the End of the 17th Century. *Dissertationes Orientales* 40, 359–404.

Kawatoko, M. 1993: On the Tombstones Found at the Badi Site: the Al-Rih Island. *Kush* 16, pp. 186–224.

Keddie, N. R. 1992: Material Culture, Technology, and Geography: Toward a Holistic Comparative Study of the Middle East. In R. Cole (ed.), *Comparing Muslim Societies: Knowledge and State in a World Civilisation*. Ann Arbor: University of Michigan Press, pp. 31–62.

Keller, W. 1965: *The Bible as History: Archaeology Confirms the Book of Books*. London: Hodder and Stoughton.

Kent, S. (ed.) 1990: *Domestic Architecture and the Use of Space*. Cambridge: Cambridge University Press.

Kessler, C. 1970: Abd Al-Malik's Inscription in the Dome of the Rock: A Reconsideration. *Journal of the Royal Asiatic Society* (unnumbered), pp. 2–14.

Khan, H-U. 1994: An Overview of Contemporary Mosques. In M. Frishman and H-U. Khan (eds), *The Mosque: History, Architectural Development and Regional Diversity*, London: Thames and Hudson, pp. 247–67.

Khan, S. F. 1976: Pakistani Women in Britain. *New Community* 5, 99–108.

Khuri, F. I. 1990: *Imams and Emirs: State, Religion and Sects in Islam*. London: Saqi Books.

Kiel, M. 1974: Some Early Ottoman Monuments in Bulgarian Thrace. *Belleten* 38, 635–54.

King, G. R. D. 1983: Two Byzantine Churches in Northern Jordan and their Re-use in the Islamic Period. *Damaszener Mitteilungen* pp. 111–36.

King, G. R. D. 1989: Islamic Archaeology in Libya, 1969–1989. *Libyan Studies* 20, 193–207.

King, G. R. D. 1994a: Introduction. In G. R. D. King and A. Cameron (eds), *The Byzantine and Early Islamic Near East, II: Land Use and Settlement Patterns*, Princeton, NJ: Darwin Press, pp. 1–15.

King, G. R. D. 1994b: Settlement in Western and Central Arabia and the Gulf in the Sixth–Eighth Centuries AD. In G. R. D. King and A. Cameron (eds), *The Byzantine and Early Islamic Near East, II: Land Use and Settlement Patterns*, Princeton, NJ: Darwin Press, pp. 181–212.

King, G. R. D. and Cameron, A. (eds) 1994: *The Byzantine and Early Islamic Near East, II: Land Use and Settlement Patterns*. Princeton, NJ: Darwin Press.

Kirkman, J. 1966: *Men and Monuments on the East African Coast*. London: Lutterworth.

Kirkman, J. 1976: *City of San'a*. London: World of Islam Festival Trust.

Kisaichi, M. 1994: The Maghrib. In M. Haneda and T. Miura (eds), *Islamic Urban Studies: Historical Review and Perspectives*. London: Kegan Paul, pp. 11–82.

Komatsu, H. C. 1994: Asia. In M. Haneda and T. Miura (eds), *Islamic Urban Studies: Historical Review and Perspectives*. London: Kegan Paul, pp. 181–328.

Kuban, D. 1974: *Muslim Religious Architecture*. Leiden: E. J. Brill.

Kubiak, W. 1982: *Al-Fustat: its Foundation and Early Development*. Warsaw: University of Warsaw.

Kuran, A. 1987: Form and Function in Ottoman Building Complexes. *Journal of the Islamic Environmental Design Research Centre* 5–6, 132–9.

Kureishi, H. 1990: *The Buddha of Suburbia*. London: Faber and Faber.

Lahiri, N. 1996: Archaeological Landscapes and Textual Images: a Study of the Sacred Geography of Late Medieval Ballabgarh. *World Archaeology* 28, 244–64.

Lane, E. W. 1883 (1987): *Arabian Society in the Middle Ages*. London: Curzon Press.

Lane, E. W. 1895 (1989): *Manners and Customs of the Modern Egyptians*. London: East and West.

Lapidus, I. M. 1973a: Traditional Muslim Cities: Structure and Change. In L. Carl Brown (ed.), *From Madina to Metropolis: Heritage and Change in the Near Eastern City*, Princeton, NJ: Darwin Press, pp. 51–69.

Lapidus, I. M. 1973b: The Evolution of Muslim Urban Society. *Comparative Studies in Society and History* 15, 21–50.

Lapidus, I. M. 1988: *A History of Islamic Societies*. Cambridge: Cambridge University Press.

Laqueur, H-P. 1992: Dervish Gravestones. In R. Lifchez (ed.), *The Dervish Lodge*. Los Angeles: University of California Press, pp. 284–95.

Lassner, J. 1970a: The Caliph's Personal Domain: the City Plan of Baghdad Re-examined. In A. H. Hourani and S. M. Stern (eds), *The Islamic City in the Light of Recent Research*. Oxford: Bruno Cassirer, pp. 103–18.

Lassner, J. 1970b: *The Topography of Baghdad in the Early Middle Ages*. Detroit: Wayne State University Press.

Lassy, I. 1916: *The Muharram Mysteries among the Azerbeijan Turks of Caucasia*. Helsinki: Helsingfors.

LaViolette, A. 1994: Masons of Mali: a Millennium of Design and Techno logy in Earthern Materials. In S. T. Childs (ed.), *Society, Culture and*

Technology in Africa: MASCA Research Papers in Science and Archaeology, vol. 11. Philadelphia: University of Pennsylvania Museum of Archaeology and Anthropology, pp. 86–97.

Layton, R. 1989: *Who Needs the Past? Indigenous Values and Archaeology.* London: Unwin Hyman.

Leach, E. 1976: *Culture and Communication: the Logic by which Symbols are Connected.* Cambridge: Cambridge University Press.

Leach, M. and Leach, J. 1977: Meydiha's *Kisir*: a Wheat Dish from Southern Turkey. In J. Kuper (ed.), *The Anthropologists' Cookbook.* London: Routledge and Kegan Paul, pp. 61–8.

Lebeuf, A. M. D. 1967: Boum Massenia: Capitale de l'Ancien Royaume du Baguirmi. *Journal des Africanistes* 37, 214–44.

Lebeuf, J. P. and Kirsch, J. H. I. 1989: *Ouara, Ville Perdue (Tchad).* Paris: Editions Recherche sur les Civilisations.

Leisten, T. 1990: Between Orthodoxy and Exegesis: Some Aspects of Attitudes in the Shari'a toward Funerary Architecture. *Muqarnas* 7, 12–22.

Levtzion, N. 1979. Patterns of Islamization. In N. Levtzion (ed.), *Conversion to Islam.* New York: Holmes and Meier, pp. 207–16.

Levtzion, N. and Hopkins, J. F. P. 1981: *Corpus of Early Arabic Sources for West African History.* Cambridge: Cambridge University Press.

Lewcock, R. and Serjeant, R. B. 1983: The Houses of San'a. In R. B. Serjeant and R. Lewcock (eds), *San'a: an Arabian Islamic City.* London: World of Islam Festival Trust, pp. 436–500.

Lewis. B. 1987: *Islam from the Prophet Muhammad to the Capture of Constantinople*, vol. 2: *Religion and Society.* Oxford: Oxford University Press.

Lewis, I. M. 1980: Introduction. In I. M. Lewis (ed.), *Islam in Tropical Africa.* London: Hutchinson, pp. 4–98.

Lewis, P. 1994: *Islamic Britain: Religion, Politics and Identity among British Muslims.* London: I. B. Tauris.

Lieber, A. E. 1981: International Trade and Coinage in the Northern Lands during the Early Middle Ages: an Introduction. In M. A. S. Blackburn and D. M. Metcalf (eds), *Viking Age Coinage in the Northern Lands* (BAR S122). Oxford: British Archaeological Reports, pp. 1–34.

Lifchez, R. (ed.) 1992: Introduction. In R. Lifchez (ed.), *The Dervish Lodge.* Los Angeles: University of California Press, pp. 1–12.

Lindholm, C. 1996: *The Islamic Middle East: an Historical Anthropology.* Oxford: Blackwell.

Lings, M. 1968: The Qoranic Symbolism of Water. *Studies in Comparative Religion* 2, 153–60.

Locock, M. (ed.) 1994: *Meaningful Architecture: Social Interpretation of Buildings.* Aldershot: Avebury.

Lodrick, D. O. 1981: *Sacred Cows, Sacred Places.* Berkeley, CA: University of California Press.

Lopez, J. B. 1992: The City Plan of the Alhambra. In J. D. Dodds (ed.), *Al-Andalus: the Art of Islamic Spain.* New York: Metropolitan Museum, pp. 153–61.

Lowick, N. 1974: The Arabic Inscriptions on the Mosque of Abu Ma'ruf at Sharwas (Jebel Nefusa). *Libyan Studies* 5, 14–19.

Lowick, N. 1985: The Religious, the Royal and the Popular in the Figural Coinage of the Jazira. In J. Cribb (ed.), *Coinage and History of the Islamic World*. London: Variorum, pp. 159–74.

Lyons, D. 1996: The Politics of House Shape: Round vs Rectilinear Domestic Structures in Déla Compounds, Northern Cameroon. *Antiquity* 70, 351–67.

McCloud, A. B. 1995: *African American Islam*. London: Routledge.

MacDougall, E. B. and Ettinghausen, R. (eds) 1976: *The Islamic Garden*. Washington: Dumbarton Oaks.

Mackie, L. W. 1985: Covered with Flowers: Medieval Floor Coverings Excavated at Fustat in 1980. *Oriental Carpet and Textile Studies* 1, 23–35.

Maclagan, I. 1994: Food and Gender in a Yemeni Community. In S. Zubaida and R. Tapper (eds), *Culinary Cultures of the Middle East*. London: Tauris, pp. 159–72.

Maclean, R. 1996: Personal communication, 10 March.

Maclean, R. 1997: Personal communication, 14 January.

Marcais, G. 1945: La conception des villes dans l'Islam. *Revue d'Alger* 2, 517–33.

Marcais, G. 1965: Dar. In *The Encyclopedia of Islam*, vol. 2, 2nd edn. Leiden: E. J. Brill, pp. 113–15.

Marcais, W. 1928: L'Islamisme et la vie urbaine. *L'Académie des Inscriptions et Belles-Lêttres, Comptes Rendus* (January–March), 86–100.

Martin, L. 1996: Personal communication, 31 July.

Marx, E. 1977: Communal and Individual Pilgrimage: the Region of Saints' Tombs in Southern Sinai. In R. P. Werbner (ed.), *Regional Cults*, London: Academic Press, pp. 29–51.

Mason, R. B. and Keall, E. J. 1990: Petrography of Islamic Pottery from Fustat. *Journal of the American Research Center in Egypt* 27, 165–84.

Masry, A. H. 1994: Archaeology and the Establishment of Museums in Saudi Arabia. In F. E. S. Kaplan (ed.), *Museums and the Making of 'Ourselves': The Role of Objects in National Identity*. London: Leicester University Press, pp. 125–67.

Mate, M. S. 1983: Daulatabad: Road to Islamic Archaeology in India. *World Archaeology* 14, 335–41.

Mathew, G. 1956: Chinese Porcelain in East Africa and on the Coast of Southern Arabia. *Oriental Art* 2, 50–5.

Mauny, R. 1951: Notes d'archéologie au sujet de Gao. *Bulletin de l'Institut Français d'Afrique Noire (B)* 13, 837–52.

Mawdudi, S. A. 1986: *The Islamic Way of Life*, ed. K. Ahmad and K. Murad. Leicester: The Islamic Foundation.

Mayer, L. A. 1956: *Islamic Architects and their Works*. Geneva: Albert Kundig.

Mercer, J. 1976: *Spanish Sahara*. London: Allen and Unwin.

Mercier, M. 1922: *La civilisation urbaine au Mzab*. Algiers: University of Algiers.

Metcalf, P. and Huntingdon, R. 1991: *Celebrations of Death: the Anthropology of Mortuary Ritual*. Cambridge: Cambridge University Press.

Michot, J. 1978: Les fresques du pèlerinage au Caire. *Art and Archaeology Research Papers* 13, 7–21.

Micklewright, N. 1991: Tiraz Fragments: Unanswered Questions about Medieval Islamic Textiles. In C. G. Fisher (ed.), *Brocade of the Pen: the Art of Islamic Writing*. Michigan: Michigan State University, pp. 31–45.

Mikami, T. 1980–1: China and Egypt: Fustat. *Transactions of the Oriental Ceramic Society* 45, 67–89.

Miles, G. C. 1948: *Early Arabic Glass Weights and Stamps*. New York: American Numismatic Society.

Miles, G. C. 1951: *Early Arabic Glass Weights and Stamps: a Supplement*. New York: American Numismatic Society.

Miles, G. C. 1952: Mihrāb and 'Anazah: a study in Early Islamic Iconography. In G. C. Miles, *Archaeologica Orientalia in Memoriam Ernst Herzfeld*. New York: J. J. Augustin, pp. 156–71.

Miner, H. 1953: *The Primitive City of Timbuctoo*. Princeton, NJ: Princeton University Press.

Momen, M. 1985: *An Introduction to Shi'i Islam: the History and Doctrines of Twelver Shi'ism*. Oxford: George Ronald.

Monod, T. 1969: Le 'Ma'den Ijafen: une epave caravaniere ancienne dans la Majabat Al-Koubra. *Actes du 1er Colloque International d'Archéologie Africaine, 1966, Fort Lamy*. Fort Lamy: Institut National Tchadien pour les Sciences Humaines, pp. 286–320.

Montet, E. 1909: *Le culte des saints Musulmans dans l'Afrique du Nord*. Geneva: University of Geneva.

Moore, H. L. 1986: *Space, Text and Gender: an Anthropological Study of the Marakwet of Kenya*. Cambridge: Cambridge University Press.

de Moraes Farias, P. F. 1990: The Oldest Extant Writing in West Africa. *Journal des Africanistes* 60 (2), 65–113.

Mortensen, I. D. 1991: From Ritual Action to Symbolic Communication. In P. Garwood, D. Jennings, R. Skeates and J. Toms (eds), *Sacred and Profane*. Oxford: Oxbow Books, pp. 80–7.

Mortensen, I. D. 1993: *Nomads of Luristan: History, Material Culture and Pastoralism in Western Iran*. London: Thames and Hudson.

Moynihan, E. B. 1980: *Paradise as a Garden in Persian and Mughal India*. London: Scolar Press.

Mujeeb, M. 1967: *The Indian Muslims*. London: Allen and Unwin.

Muniz, A. M., Riquelme, J. A. and Von Lettow-Vorbeck, C. L. 1995: Dromedaries in Antiquity: Iberia and Beyond. *Antiquity* 69, 368–75.

Murphy, C. 1986: Piety and Honour: the Meaning of Muslim Feasts in Old Delhi. In R. S. Khare and M. S. A. Rao (eds), *Food, Society and Culture*, Durham: Carolina University Press, pp. 85–119.

Nasr, S. H. 1991: *Islamic Spirituality*, vol. 2: *Manifestations*. London: SCM Press.

Nasr, A. M. 1993: The Structure of Society in Pre-Islamic Arabia and the Impact of the Hijra: a Traditional Archaeology. In I. R. Netton (ed.), *Golden Roads: Migration, Pilgrimage and Travel in Medieval and Modern Islam*. Richmond: Curzon Press, pp. 3–10.

Nath, R. 1970: *Colour Decoration in Mughal Architecture*. Bombay: Taraporevala.

Needham, J. 1954: *Science and Civilisation in China*. Cambridge: Cambridge University Press.

Netton, I. R. 1993: Preface. In I. R. Netton (ed.), *Golden Roads: Migration, Pilgrimage and Travel in Medieval and Modern Islam*. Richmond: Curzon Press, pp. x–xv.

Nevett, L. 1994: Separation or Seclusion? Towards an Archaeological Approach to Investigating Women in the Greek Household in the Fifth to Third Centuries BC. In M. Parker Pearson and C. Richards (eds), *Architecture and Order: Approaches to Social Space*. London: Routledge, pp. 98–112.

Nicolaisen, J. 1963: *Ecology and Culture of the Pastoral Tuareg*. Copenhagen: National Museum.

Nicolle, D. 1976: *Early Medieval Islamic Arms and Armour*. Madrid: Instituto de Estudios Sobre Armas Antiguas.

Nicolle, D. 1993: *Armies of the Muslim Conquest*. London: Osprey.

Nielsen, J. 1995: *Muslims in Western Europe*. Edinburgh: Edinburgh University Press.

Niezen, R. W. 1987: Diverse Styles of Islamic Reform among the Songhay of Eastern Mali. Unpublished PhD dissertation, University of Cambridge.

Noonan, T. 1981: Ninth Century Dirham Hoards from European Russia: a Preliminary Analysis. In M. A. S. Blackburn and D. M. Metcalf (eds), *Viking Age Coinage in the Northern Lands* (BAR S122). Oxford: British Archaeological Reports, pp. 47–118.

Northedge, A. and Falkner, R. 1987: The 1986 Survey Season at Samarra. *Iraq* 49, 143–73.

Northedge, A., Wilkinson, T. J. and Falkner, R. 1990: Survey and Excavations at Samarra 1989. *Iraq* 52, 121–47.

Nuseibeh, S. and Grabar, O. 1996: *The Dome of the Rock*. London: Thames and Hudson.

Oliver, P. 1987: *Dwellings: the House across the World*. Oxford: Phaidon.

Ortiz, A. 1969: *The Tewa World: Space, Time, Being, and Becoming in a Pueblo Society*. Chicago: Chicago University Press.

Ory, S. 1991: Maḵbara (Central Arab Lands). In *The Encyclopedia of Islam*, vol. 6, 2nd edn. Leiden: E. J. Brill, pp. 122–3.

O'Shea, J. 1984: *Mortuary Variability: an Archaeological Investigation*. New York: Academic Press.

Ozanne, P. 1971: Ghana. In P. L. Shinnie (ed.), *The African Iron Age*. Oxford: Clarendon Press, pp. 36–65.

Papanek, H. 1973: Purdah: Separate Worlds and Symbolic Shelter. *Comparative Studies in Society and History* 15, 289–325.

Park, M. 1807: *Travels in the Interior Districts of Africa, 1795, 1796 and 1797*. London: W. Bulmer.

Parker Pearson, M. 1993: The Powerful Dead: Archaeological Relationships between the Living and the Dead. *Cambridge Archaeological Journal* 3, 203–29.

Parker Pearson, M. and Richards, C. (eds) 1994: *Architecture and Order: Approaches to Social Space*. London: Routledge.

Parry, V. J. 1970: Warfare. In P. M. Holt, A. Lambton and B. Lewis (eds), *The Cambridge History of Islam*, vol. 2b. Cambridge: Cambridge University Press, pp. 824–50.

Parry, V. J. and Yapp, M. E. (eds) 1975: *War, Technology and Society in the Middle East*. London: Oxford University Press.

Paul, A. 1955: Aidhab: a Medieval Red Sea Port. *Sudan Notes and Records* 36, 64–70.

Pedersen, J. 1986: Madrasa. In *The Encyclopedia of Islam*, vol. 6, 2nd edn. Leiden: E. J. Brill, pp. 1123–34.

Pedersen, P. 1995: Nature, Religion and Cultural Identity: the Religious Environmentalist Paradigm. In O. Bruun and A. Kalland (eds), *Asian Perceptions of Nature: a Critical Approach*. Richmond: Curzon Press, pp. 258–76.

Pellat, Ch. 1965: Ghurāb. In *The Encyclopedia of Islam*, vol. 2, 2nd edn. Leiden: E. J. Brill, pp. 1096–7.

Pellat, Ch. 1971a: Hayawān. In *The Encyclopedia of Islam* vol. 3, 2nd edn. Leiden: E. J. Brill, pp. 304–9.

Pellat, Ch. 1971b: Ibil. In *The Encyclopedia of Islam*, vol. 3, 2nd edn. Leiden: E. J. Brill, pp. 665–8.

Peters, F. E. 1994: *The Hajj: the Muslim Pilgrimage to Mecca and the Holy Places*. Princeton, NJ: Princeton University Press.

Peters, R. 1977: *Jihad in Medieval and Modern Islam*. Leiden: E. J. Brill.

Petersen, A. 1994: The Archaeology of the Syrian and Iraqi Hajj Routes. *World Archaeology* 26, 47–56.

Petersen, A. 1996: *Dictionary of Islamic Architecture*. London: Routledge.

Petersen, A. 1997: Personal communication, 11 December.

Petherbridge, G. T. 1978: The House and Society. In G. Michell (ed.), *Architecture of the Islamic World*. London: Thames and Hudson, pp. 193–208.

Petrushevsky, I. P. 1985: *Islam in Iran*. London: Athlone Press.

Petsopoulos, Y. 1982: Introduction: the Ottoman Style. In Y. Petsopoulos (ed.), *Tulips, Arabesques and Turbans: Decorative Arts from the Ottoman Empire*. London: Alexandria Press, pp. 6–9.

Philby, H. St J. B. 1920: Southern Najd. *The Geographical Journal* 55 (3), 161–91.

Philon, H. 1980: *Islamic Art*. Athens: Benaki Museum.

Pinder-Wilson, R. (ed.) 1969: *Paintings from Islamic Lands*. Oxford: Bruno Cassirer.

Pinder-Wilson, R. 1976: The Persian Garden. In E. B. MacDougall and R. Ettinghausen (eds), *The Islamic Garden*. Washington: Dumbarton Oaks, pp. 71–85.

Possehl, G. L. 1981: Cambay Beadmaking. *Expedition* (summer), pp. 39–47.

Prins, A. H. J. 1967: *The Swahili-speaking Peoples of the East African Coast*. London: International African Institute.

Prominska, E. 1971: Paleopathology According to Age at the Moslem Necropoles at Kom el-Dikka in Alexandria (Egypt). *Africana Bulletin* 14, 171–3.

Qaisar, A. J. 1988: *Building Construction in Mughal India: the Evidence from Painting*. Delhi: Oxford University Press.

Ragib, Y. 1970: Les premières monuments funeraires de l'Islam. *Annales Islamologiques* 9, 21–36.

Rahman Zakry, A. 1965: On Islamic Swords. In Geddes, C. L. (ed.) *Studies in Islamic Art and Architecture in Honour of Professor K. A. C. Creswell*. Cairo: American University in Cairo Press, pp. 270–91.

Rapoport, A. 1969: *House Form and Culture*. Englewood Cliffs, NJ: Prentice-Hall.

Rapoport, A. 1980: Vernacular Architecture and the Cultural Determinants of Form. In A. D. King (ed.), *Buildings and Society: Essays on the Social Development of the Built Environment*. London: Routledge, pp. 283–305.

Rathjens, C. 1957: *Jewish Domestic Architecture in San'a, Yemen*. Jerusalem: Israel Oriental Society.

Raza, M. S. 1993: *Islam in Britain: Past, Present and the Future*. Leicester: Volcano Press.

Redman, C. L. 1986: *Qsar es-Seghir: an Archaeological View of Medieval Life*. London: Academic Press.

Renfrew, C. 1994: The Archaeology of Religion. In C. Renfrew and E. Zubrow (eds), *The Ancient Mind: Elements of Cognitive Archaeology*. Cambridge: Cambridge University Press, pp. 47–54.

Reygasse, M. 1950: *Monuments funéraires pré-Islamiques de l'Afrique du Nord*. Paris: Arts et Métiers Graphiques.

Ricklefs, M. C. 1979: Six Centuries of Islamization in Java. In N. Levtzion (ed.), *Conversion to Islam*. New York: Holmes and Meier, pp. 100–128.

Rielly, K. 1996: Personal communication, 15 September.

Roche, M. 1970: *Le M'zab: Architecture Ibadite en Algerie*. Paris: Arthaud.

Rogers, J. M. 1976: Waqf and Patronage in Seljuk Anatolia: the Epigraphic Evidence. *Anatolian Studies* 26, 69–103.

Rogers, J. M. and Ward, R. M. 1988: *Suleyman the Magnificent*. London: British Museum.

Roman, S. 1990: *The Development of Islamic Library Collections in Western Europe and North America*. London: Mansell.

Rosen, S. A. and Avni, G. 1993: The Edge of the Empire: the Archaeology of Pastoral Nomads in the Southern Negev Highlands in Late Antiquity. *Biblical Archaeologist* 56, 188–99.

Rosenthal, F. 1971: Intihār. In *The Encyclopedia of Islam*, vol. 3, 2nd edn. Leiden: E. J. Brill, pp. 1246–48.

Rowley-Conwy, P. 1989: Nubia AD 0–550 and the 'Islamic' Agricultural Revolution: Preliminary Botanical Evidence from Qasr Ibrim. *Archéologie du Nil Moyen* 3, 131–8.

Rudofsky, B. 1981: *Architecture without Architects*. London: Academy Editions.

Ruggles, D. F. 1993: The Gardens of the Alhambra and the Concept of the Garden in Islamic Spain. In J. D. Dodds (ed.), *Al-Andalus: the Art of Islamic Spain*. New York: Metropolitan Museum, pp. 163–71.

Rykwert, J. 1976: *The Idea of a Town*. London: Faber and Faber.

Saad, E. N. 1983: *Social History of Timbuktu: the Role of Muslim Scholars and Notables 1400–1900*. Cambridge: Cambridge University Press.

Sabra, A. I. 1976: The Scientific Enterprise. In B. Lewis (ed.), *The World of Islam*. London: Thames and Hudson, pp. 181–92.

Sadan, J. 1991. Mashrūbāt. In *The Encyclopedia of Islam*, vol. 6, 2nd edn. Leiden: E. J. Brill, pp. 720–3.

Said, E. W. 1978: *Orientalism*. London: Routledge and Kegan Paul.

Saitowitz, S. J., Reid, D. L. and Van der Merwe, N. J. 1996: Glass Bead Trade from Islamic Egypt to South Africa c.AD 900–1250. *South African Journal of Science* 92, 101–4.

Sakhai, E. 1991: *The Story of Carpets*. London: Studio.

Salim, S. M. 1962: *Marsh Dwellers of the Euphrates Delta*. London: Athlone Press.

Salman, I. 1969: Islam and Figurative Art. *Sumer* 25, 59–96.

Samson, R. (ed.) 1990: *The Social Archaeology of Houses*. Edinburgh: Edinburgh University Press.

Sanogo, K. 1991: La mission d'inventaire dans la zone de retenue du barrage de Manantali. In M. Raimbault and K. Sanogo (eds), *Recherches archéologiques au Mali*. Paris: Karthala, pp. 151–63.

Sanseverino, H. 1983: Archaeological Remains on the Southern Somali Coast. *Azania* 18, 151–64.

Sauvaget, J. 1940: Caravansérais Syriens du Moyen Age, II: Caravansérais Mamelouks. *Ars Islamica* 7, 1–19.

Sauvaget, J. 1950: Les epitaphes royales de Gao. *Bulletin de l'Institut Français de l'Afrique Noire* 12, 418–40.

Scanlon, G. T. 1970a: Housing and Sanitation: Some Aspects of Medieval Egyptian Life. In A. H. Hourani and S. M. Stern (eds), *The Islamic City in the Light of Recent Research*. Oxford: Bruno Cassirer, pp. 185–94.

Scanlon, G. T. 1970b: Egypt and China: Trade and Imitation. In D. S. Richards (ed.), *Islam and the Trade of Asia*. Oxford: Bruno Cassirer, pp. 81–95.

Scarce, J. 1987: *Women's Costume of the Near and Middle East*. London: Unwin Hyman.

Scerrato, U. 1981: Survey of Wooden Mosques and Related Wood Carvings in the Swat Valley: ISMEO Activities. *East and West* 31, 178–81.

Scerrato, U. 1983: Labyrinths in the Wooden Mosques of North Pakistan: a Problematic Presence. *East and West* 33, 21–9.

Schacht, J. 1954: Sur la diffusion des formes d'architecture religeuse Musulmane à travers le Sahara. *Travaux de l'Institut de Recherches Sahariennes* 11, pp. 11–27.

Schacht, J. 1961: Further Notes on the Staircase Minaret. *Ars Orientalis* 4, pp. 137–41.

Schacht, J. 1964: *An Introduction to Islamic Law*. Oxford: Clarendon Press.

Schimmel, A. 1970: *Islamic Calligraphy*. Leiden: E. J. Brill.

Schimmel, A. 1975: *Mystical Dimensions of Islam*. Chapel Hill: University of North Carolina Press.

Schimmel, A. 1976: The Celestial Garden in Islam. In E. B. MacDougall and R. Ettinghausen (eds), *The Islamic Garden*. Washington: Dumbarton Oaks, pp. 13–39.

Schimmel, A. 1980: *Islam in the Indian Subcontinent*. Leiden: E. J. Brill.

Schimmel, A. 1990: *Calligraphy and Islamic Culture*. London: I. B. Tauris.

Schimmel, A. 1991: Sacred Geography in Islam. In J. Scott and P. Simpson-Housley, (eds), *Sacred Places and Profane Spaces: Essays in the Geographics of Judaism, Christianity and Islam*. New York: Greenwood, pp. 163–75.

Schneider, M. 1983: *Steles funéraires Musulmanes des Iles Dahlak (Mer Rouge)*. Cairo: Institut Français d'Archéologie Orientale.

Schumacher, C. E. 1888: *The Jaulân*. London: Bentley.

Serjeant, R. B. 1959: Mihrab. *Bulletin of the School of Oriental and African Studies* 22, 439–53.

Serjeant, R. B. and Lewcock, R. (eds) 1983: *San'a: an Arabian Islamic City*. London: World of Islam Festival Trust.

Shakespear, S. 1995: Personal communication, 7 November.

Shali, S. L. 1993: *Kashmir: History and Archaeology through the Ages*. Delhi: Indus.

Shawesh, A. M. 1995: Traditional Settlement in the Oasis of Ghadames in the Libyan Arab Jamahiriya. *Libyan Studies* 26, 35–47.

Sheriff, A. 1992: Mosques, Merchants and Landowners in Zanzibar Stone Town. *Azania* 27, 1–20.

Sherratt, A. 1992: What Can Archaeologists Learn from *Annalistes*? In A. B. Knapp (ed.), *Archaeology, Annales and Ethnohistory*. Cambridge: Cambridge University Press, pp. 135–42.

Shiloah, A. 1995: *Music in the World of Islam: a Socio-Cultural Study*. Aldershot: Scolar Press.

Silverman, R. 1991: Arabic Writing and the Occult. In C. G. Fisher (ed.), *Brocade of the Pen: the Art of Islamic Writing*. Michigan: Michigan State University, pp. 19–30.

Simoons, F. J. 1981: *Eat Not this Flesh*. Westport, Conn.: Greenwood.

Simpson, St J. 1995: Death and Burial in the Late Islamic Near East: Some Insights from Archaeology and Ethnography. In S. Campbell and A. Green (eds), *The Archaeology of Death in the Ancient Near East*. Oxford: Oxbow Books, pp. 240–51.

Sims, E. 1978: Markets and Caravanserais. In G. Michell (ed.), *Architecture of the Islamic World*. London: Thames and Hudson, pp. 97–111.

Sjöström, I. 1993: *Tripolitania in Transition: Late Roman to Early Islamic Settlement*. Aldershot: Avebury.

Smith, J. I. and Haddad, Y. Y. 1983: *Islamic Understanding of Death and Resurrection*. New York: State University of New York Press.

Sopher, D. E. 1967: *Geography of Religions*. Englewood Cliffs, NJ: Prentice-Hall.

Soucek, P. P. 1988: The Life of the Prophet: Illustrated Versions. In P. P. Soucek (ed.), *Content and Context of Visual Arts in the Islamic World*. University Park: Pennsylvania University Press, pp. 193–219.

Soundara Rajan, K. V. 1980: *Ahmadabad*. New Delhi: Archaeological Survey of India.

Sourdel-Thomine, J. 1971: Ḥammām. In *The Encyclopedia of Islam*, vol. 3, 2nd edn. Leiden: E. J. Brill, pp. 139–44.

Stephen, C. 1876 (1967): *Archaeology and Monumental Remains of Delhi*. Allahabad: Kitab Mahal.

Stern, S. M. 1970: The Constitution of the Islamic City. In A. H. Hourani and S. M. Stern (eds), *The Islamic City in the Light of Recent Research*. Oxford: Bruno Cassirer, pp. 25–50.

Stowasser, B. F. 1984: The Status of Women in Early Islam. In F. Hussain (ed.), *Muslim Women*. London: Croom Helm, pp. 11–43.

Talbot Rice, D. 1971: *Islamic Painting: a Survey*. Edinburgh: Edinburgh University Press.

Talbot Rice, D. 1993: *Islamic Art*. London: Thames and Hudson.

Talib, K. 1984: *Shelter in Saudi Arabia*. London: Academy.

Tampoe, M. 1989: *Maritime Trade between China and the West* (BAR Int. S555). Oxford: British Archaeological Reports.

Taphoo, R. 1974: The Origin and Development of Islamic Tombs in India (I). *Quarterly Review of Historical Studies* 14, 173–82.

Taphoo, R. 1975: The Origin and Development of Islamic Tombs in India (II). *Quarterly Review of Historical Studies* 15, 20–30.

Tapper, R. and Zubaida, S. 1994: Introduction. In S. Zubaida and R. Tapper (eds), *Culinary Cultures of the Middle East* London: Tauris, pp. 1–17.

Tarlow, S. and Boyd, B. 1992: Editorial. *Archaeological Review from Cambridge* 11 (1), pp. 1–9.

Tate, G. P. 1910: *Seistan: a Memoir on the History, Topography, Ruins and People of the Country*. Calcutta: Superintendent Government Printing.

Thesiger, W. 1954: The Marshmen of Southern Iraq. *Geographical Journal* 120, pp. 272–81.

Thesiger, W. 1980: *The Marsh Arabs*. London: Penguin.

Thomassey, P. and Mauny, R. 1951: Campagne de Fouilles à Koumbi Saleh. *Bulletin de l'Institut Français de l'Afrique Noire (B)* 13, 438–62.

Thomassey, P. and Mauny, R. 1956: Campagne de Fouilles de 1950 à Koumbi Saleh. *Bulletin de l'Institut Français de l'Afrique Noire (B)* 18, pp. 117–40.

Thompson, J. 1993: *Carpets from the Tents, Cottages and Workshops of Asia*. London: Laurence King.

Tillotson, G.H.R. 1990: *Architectural Guides for Travellers: Mughal India*. London: Penguin.

Tjandrasamita, U. 1978: The Introduction of Islam and the Growth of Moslem Coastal Cities in the Indonesian Archipelago. In H. Soebadio and C. A. du Marchie Sarvaas (eds), *Dynamics of Indonesian History*. Oxford: North-Holland, pp. 141–60.

Torres Balbás, L. 1942: Gibraltar: Ilave y Guarda de Espāna. *Al-Andalus* 7, 168–216.

Triano, A. V. 1992: Madinat al-Zahra: the Triumph of the Islamic State. In J. D. Dodds (ed.), *Al-Andalus: the Art of Islamic Spain*. New York: Metropolitan Museum of Art, pp. 27–39.

Trigger, B. G. 1989: *A History of Archaeological Thought*. Cambridge: Cambridge University Press.

Trigger, B. G. and Glover, I. (eds) 1981: Regional Traditions of Archae ological Research 1. *World Archaeology* 13 (2).

Trigger, B. G. and Glover, I. (eds) 1982: Regional Traditions of Archaeological Research 2. *World Archaeology* 13 (3).

Trimingham, J. S. 1949: *Islam in the Sudan*. London: Oxford University Press.

Trimingham, J. S. 1959: *Islam in West Africa*. Oxford: Clarendon Press.

Trimingham, J. S. 1971: *The Sufi Orders in Islam*. London: Oxford University Press.

Tsafrir, Y. and Foerster, G. 1994: From Scythopolis to Baysan: Changing Concepts of Urbanism. In G.R.D. King and A. Cameron (eds), *The Byzantine and Early Islamic Near East, II: Land Use and Settlement Patterns*. Princeton, NJ: Darwin Press, pp. 95–115.

Vardjavand, P. 1979: La découverte archéologique du complexe scientifique de l'Observatoire de Maraqe. In *Akten des VII Internationalen Kongresses für Iranische Kunst und Archaäologie*. Berlin: Dietrich Reimer Verlag, pp. 526–36.

Vercoutter, J. 1958: Excavations at Sai 1955. *Kush* 6, 144–69.

Verin, P. 1986: *The History of Civilisation in North Madagascar*. Rotterdam: A. A. Balkema.

Verity, P. 1971: Kababish Nomads of Northern Sudan. In P. Oliver (ed.), *Shelter in Africa*. London: Barrie and Jenkins, pp. 25–35.

Vickers, M. 1995: Arab Mosques Call Albanians Back to Prayer. *The European Magazine*, 28 September – 4 October, 3.

Violich, F. 1962: Evolution of the Spanish City. *Journal of the American Institute of Planners* 28 (3), 170–9.

Vire, M. M. 1958: Notes sur trois epitaphes royales de Gao. *Bulletin de l'Institut Français de l'Afrique Noire (B)* 20, 368–76.

Vogelsang-Eastwood, G. 1993: Unearthing History: Archaeological Textiles from Egypt. *Hali* 15, 85–9.

Volwahsen, A. 1970: *Living Architecture: Islamic Indian*. London: Mac-Donald.

Von Grunebaum, G. E. 1955: The Structure of the Muslim Town. In *Islam: Essays in the Nature and Growth of a Cultural Tradition* (American Anthropological Association Memoir 81). Ann Arbor: American Anthropological Association.

Von Grunebaum, G. E. 1976: *Muhammadan Festivals*. London: Curzon Press.

Von Wartburg, M-L. 1983: The Medieval Cane Sugar Industry in Cyprus: Results of Recent Excavations. *The Antiquaries Journal* 63, 298–314.

Wagstaff, J. M. (ed.) 1987: *Landscape and Culture: Geographical and Archaeological Perspectives*. Oxford: Blackwell.

Waines, D. 1991: Maṭbak̲h̲. In *The Encyclopedia of Islam*, vol. 6, 2nd ed. Leiden: E. J. Brill, pp. 807–9.

Waines, D. 1995: *An Introduction to Islam*. Cambridge: Cambridge University Press.

Wansbrough, J. 1977: *Quranic Studies: Sources and Methods of Scriptural Interpretation*. Oxford: Oxford University Press.

Wansbrough, J. 1978: *The Sectarian Milieu: Content and Composition of Islamic Salvation History*. Oxford: Oxford University Press.

Wasserstein, D. J. 1993: Coins as Agents of Cultural Definition in Islam. *Poetics Today* 14, 303–22.

Watson, A. M. 1983: *Agricultural Innovation in the Early Islamic World*. Cambridge: Cambridge University Press.

Watson, K. 1972: French Romanesque and Islam: Influences from Al-Andalus on Architectural Decoration. *Art and Archaeology Research Papers* 2, 1–27.

Watson, K. 1989: The Kufic Inscription in the Romanesque Cloister of Moissac in Quercy: Links with Le Puy, Toledo and Catalan Woodworkers. *Arte Medieval* 3 (1), pp. 7–27.

Webb, S. 1987: Re-burying Australian Skeletons. *Antiquity* 61, 292–6.

Weber, M. 1958: *The City*. New York: Free Press.

Webster, S. 1984: *Ḥarīm* and *Ḥijāb*: Seclusive and Exclusive Aspects of Traditional Muslim Dwelling and Dress. *Women's Studies International Forum* 7, 251–57.

Weir, S. 1985: *Qat in Yemen: Consumption and Social Change*. London: British Museum.

Weisgerber, G. 1980: Patterns of Early Islamic Metallurgy in Oman. *Proceedings of the Seminar for Arabian Studies* 10, 115–26.

Welch, A. 1979: *Calligraphy in the Arts of the Muslim World*. Folkestone: Dawson.

Wenzel, M. 1972: *House Decoration in Nubia*. London: Duckworth.

Westermarck, E. 1933: *Pagan Survivals in Mohammedan Civilisation*. London: Macmillan.

Whalen, N., Killick, A., James, N., Morsi, G. and Kamel, M. 1981: Saudi Arabian Archaeological Reconnaissance 1980: Preliminary Report on the Western Province Survey. *Atlal* 5, 43–58.

Wheatcroft, A. 1995: *The Ottomans: Dissolving Images*. London: Penguin.

Wheatley, P. 1971: *The Pivot of the Four Quarters: a Preliminary Enquiry into the Origins and Character of the Ancient Chinese City*. Edinburgh: Edinburgh University Press.

Whitcomb, D. S. 1979: Imported Far Eastern Wares. In D. S. Whitcomb and J. H. Johnson (eds), *Quseir al-Qadim 1978: Preliminary Report*. Cairo: American Research Centre in Cairo, pp. 108–9.

Whitcomb, D. S. 1988: Islamic Archaeology in Aden and the Hadhramaut. In D. T. Potts (ed.), *Araby the Blest: Studies in Arabian Archaeology*. Copenhagen: Museum Tusculanum Press, pp. 177–263.

Whitcomb, D. S. 1990–1: Glazed Ceramics of the Abbasid Period from the Aqaba Excavations. *Transactions of the Oriental Ceramic Society* 55, 43–65.

Whitcomb, D. S. 1992: The Islamic Period as Seen from Selected Sites. In B. MacDonald (ed.), *The Southern Ghors and Northeast Arabah Archaeological Survey*. Sheffield: J. R. Collis, pp. 113–18.

Whitcomb, D. S. 1995: Islam and the Socio-cultural Transition of Palestine: Early Islamic Period (638–1099 CE). In T. E. Levy (ed.), *The Archaeology of Society in the Holy Land*. London: Leicester University Press, pp. 488–98.

Whitcomb, D. S. 1996: Urbanism in Arabia. *Arabian Archaeology and Epigraphy* 7, 38–51.

Whitehouse, D. 1968: Excavations at Siraf: First Interim Report. *Iran* 6, 1–22.

Whitehouse, D. 1970: Siraf: a Medieval Port on the Persian Gulf. *World Archaeology* 2, 141–58.

Whitehouse, D. 1971: The Houses of Siraf, Iran. *Archaeology* 24 (3), 255–62.

Whitehouse, D. 1972: Staircase Minarets on the Persian Gulf. *Iran* 10, 155–58.

Whitehouse, D. 1973: Chinese Stoneware from Siraf: the Earliest Finds. In N. Hammond (ed.), *South Asian Archaeology*. Park Ridge: Noyes Press, pp. 241–55.

Whitehouse, D. 1974: Excavations at Siraf: Sixth Interim Report. *Iran* 12, 1–30.

Whitehouse, D. 1976: Kish. *Iran* 14, 146–7.

Whitehouse, D. 1980: *Siraf III: the Congregational Mosque and Other Mosques from the Ninth to the Twelfth Centuries*. London: British Institute of Persian Studies.

Wiedemann, E. 1986: al-Kuḥl. In *The Encyclopedia of Islam*, vol. 5, 2nd ed. Leiden: E. J. Brill, pp. 356–7.

Wijayapala, W. and Prickett, M. E. 1986: *Sri Lanka and the International Trade: an Exhibition of Ancient Imported Ceramics found in Sri Lanka's Archaeological Sites*. Colombo: Archaeological Department.

Wilber, D. N. 1979: *Persian Gardens and Garden Pavilions*. Washington, DC: Dumbarton Oaks.

Wilkinson, T. J. 1975: Sohar Ancient Fields Project: Interim Report no. 1. *Journal of Oman Studies* 1, 75–80.

Wilkinson, T. J. 1977: Sohar Ancient Fields Project: Interim Report no. 3. *Journal of Oman Studies* 3, 13–16.

Williamson, A. 1974: Harvard Archaeological Survey of Oman 1973, III: Sohar and the Sea Trade of Oman in the Tenth Century. *Proceedings of the Seminar for Arabian Studies* 4, 78–95.

Wilson, R. T. 1984: *The Camel*. Harlow: Longman.

Wilson, T. 1979: Swahili Funerary Architecture of the Northern Kenya Coast. *Art and Archaeology Research Papers* (December), 33–46.

Woodward, M. R. 1989: *Islam in Java: Normative Piety and Mysticism in the Sultanate of Yogyakarta*. Tucson: University of Arizona Press.

Woolley, C. L. and Lawrence, T. E. 1936: *The Wilderness of Zin*. London: Jonathan Cape.

Xiaowie, L. 1994: China. In M. Frishman and H-U. Khan (eds), *The Mosque: History, Architectural Development and Regional Diversity*. London: Thames and Hudson, pp. 209–23.

Young, G. and Wheeler, N. 1977: *Return to the Marshes: Life with the Marsh Arabs of Iraq*. London: Collins.

Zeyadeh, A. 1994: Settlement Patterns: an Archaeological Perspective. Case Studies from Northern Palestine and Jordan. In G.R.D. King and A. Cameron (eds), *The Byzantine and Early Islamic Near East, II: Land Use and Settlement Patterns*. Princeton, NJ: Darwin Press, pp. 117–31.

Ziadeh, G. 1995: Ethno-history and 'Reverse Chronology' at Ti'innik, a Palestinian Village. *Antiquity* 69, 999–1008.

Index